Canadian Women **Writing Fiction**

CANADIAN WOMEN
Writing Fiction

Edited by Mickey Pearlman

University Press of Mississippi
JACKSON

813
CAN

Library of Congress Cataloging-in-Publication Data

Canadian women writing fiction / edited by Mickey Pearlman.
　　　p.　　cm.
　　Includes index.
　　ISBN 0-87805-636-X
　　1. Canadian fiction—Women authors—History and criticism.
　　2. French-Canadian fiction—Women authors—History and criticism.
　　3. Women and literature—Canada.　I. Pearlman, Mickey, 1938–
　　PR9188.C36　1993
　　813.009′9287—dc20　　　　　　　　　　　　　　　92-44969
　　　　　　　　　　　　　　　　　　　　　　　　　　　CIP

British Library Cataloging-in-Publication data available

Contents

Canadian Women **Writing Fiction**

Introduction

To some degree, this collection of critical essays about contemporary Canadian writing women, commissioned specifically for this volume, was energized by another book I edited. *American Women Writing Fiction* examined several pervasive themes—memory, identity, family, space—that permeate the fiction of the ten women in the United States whose work we chose to examine: Toni Cade Bambara, Alison Lurie, Joyce Carol Oates, Mary Lee Settle, Mary Gordon, Jayne Anne Phillips, Susan Fromberg Schaeffer, Joan Didion, Louise Erdrich and Gail Godwin.

Originally, our aim here was to see how these ideas resonated in the work of what we hoped was a similarly representative group of Canadians: Alice Munro, Mavis Gallant, Anne Hébert, Margaret Atwood, Marie Claire Blais, Janette Turner Hospital, Isabel Huggan, Jane Urquhart, Audrey Thomas, Sandra Birdsell, Carol Shields, Marlene Nourbese Philip, Joy Kogawa, and Beatrice Culleton. How would Canadians, some hyphenated (Japanese-Canadian, for example) and some not, from both coasts, who write in English and French, mirror in their work the usually debilitating effects of enclosed or limited emotional and physical spaces in the lives of women? Would supposedly nest-like space emerge, as it does in most fiction by American women, as both a trap and an antithesis to Mark Twain's "territory," to which American fictional men, at least, light out? How would the French Canadians, or the hyphenated, or nonwhite, or the perhaps more stereotypical English-speaking, native-born, white Canadian writers be affected by the often negative and imprisoning power of memory? Would the novels and short stories of these women reflect the labyrinthine complications of family and their accompanying influence on the identities of women—largely as someone's mother, daughter, wife, or sister?

Our problems began immediately, when it became clear to the ten critics in this collection that, while the concepts of memory, family, and space resonated throughout the work of these writers, the issue of identity was the linchpin of Canadian writing by women—at least as we were seeing it. And the concept of identity, always and everywhere in flux, was shaped by ethnicity, race, culture, habit, and even social policy. For example, the *New York Times* recently stated that "although Canadians generally consider themselves more progressive than Americans on social issues, many here see the United States ahead on [issues concerning indecency]. 'One of the problems may be that while it's hard to generalize because both countries are so big and diverse, Canadian culture, with its strong Protestant ethic, tends to be more prudish than American,' [University of Toronto law professor Denise] Reaume said."

While the American authors in the previous collection were, of course, of diverse racial, religious, and ethnic backgrounds, they were all born, to borrow a phrase, in the USA. In the case of the fourteen Canadians, we soon found that, to use Heather Zwicker's comments about those Canadians she calls "women of color," "Making oneself at home in the new world necessitates a radical rethinking of national identity. History, natality, family and place no longer fall neatly into the territorial and historical entity that we know as Canada." She adds that Canadians "are by and large a border people," most of whom live in a hundred-mile strip along the United States border.

It became apparent immediately that Zwicker's insights were applicable not only to the entire discussion about what constitutes "Canadianness" in Canadian writers (if such a label can be defined) but to the question of identity in general. Identity, Zwicker says, necessitates not only "expanding the term 'Canadian' to include women of color in a pluralistic sense, but . . . blowing wide open any easy notion of what constitutes a national tag like 'Canadian'. . . . Women of color [a term widely used in the United States] is a relatively new category designed to provide a basis for solidarity among women of various racial and ethnic identities different from the white, Protestant, Euro-Canadian popularly believed to characterize Canada. The term does not denote visible difference—many women of color are fair-skinned, mixed-blood, or can 'pass' as white—but is a form of self-identification that recognizes marginalization and affirms difference." She explains that Joy Kogawa, for instance, "writes about the Nisei, second-generation Japanese Canadians for whom relocation is a matter not of choice but of racist governmental policy. The problem Kogawa addresses is, 'How do you make a country your own when it disowns you?'" Zwicker also notes that Beatrice Culleton, who writes primarily about the Metis (which *Webster's* defines as "the offspring of a French Canadian and an American Indian"), "radically revises conventional notions of the family and its relation to the nation, and argues, like Kogawa, for the importance of personal history in the construction of the national." Culleton's settings are "reminiscent of Marlene Nourbese Philip's choice of the Caribbean rather than Africa as a site of return: there is no going back to any pure origin. Metis and Creole, not Indian or African, symbolize survival in the 'new world'."

Identity, then, evolves not only from place and site, from birth and perception, but in reaction to someone else's perception of you. For instance, gender and race—as components of identity—play a part in the discussion of Audrey Thomas and her work, although Thomas has an additional issue that affects her sense of national identity. As Virginia Tiger relates, Thomas "has more than once indicated her displeasure at being described as an American living in Canada. Some 26 years after emigrating to the Canadian west coast, [Thomas] queried, 'Why don't [reviewers] say a Canadian born in the States?'" In Tiger's view, Audrey Thomas would be better described as "British Columbia's answer to Colette . . . a writer of very specific witness whose world is bounded by family, flora, fauna, and that intertidal life whose symbolic soundings resonate especially distinctly for women and upon whose meanings she has both predicated and titled one novel. Part of her interest (possibly even a large part) lies in her public invitation to have the heroines of her prose be identified with the author of that prose." Tiger reports that Thomas told one critic, "'I never write about anybody but myself.' . . . The presiding figure of the author's imagination [is] a woman longing for the pastoral domesticity of husband, children, and [Caribbean] island life, yet bolted into voyage and action by sexual love and an equally uncontrollable passion for words, words as puzzles, words as refrains, words as wizards."

Carol Shields, who was also born in the States but has lived in Canada since 1957, "moves easily [and fictionally] back and forth across the border," writes Abby Werlock. "Shields seems less concerned with the Canadianness of her characters. Hers is a humanist approach, which blurs both national boundaries and, in postmodern fashion, the lines separating literary genres." Werlock feels that Shields seems more interested in "women's identity" than in Canadian identity, and in *Various Miracles*, a collection of short stories, Shields "underscores the themes of women's identity" by stressing "the closeness of women's relationships." As

Shields said in a previous interview, "Where were the novels about the kind of women I knew, women who had a reflective life, a moral system, women who had a recognizable domestic context, a loyalty to their families, a love for their children?," and Werlock says that when Shields "illuminates the reality of women's history of entrapment and violation, as well as its obverse—the reality of women's achievements and contributions to revisioning the status quo—the very difference in their voices is essential." Those are her subjects.

Werlock contrasts the work of Carol Shields with that of the native-born Sandra Birdsell, whose vision of Canada "is filled with anger, prejudice, and a sense that the experiment [of Canada] is not working." Birdsell invents the "mythical Canadian town [of Agassiz] as her setting, presents a microcosm peopled largely by first- and second-generation immigrants who move as essentially solitary individuals lacking meaningful relationships with family and community. . . . Birdsell's two published novels to date depict the residents of Agassiz . . . a mixture of all the ethnic Canadians—particularly native Americans, Metis, Mexicans, South Americans, French, British, German, and Russians."

She uses this community as an antithesis to "the traditional fictional use of the Canadian wilderness theme as noted by Northrup Frye and others. The town becomes a metaphor for Canada itself . . . with its vast ethnic population and its 'undesirable' ethnics lurking around the fringes. The town invokes the 'garrison mentality of the whites, who even in the 1950s look nervously over their shoulders when an Indian walks into town.'" Werlock says that both of Birdsell's novels "depict the residents of Agassiz as . . . working-class people, primarily women immigrants and their daughters trying to define themselves both in relation to their contemporary English-speaking world and to their ethnic heritage. . . . if in Birdsell's work the major women characters are, in fact, metaphors for the problems that plague Canada, the implications are bleak indeed. . . . the characters are still unsure of themselves, still searching, unable or unwilling to communicate their thoughts and to make sense of their experiences and feelings."

Birdsell has reaffirmed this in interviews: "A lot of things that happen to us are inevitable; we don't do anything about them, especially as women," and Werlock makes clear that "like their mothers, the daughters live lives bereft of any sense of achievement or fulfillment, ultimately seeming able merely to endure." Birdsell's novel, *The Missing Child*, is a "relentlessly dark, harrowing, apocalyptic novel of Agassiz women whose childhood memories reveal male violence, sexual abuse and murder . . . a novel which again unfolds during a flood—purposely caused by angry dispossessed native Americans—which, by the end, engulfs everyone in the entire town." Curiously, that image of uncontrolled, destructive water—floods, whirlpools, dangerous waterfalls, recurs often in the work of several writers in this volume.

As Marilyn Wesley points out, the fiction of Anne Hébert, little known in the United States, also focuses on the impact of community on identity: "Hébert's fiction conceives of space in terms of the effect of the restrictive mores of small, tightly knit communities on the options of her protagonists, both male and female. That influential space is further contracted because community influence conditions individuals through the miniaturized world of family relationship. The effect of this process is most frequently experienced as the inadequacy of gender roles to the fulfillment of human needs and to the completion of personal identity."

And it is in one of Hébert's novels that "the waterfall is presented as an object of [a] young man's physical environment, and also as a representation of the roaring that he has been aware of inside his head . . . the torrent is a summarizing emblem for [the character's] internal confusion and anger and his external submersion in the deterministic world of his mother's destructive religiosity." Wesley makes the point that "the needs and desires of [Hébert's] heroes and heroines relentlessly collide with larger pressures they can neither comprehend, contain, nor disregard. . . . [That] very irresolvability of conflict, registered in the symbolic expression of her character's dilemmas, of which the waterfall is a good example, lends Hébert's work its tragic dimension."

In different ways Margaret Atwood is also involved with issues of identity as they are formed by communities and spaces. Roberta White points out that "although most of [Atwood's] novels are set in Toronto, a city she establishes on the map of world literature as Joyce did Dublin, Atwood never enters the same fictional world twice." Atwood herself, says White, "characterizes earlier Canadian literature as a dreary record of victimization and struggle whose 'true and only season' is winter. Seeing herself as working against a literary tradition dismal as a continent of snow, Atwood writes novels filled with color, wit, transformation, and surprise while retaining that key theme of the national literature, the struggle to survive."

That "struggle to survive" is, of course, paramount in the short stories of Alice Munro, peopled as they are with "Calvinists, Polish and Croatian immigrants, ministers, gypsies, Scots, divorcees, teachers, laborers, each caught at different stages of life," and Georgeann Murphy astutely points out that "change is often remarked as a significant theme in Munro's work, [but] her focus is always on the connection between what went before and what comes after the change. . . . Initiating change and trying to recreate themselves do not break characters' connection to the past and the identities shaped there. As Munro writes in 'Differently,' 'People make momentous shifts, but not the changes they imagine.' Her stories are filled with men and women who have 'smelled love and hope' and suffer for it." For Munro, says Murphy, "connection is a consuming theme."

Once again, identity and biography are interwoven: "Born in 1931 to a farmer who raised silver foxes, Munro grew up in relative poverty near Wingham, Ontario, not far from Lake Huron, lived in British Columbia for twenty-five years, and moved back to Ontario." Her stories "reiterate a life pattern of departure and return, often depicting the brutality and squalor of life on the edge of a small rural community." Munro has herself addressed this sense of displacement, and Murphy says that Munro is "not sure she acquired an authentic feel for British Columbia, even after twenty years of living there: 'I always felt that when I lived in Vancouver and Victoria that I had to go home to die, because life on the west coast wasn't real in the same way.'"

While no legitimate critic, Canadian or otherwise, would characterize the work of these writers as only an amalgamated ouevre about the problems of identity and their attendant components of family, space, and memory, it would be similarly illegitimate to ignore the ideas about sanctity, exile, homelessness, refuge, and displacement—all related ideas—which so much of their work engenders. As Martha Vertreace writes, the French Canadian author Marie Claire Blais, in *Deaf to the City*, "presents several characters who long for an ideal lover and for sanctity."

Ideas about exile and sanctity dominate the work of Janette Turner Hospital, who is truly a multinational writer. Born in Melbourne, she lives in Canada one-third of each year but teaches at an Australian university during the summer and in Boston during the fall. "Her characters," writes Margaret Schramm, "tend to be nomads like herself, and she writes about crossing boundaries rather than about Canadian settings. . . . The internationalism in Hospital's fiction is, however, distinctively Canadian, for it reflects what Coral Ann Howells calls 'that mixture of cultures which is characteristic of Canadian social geography. Even the nomadic lives of Hospital's protagonists are typically Canadian,' for according to Robert

Kroetsch, 'Canadians are supremely at home when they travel . . . and the urban figures in Canadian literature are, typically, traveling.'"

"As often happens in Hospital's novels," Schramm observes, "taking responsibility for the plight of another character (particularly a double) becomes a means of redemption," and "Hospital's moral aesthetic [is] her commitment to breaking down the borders separating nationalities, classes, and individuals." Schramm identifies as the major dilemma, for Hospital and her characters, that "Hospital repeatedly undermines the notion of a unified, knowable self, instead presenting the self as fragmented and enigmatic. . . . Her more recent novels portray the family as fragmented, with a physically or emotionally absent father the object of the protagonist's quest"; in fact, major characters in *The Ivory Swing*, *Borderline*, *Charades* and *The Last Magician* "feel deeply responsible for women who exist on the margins of society and are victims of violence."

Similar sensitivities to the precariousness of women's lives (in and out of Canada) emerge in the writers discussed by Katherine Gottschalk. "Isabel Huggan [who lives in France] and Jane Urquhart are very different writers, but in their fiction the familiar difficulties arise: while placed in spaces determined and controlled by others, women struggle to shape or at least to understand their identities. They seek to increase and shape the space available in which to conduct their lives."

In Huggan's *The Elizabeth Stories*, set in 1950s Canada, "as has so often been the plan for women, sexual development means increasing repression, means being silenced and controlled by men—means feeling a failure at being feminine and becoming secretive about real feelings." It was "a time when men firmly placed women in the enclosed 'landscape of the kitchen.'" In contrast, Jane Urquhart "sets her first novel, *The Whirlpool*, in 1889 Niagara Falls, Ontario, . . . [and] for Maud Grady, a character in this novel . . . Maud Grady's is a circular, death-centered world."

In *Changing Heaven*, writes Gottschalk, Urquhart continues to explore her intensely poetic interest in landscape and weather, but with deleterious results. She agrees with the critic Kathryn Chittick, who says that "in the 1980s . . . the contemporary Canadian heroine . . . gives a sense of being completely encompassed by her own impotence," and Gottschalk adds that "Urquhart's female characters find themselves placed in constricting and silencing spaces."

One who has left the space, and has not lived in Canada for over thirty years, is the Paris-based Mavis Gallant. "After probing various mysteries about her family and her past, such as the circumstances of her father's death, Linnet, a character in *Home Truths* will, like Gallant, leave Canada permanently for France." Gallant, says Diane Simmons, "describes something she sees in the Canadian personality. Here everyone seems to feel a sense of loss; it is a country of children pushed from some all-but-forgotten nest: 'I've never been in a country where there was so much gap between reality and dream,' Gallant said of Canada in an interview. 'The people's lives don't match up to what they seem to think they were and the people invent things or they invent background or they invent families. . . . In Europe you can't invent because everyone knows too much.'" Many of Gallant's adult characters, Simmons adds, are "given the dangerous opportunity to see through [their] own pretenses to [their] real selves beneath."

Several of the critics in this collection refer to the writing of W. H. New in *A History of Canadian Literature*: "Canada appears repeatedly as a place of exile; . . . it is not so much that the country houses exiles, though that is part of the 'exile syndrome', but that Canada is a society in which foreigness [sic] and familiarity are one." Others allude to Northrup Frye's question, "Where is here?" and his belief that Canadians entered the twentieth century uncertain of "what kind of people we were—or even, whether a Canadian could be identified." Margaret Atwood has answered Frye's question by emphasizing the central role of literature in Canada: "We need to know about here, because here is where we live. . . . Without that knowledge we will not survive." As Linda Hutcheon points out, Canadian writers must certainly grapple with the questions of Canadian identity because individuals may assume selfhood "only when [they] have attained it," and she believes that women have long been denied the dominant male power bases which enable self-assertiveness and a strong sense of self. Lorna Irvine concurs: "The female voice politically and culturally personifies Canada," and Coral Ann Howells notes the "close parallels between the historical situation of women and of Canada as a nation, for women's experience of the power politics of gender and their problematic relation to patriarchal traditions of authority have affinities with Canada's attitude to the cultural imperialism of the United States as well as its ambivalence towards its European inheritance." Unlike the United States, which has an identity, Howells writes, Canada's "problem of identity may not be the problem of having no identity but rather of having multiple identities, so that any single national self-image is reductive and always open to revision."

In spite of our mutual and individual attempts to map the themes of memory, space, and family in the work of these writers, the ten essays have finally concentrated much more on the undeniably pervasive discussions of identity in the Canadian literature we examined. These fourteen Canadian women, stirred by their own personal and fictional struggles with identity and energized by what seems to be the internal Canadian preoccupation with this subject, seem poised to answer—to the extent that an answer is possible—both the questions of what constitutes a Canadian writer and the larger, more important question of Canadian identity.

1. The Art of Alice Munro: Memory, Identity, and the Aesthetics of Connection

Alice Munro's first collection of stories, *Dance of the Happy Shades*, published in 1968, won her the Canadian Governor General's Award but little fame. Her second book, however, *Lives of Girls and Women*, found in 1971 a wider audience, one ready to declare her "an important new talent"—even though she had been publishing fiction for nearly twenty years. Since then she has enjoyed, perhaps more than any of her contemporaries, a consistently high degree of both popular and critical success,[1] inspiring more book-length studies of her work than she has published books. Her most recent collection, *Friend of My Youth* (1990), was glowingly reviewed on both sides of the Atlantic: Peter Kemp in the London *Sunday Times* pronounced her "an unrivalled chronicler of human nature."[2] Such praise prompts readers to return to Munro's earlier stories, each so well crafted as to reward second and third readings, in order to search out new meaning in light of later developments. This critical approach is especially appropriate to a study of Alice Munro's writing, for returning to and re-evaluating what has gone before is both Munro's method and her great theme.

To an extraordinary extent, the raw material of Munro's work comes from her own life, a fact she readily admits.[3] Born in 1931 to Robert Eric Laidlaw, a farmer who raised silver foxes, and Ann Chamney Laidlaw, Munro grew up in relative poverty near Wingham, Ontario, not far from Lake Huron. Married in 1951 to James Munro, she took her B.A. at the University of Western Ontario in 1952 and moved with her husband to British Columbia, where he opened a successful bookstore in Victoria. They had three daughters. Her mother, Ann Laidlaw, died after a long struggle with Parkinson's disease in 1959. Following her divorce in 1976, Munro remarried and moved back to Ontario, where she now lives.

The chronological and geographical settings of Munro's stories roughly reiterate this life pattern of departure and return. Many of the earliest, appearing in *Dance of the Happy Shades* and *Lives of Girls and Women* (a novel that is itself a progression of connected stories), are set in the "quasi-pioneer environment"[4] of southern Ontario, often depicting the brutality and squalor of life on the edge of a small rural community. Frequently, their point of view is that of a young girl scrutinizing the incomprehensible behavior of adults. Munro never abandons southern Ontario as a setting; many consider it the inspiration for her best work. But stories from her middle period, collected in *Something I've Been Meaning to Tell You* (1974), more frequently present young, troubled married life on the Canadian West Coast during an ironically rendered beat era, early feminist consciousness-raising, and the bewildering changes of the sixties. Munro acknowledges that she is "not at all sure" she acquired an authentic feel for British Columbia, even after twenty years of living there[5]: "I always felt when I lived in Vancouver and Victoria that I had to go home to die, because life on the west coast wasn't real in the same way."[6] Her collection *The Beggar Maid* (1978—published in Canada as *Who Do You Think You Are?*) begins and ends back in Ontario, following the progress of the protagonist Rose, whose life parallels Munro's in many ways. Munro's plots since 1978, often set near her childhood home, regularly concern strategies of coping and acceptance; in her own words, "I write about where I am in life."[7]

Because her work is so closely related to her life, and so thematically consistent (she has been criticized for her "continual elaboration of the similar"[8]), generalizations about setting and subject are possible and sometimes illuminating. They should not, however, obscure the variety in Munro's characterization. *Friend of My Youth*, for example, swells with a population of intensely realized characters—Calvinists, Polish and Croatian immigrants, ministers, gypsies, Scots, divorcees, teachers, laborers—each caught at different stages of life.[9] Some, while not exactly types, function symbolically: pilots stand for romantic, exciting, and irresponsible sex in "How I Met My Husband" (*SIBMTY*),[10] "White Dump" (*PL*), and "Hold Me Fast, Don't Let Me Pass" (*FMY*), and brassy, husband-hunting nurses in "Images" (*DHS*) and "Friend of My Youth" (*FMY*) embody coarse intrusions of the outside world on the sequestered, delicately balanced power structure of home. Fathers in Munro's stories are often strong, courageous, traditionally masculine, and capable of transforming hardship with humor, like Ben Jordan in "Walker Brothers Cowboy" (*DHS*) or Fleming in "The Stone in the Field" (*MJ*). Typically, they are also intelligent and have a love of language, like Rose's father in

"Royal Beatings" (*BM*, 5–6), or of astronomy, like the narrator's father in "The Moons of Jupiter," published two years after Munro's own father died during cardiac surgery.[11] Mothers, however, are more frequent and powerful figures in Munro's stories, a fact the narrator of "The Ottawa Valley" (*SIBMTY*), herself a writer, appears to acknowledge as she frets that she can never "*get rid*" of her mother. This plaint concludes both that story and the collection: "[My mother] has stuck to me as close as ever and refused to fall away, and I could go on, and on, applying what skills I have, using what tricks I know, and it would always be the same" (246). Munro's stories, taken collectively, provide a cohesive portrait of Munro's mother, most notably the exquisitely painful "Peace of Utrecht" (*DHS*), written the year Ann Laidlaw died. Mother figures in Munro, like Ada Johnson of *LGW*, are frequently martyrs to a disease either named as or similar to Parkinson's. They are dreadful housekeepers, visibly constrained by poverty and family obligations, independent, proud, and eager for their daughters to become even more so. Narrators speak of them with a mixture of exasperation, guilt, pride, and longing, like that of the narrator of "Friend of My Youth," who dreams of her dead mother "looking quite well" and saying she was always sure she would see her daughter again one day (3–4).

A character who appears with even more frequency than the mother who refuses "to fall away" from the narrator's memory and writing is the narrator herself. Munro's work is full of first-person retrospective narrators and third-person protagonists who are, themselves, writers or artists with "a need to picture things, to pursue absurdities" ("Royal Beatings," *BM*, 3). Often they are intelligent women[12] with lives animated by conflicts arising from a repressive Scotch-Irish Protestant upbringing; frequently they are torn by competing but equally compelling needs for freedom and domesticity. Rose in "Providence" (*BM*), kept from adventure and her lover Tom by her love and responsibility for her daughter Anna, is a good example. This double bind so common in women's lives since the sixties often reveals itself in Munro's protagonists' bifurcated attitude toward writing: they love language, but, like the narrator of "The Office" (*DHS*), they are tentative about writing as an activity: "I am a writer. That does not sound right. Too presumptuous; phoney, or at least unconvincing. Try again. I write. Is that better? I *try* to write. That makes it worse. Hypocritical humility" (59). Munro herself has always written in a room with a function other than simply providing her a place to write and has felt "less uneasy about writing because [she] was doing it in a room that wasn't a study." She wrote *Lives of Girls and Women*, for example, in her laundry room. [13]

Despite their attendant uneasiness about doing so, Munro's protagonists are driven to listen and watch, record, and reshape what they see around them. Mary in "The Shining Hours" (*DHS*) draws Mrs. Fullerton's story out of her by pretending to know less than she really does; Dorothy in "Marrakesh" is a retired schoolteacher driven to observe whatever is before her: "Beautiful or ugly had ceased to matter, because there was in everything something to be discovered" (*SIBMTY*, 163). Del Jordan, at the end of "Heirs of the Living Body" (*LGW*, 52), removes her dead Uncle Craig's historical manuscript from its fireproof and padlocked tin box and replaces it with her own writing, some poems and the beginning of a novel; she carries her uncle's perfectly typed thousand pages to the cellar, where they are ruined in a spring flood. Del's memory of the past and her connection to her family are linked to, but displaced by, her need to forge an identity in the present, and that identity, for Del—and for all of Munro's artist/protagonists—is connected to "the elegant channels of language" ("Age of Faith," *LGW*, 83). Munro's writers recognize that writing can be a strategy for dealing with life: Del carries with her the idea of her novel, her reshaping of a community tragedy, like "one of those magic boxes a favored character gets hold of in a fairy story: touch it and his troubles disappear" ("Epilogue: The Photographer," *LGW*, 204). Hugo in "Material" (*SIBMTY*) has reinvented his life, his ex-wife ruefully discovers, in his book-jacket biography, aggrandizing the enviable and eliminating the painful.

If writing can transform and re-create—"It is an act of magic . . . of a special, unsparing, unsentimental love" ("Material," *SIBMTY*, 43)—it is also a challenging covenant between the writer and the world, one the narrator of "The Stone in the Field" despairs of getting right: "I no longer believe that people's secrets are defined and communicable, or their feelings full-blown and easy to recognize. I don't believe so." (*MJ*, 35). Furthermore, any failure of talent undercuts the artist's identity: Rose, an actress returning home to care for her senile stepmother Flo, is ashamed of a failure to accurately portray her characters in her acting, an especial embarrassment in a community where people might remember when her schoolgirl pride in performance resulted in her teacher's humiliating question, "Who do you think you are?" (*BM*, 200). Even in middle age, Rose is still unsure of the answer to that question. She struggles to reconcile her memories and her identity.

Writing can be that act of reconciliation for Munro's writers; writing is an act of magic and of love. But a love affair can impair a protagonist's ability to write, and thus imperil her identity. Lydia, the poet/editor of "Dulse" (*MJ*), is so devastated by the collapse of an affair that she believes she will probably write no more poems; she wonders how much money she could make as a cleaning lady (37). Writing, identity, and love are also problematically connected in "Bardon Bus" (*MJ*), when the writer/narrator recognizes in her friend Kay—as well as in herself—the tendency to reinvent her identity for a man (116): if the self can be forged by the act of writing, it can be lost in attraction to the opposite sex. Almeda Joynt Roth, Munro's turn-of-the-century "poetess" in the Canadian wilderness of "Meneseteung" (*FMY*), also recognizes a link between loving and loss of creative power, noticing that a married woman's creativity is focused on reinventing a man as a husband (60)—a task she herself does not want. At the end of her life, she channels the last of her creative juices not into the pursuit of Jarvis Poulter but into a poem.

The typical writer in Munro's fiction is, then, ambivalent about her work but driven to do it. She struggles for representative accuracy, which failures of love and/or talent undercut. Munro's writers labor to connect memory and identity, and the problems inherent in such connection provide the central conflicts of Munro's fiction. But always, connection itself is the subsuming theme. Three kinds of connection are especially important to the Munro *Weltanschauung*: travel, the connection of one place to another in a journey replete with metaphorical meaning; change, the connection between past and present; and sexual love, probably the most fundamental and highly problematic of human connections.

Eudora Welty has written that "writers and travelers are mesmerized alike by knowing of their destinations."[14] In this state of something like highway hypnosis, several of Alice Munro's characters experience significant realizations: the process of travel, involving as it does removal from quotidian obligations and attachments, focuses attention on the essential. A journey can thus be made toward a revelation as much as toward a destination, and not infrequently, Munro's characters make those journeys simultaneously. On a train to Vancouver, the narrator of "The Spanish Lady" (*SIBMTY*) reviews the disintegration of her marriage and meets a Rosicrucian who believes he knew her in a previous life; her unmet arrival in the station, coinciding with the sudden death of an old man who had been sitting on a bench there, is a "message" putting her life in sudden, graphic perspective (190–91). Rose Jordan has her first sexual pleasure from a man on board a train to Toronto in "Wild Swans" (*BM*). And Mary Jo of "Eskimo" (*PL*) encounters an unexpected—and unwelcome—reflection of her devotion to her lover/employer, Dr. Steeter, on board a winter flight to Tahiti. Munro herself finds train travel conducive to writing:

> One of the problems I used to have is getting really sort of seized up and not being able to write at all, not doing anything and nothing happening. But if you are in the train you are going from place to place with no effort on your part. Something is being achieved, and so I don't think you get that really tight feeling about it. So I relax and write.[15]

What dislodges Munro's writer's block and what inspires her characters' epiphanies amount to the same thing: being in the process of making a physical connection between two places can lubricate intellectual and emotional connections as well.

Connection in Munro is both a hedge against and a barrier to change, that sometimes fearful and sometimes desirable fact of human life. While change is often remarked as a significant theme in Munro's work,[16] her focus is always on the connection between what went before and what comes after the change. Connection with the past is undeniably strong in Munro's writing, and characters who wish to sever their connections with the past discover they cannot. Maddy, the older sister in "The Peace of Utrecht" (*DHS*), finds that though her ten-year obligation of caring for her mother has ended, she can't retrieve her life from her guilt over putting her mother in the hospital where she died. Helena in "Executioners" (*SIBMTY*) longs for the time when everyone who remembers the terrible killing fire of her childhood will be dead so that it will finally and forever be over. Even Del, as she replaces that manuscript of Uncle Craig's with her own in "Heirs of the Living Body" (*LGW*), is not so much disposing of her past as she is confirming her familial destiny of becoming a writer herself—like the uncle whose work she tried to put behind her, work she will herself write about one day.

Familial connection is strong in Munro's stories, and it militates against change. Del Jordan believes that despite their apparent differences, her father, mother, and uncle are connected to each other and to their home: "This connection was plain as a fence . . . it would stay between us and anything" ("The Flat Roads," *LGW*, 22). Blood ties may sometimes be inscrutable, as they are to Mildred in "Visitors" (*MJ*), but they are undeniable. And in challenging situations when characters lack the protection of a present family, they form their own, no matter what their ages. Helen, the sixth-grader in "Day of the Butterfly" (*DHS*), betrays the only other outsider at school in her effort to be part of a group; "Mrs. Cross and Mrs. Kidd" (*MJ*) survive the indignities of old age through their connection to each other. In both cases, change, in the form of new friendships, threatens the old order, but the old order wins out. Teenagers threatened by the death of a classmate form an artificial and ceremonial connection in "Circle of Prayer" (*PL*): girls who don't know each other or the deceased at all well sing in unison and drop their jewelry into her open casket. Connection here is the only solace for the specter of the ultimate change, death.

Death as a violent, transforming upheaval is also at the center of "Accident" (*MJ*). When her lover Ted's son is killed, Frances's life changes forever: she ends up married with children of her own as a direct result of Ted's loss. Frances meditates, however, not on the changes made in her life but on how she has remained the same despite those changes (109). While Frances has change thrust upon her, other Munro characters try actively to impose changes, but with little success: they remain connected to what went before. "Jesse and Meribeth" (*PL*) attempt to re-create themselves by spelling their names in a new way; Jessie later marvels, like Frances, that she has stayed the same, even though she had thought she "could turn [herself] inside out, over and over again, and tumble through the world scot free" (188). Initiating change and trying to re-create themselves do not break characters' connection to the past and their identities shaped there: "People make momentous shifts, but not the changes they imagine" ("Differently," *FMY*, 242). Margot in "Wigtime" (*FMY*) breaks up the marriage of Reuel and Teresa while she is still a high-school student; later, Reuel's infidelity with another high-school student threatens to break up Margot's own marriage to him. She finds herself visiting Teresa, the woman she had earlier wronged, who is now a patient at the County Home and forever lost in the time when she was a war bride on the boat sailing to meet her husband in America. Margot recognizes that despite the momentous choices of her life—to seduce, marry, and then remain with Reuel—she is connected to a past pattern she cannot change: "'We're all on the boat,' says Margot" (274).

Margot's friend and confidant Anita mentally connects "war brides" with "war bonnets" when she hears this story. Her association suggests another sort of connection, one of key thematic importance in Munro's work: sexual love, as ever-present in Munro's writing as the image of flowing water, and just as dangerous.[17] Sex is a compelling but fearful mystery to the adolescent Del (*LGW*) and Rose (*BM*): Del's curiosity leads her to potential rape by Mr. Chamberlain, who masturbates in front of her ("Lives of Girls and Women"), while Rose's curiosity impels her to watch Shortie McGill raping his deformed sister Franny ("Privilege"). The dangers of sex for women especially impress the young in Munro's stories. Del scents coming from her Aunt Moira "a gynecological odor," marking her as "a likely sufferer from varicose veins, hemorrhoids, a dropped womb, cysted ovaries, inflammations, discharges, lumps and stones in various places, one of those heavy, cautiously moving, wrecked survivors of the female life, with stories to tell" ("Heirs of the Living Body," *LGW*, 34). Moira's daughter Mary Agnes, brain-damaged from being deprived of oxygen in the birth canal, has been assaulted by five boys who stripped her and left her lying naked in the cold mud of the fairgrounds (36). Ada Jordan's beloved teacher, Miss Rush, dies of childbirth in "Princess Ida" (*LGW*), as Callie's mother horrifically does in "The Moon in the Orange Street Skating Rink" (*PL*, 150); Ellie Grieves suffers constant pregnancies "full of vomiting fits that lasted for days, headaches, cramps, dizzy spells," terminating in miscarriages and stillbirths after "long, tearing labor[s]" ("Friend of My Youth," *FMY*, 11); Dotty in "Material" (*SIBMTY* 32) and Teresa in "Wigtime" (*FMY* 248) also report gory miscarriages. No wonder Jessie is "scared" when she sees Mrs. Cryderman's baby kick from inside her blotchy, swollen belly with its distended naval ("Jesse and Maribeth," *PL* 180).

As if rape and childbirth were not enough sexual danger, the female body itself is forever threatening Munro's characters with humiliation and exposure. The fear of tell-tale blood on the back of a skirt haunts the narrator of "Red Dress—1946" (*DHS* 150) just as it does Margot and Anita in "Wigtime," *FMY* 252; Rose fears the humiliation of dropping a Kotex pad in the high-school hall ("Half a Grapefruit," *BM*, 41). Dennis in "Bardon Bus" grotesquely reports that he envies women because "they are forced to live in the world of loss and death! Oh, I know, there's face-lifting, but how does that really help? The uterus dries up. The vagina dries up" (*MJ*, 122). Dawn Rose of "A Queer Streak" is so "affronted" by the onset of menstruation that she stops the flow for a year by sitting in the shallow, icy water of the creek; the neighbors believed the blocked, "bad blood" has affected her brain (*PL*, 215). The lonely Maria of "Five Points" endures the humiliation of paying boys to have sex with her in the shed behind her parents' store; her libido bankrupts her family and lands her in jail—while nothing is done about the boys who prostituted themselves (*FMY*, 40). Worse off yet are Marion Sherriff and Miss Farris (*LGW*), whose frustrated love lives lead them to drown themselves in the Wawanash River. Appropriately, it seems, Ada Jordan warns her daughter Del to use her brains and not be distracted by a man, lest she "get the burden, a woman always does" ("Lives of Girls and Women," *LGW*, 147).

The longing for sexual connection inflicts psychic as well as physical pain in Munro's fiction. Betrayal is common. From the high-school girl of "An Ounce of Cure" (*DHS*), so mortally depressed over being dropped by the boy who played Darcy in the Christmas production of *Pride and Prejudice* that she gets hugely drunk, to Prue, a woman in her forties who practices cynicism in a winningly lighthearted way and drowns her sorrow in a small revenge strategy of pilferage ("Prue," *MJ*), Munro's stories are filled with women—and sometimes men—who have "smelled love and hope" ("Providence," *BM*, 151) and suffer for it. Driven by a pursuit they may even view with disdain—Rose, for example, ruefully admits to herself that "nothing would do anymore but to lie under Simon, nothing would do but to give way to pangs and convulsions" ("Simon's Luck," *BM*, 170)—Munro's protagonists, like those in "Bardon Bus" (*MJ*), "Lichen" (*PL*), and "Circle of Prayer" (*PL*), often achieve only the loneliness and humiliation of being left. The spectacle of a woman waiting to hear from a man is a common occurrence: Edie lingers by the mailbox longing for a letter from her pilot ("How I Met My Husband," *SIBMTY*); at least one other woman besides the narrator writes desperate, unanswered letters to the same man in "Tell Me Yes or No" (*SIBMTY*); Rose's arranged tryst with Clifford in "Mischief" (*BM*) fizzles as she waits for him at an old logger's home; Matilda puts her life on hold for her English bigamist husband in "Oh, What Avails" (*FMY*). Once consummated, love brings an escalating sexual aphasia[18]: women under its influence can't study, like Del in *LGW*; can't read, like Rose in *BM*; can't work, like Roberta in "Labor Day Dinner" (*MJ*).[19] At its worst, sexual passion can leave behind an appalling residue of hatred: Rose's exhusband Patrick turns on her a "savagely warning face . . . a timed explosion of disgust and loathing" ("Beggar Maid," *BM* 100), and the sexually jealous Et in "Something I've Been Meaning to Tell You" (*SIBMTY*) may well have hastened her sister's suicide, poisoning her with invented stories of her ex-lover's exploits.

Despite its risks, though, connection is a subsuming theme of Munro's fiction. Her characters, particularly the writers among them, struggle to forge their identities in a crucible of connections: of one place to the next, of the past to the present, and of one sexual being to another. Her settings and plots rely heavily on Munro's memories of her own past, connected to and reassessed by her narrative personae. Munro's story-telling style, too, is a function of connection, its four coordinates a modernist narrative technique, a lapidary attention to point of view, a persistent undercutting of meaning, and a riveting attention to detail. Munro's narrative technique follows the modernist tradition of juxtaposing seemingly unconnected incidents to evoke a new meaning.[20] Contradictory narration, multiple storytellers, and leaps in time require the reader actively to connect and interpret divergent material. This is especially true of Munro's later stories, for her narrative strategies have grown more complex over time. "Labor Day Dinner" (*MJ*), for example, introduces multiple points of view. "The Progress of Love," title story of the 1986 collection, shifts the narrative action across three generations of contradictory stories, and "Fits" demonstrates virtuosic mastery of suspense, a technique put to good advantage throughout *FMY*.

Who tells the story is as important as how it is told, and Munro takes great care over point of view, frequently writing a story from both third- and first-person points of view before coming to a final decision about which is best.[21] Of special importance in her first-person narratives is the distance between the former (narrated) self and the present (narrating) self: for these retrospective narrators, realizations come only after the fact, if at all. Narrators, single or multiple, are likely to prove unreliable in Munro's fiction; she repeatedly considers where meaning lies,[22] and frequently undercuts even the epiphany-like closure of her earlier stories with speculation about the tricks memory plays. Rearranging details, confusing fact and fantasy, and simply mistrusting perception, Munro's characters stumble upon moments of "accidental clarity" ("Differently," *FMY*, 243) which lead nowhere and prove nothing.[23] Ada Jordan's stories of her mother, for example, differ from those of her brother Bill ("Princess Ida," *LGW*); her daughter Del does not know whom to believe.

A writing narrator in a Munro story, like the one in "Winter Wind," is likely to question the truth of her own tale:

And how is anybody to know, I think as I put this down, how am I to know what I claim to know? I have used these people, not all of them, but some of them, before. I have tricked them out and altered them and shaped them any way at all, to suit my purposes. I am not doing that now, I am being as careful as I can, but I stop and wonder, I feel compunction. (*SIBMTY*, 201)

The narrator of "The Progress of Love" realizes she has made up a memory, a vivid image of her father's protecting her mother as she fed her inherited money into the kitchen wood stove. Though the narrator knows the scene could not have occurred—her father did not even hear about the incineration until much later—"it seems so much the truth it is the truth" (*PL*, 30). Furthermore, this narrator allows her companion, Bob, to misapprehend her distress over his mentioning "sexual shenanigans" in her old home because, she says, "moments of kindness and reconciliation are worth having"—even when they're based on a lie (30). Needing to find the truth in a person or a situation, even when that "truth" contradicts the facts, Munro's characters, like most of us, "tell [themselves] stories in order to live."[24]

Balancing the uncertainty of meaning and truth in Alice Munro's fiction is her use of epitomizing detail, observation so meticulously acute that it gives the illusion of real life. The catalog is one of her techniques: the lists of what Ben Jordan, the "Walker Brothers Cowboy," sells (*DHS*, 3–4) and the detritus of Flo's life described in "Spelling" (*BM*, 180–81) clearly evoke one life in progress and one at its end. Catalogs can function as both vivid place descriptions and telling metaphors; Munro renders the emotional sterility of a bereaved couple's lives, for example, by revealing their collection of politically correct bibelots: "Eskimo prints and carvings, Indian wall hangings, ash trays, and bowls, and some gray porous-looking pots made by a former convict now being sponsored as a potter by the Unitarian Church" ("Memorial," *SIBMTY*, 211). Most memorable of all are Munro's arresting similes: "roots . . . like crocodiles" ("Walker Brothers Cowboy," *DHS*, 1); the grandmother who smells like "an old apple peel going soft" ("A Trip to the Coast," *DHS*, 183); a dead cow's open eye, like "an orange stuffed in a black silk stocking" ("Heirs of the Living Body," *LGW*, 37).

That the striking simile is the hallmark of Munro's style should come as no surprise: connection is her forte. Like the writer/narrator of "Meneseteung," Munro is curious, "driven to find things out, even trivial things. [Such people] will put things together. You see them going around with notebooks, scraping the dirt off gravestones, reading microfilm, just in the hope of seeing this trickle in time, making a connection, rescuing one thing from the rubbish" (*FMY*, 73). Munro's memories of her Ontario home, the Precambrian rock under her art, connect with her keen observation and descriptive skill to produce an uncannily accurate portrayal of how people conduct their lives. If she calls her identity as a writer into question with her series of ambivalent, self-conscious narrators, it is only because she would have us realize that none of us can be smug about labeling what we see "the truth." Like Millicent in Munro's recently published story, "A Real Life,"[25] we are bound to our past in ways we can't explain, ways which nevertheless shape our lives. And when it comes time to tell what has happened to us, as Munro herself has observed,[26] we edit the story as we go along.

Writings by Alice Munro

STORIES

"The Dimensions of a Shadow." *Folio*, April 1950: 4–10.
"Story for Sunday." *Folio*, December 1950: 4–8.
"The Widower." *Folio*, April 1951: 7–11.
"A Basket of Strawberries." *Mayfair*, November 1953: 32–33, 78–80, 82.
"The Idyllic Summer." *Canadian Forum*, August 1954: 106–07, 109–10.
"At the Other Place." *Canadian Forum*, September 1955: 131–33.
"The Edge of Town." *Queen's Quarterly* 62 (1955): 368–80.
"How Could I Do That?" *Chatelaine*, March 1956: 16–17, 65–70.
"The Time of Death." *Canadian Forum*, June 1956: 63–66.
"Good-By, Myra." *Chatelaine*, July 1956: 16–17, 55–58.
"Thanks for the Ride." *Tamarack Review* 2 (1957): 25–37.
"The Dangerous One." *Chatelaine*, July 1957: 48–51.
"Sunday Afternoon." *Canadian Forum*, September 1957: 127–30.
"The Peace of Utrecht." *Tamarack Review* 15 (1960): 5–21.
"The Trip to the Coast." In *Ten for Wednesday Night*, ed. Robert Weaver, 74–92. Toronto: McClelland and Stewart, 1961.
"Dance of the Happy Shades." *Montrealer*, February 1961: 22–26.
"An Ounce of Cure." *Montrealer*, May 1961: 26–30.
"The Office." *Montrealer*, September 1962: 18–23.
"Boys and Girls." *Montrealer*, December 1964: 25–34.
"Red Dress—1946." *Montrealer*, May 1965: 28–34.
"Postcard." *Tamarack Review* 47 (1968): 22–31, 33–39.
Dance of the Happy Shades. New York: McGraw-Hill, 1968. Includes "Walker Brothers Cowboy," "The Shining Houses," "Images," "Thanks for the Ride," "The Office" (revised), "An Ounce of Cure," "The Time of Death" (revised), "Day of the Butterfly"

(revision of "Good-By, Myra"), "Boys and Girls," "Postcard," "Red Dress—1946," "Sunday Afternoon," "A Trip to the Coast" (revised), "The Peace of Utrecht" (revised), and "Dance of the Happy Shades."

Lives of Girls and Women. Toronto: McGraw-Hill Ryerson, 1971. Includes "The Flats Road," "Heirs of the Living Body," "Princess Ida," "Age of Faith," "Changes and Ceremonies," "Lives of Girls and Women," "Baptizing," and "Epilogue: The Photographer."

"Material." *Tamarack Review* 61 (November 1973): 7–25.

"Home." In *New Canadian Stories: 74*, ed. David Helwig and Joan Harcourt, 133–53. Ottawa: Oberon, 1974.

"How I Met My Husband." *McCall's*, February 1974: 84–85, 123–27.

"Tell Me Yes or No." *Chatelaine*, March 1974: 34–35, 54, 56–60, 62.

"Forgiveness in Families." *McCall's*, April 1974: 92–93, 138, 140, 142, 144, 146.

Something I've Been Meaning to Tell You. Toronto: McGraw-Hill Ryerson, 1974. Includes "Something I've Been Meaning to Tell You," "Material," "How I Met My Husband" (revised), "Walking on Water," "Forgiveness in Families," "Tell Me Yes or No," "The Found Boat," "Executioners," "Marrakesh," "The Spanish Lady," "Winter Wind," "Memorial," and "The Ottawa Valley."

"Privilege." *Tamarack Review* 70 (1977): 14–28.

"Royal Beatings." *New Yorker*, 14 March 1977: 36–44.

"The Beggar Maid." *New Yorker*, 27 June 1977: 31, 35–41, 44–47.

"Providence." *Redbook*, August 1977: 98–99, 158–63.

"Accident." *Toronto Life*, November 1977: 61, 87–90, 92–95, 149–50, 153–56, 159–60, 162–65, 167, 169–73.

"Mischief." *Viva*, April 1978: 99–109.

"Wild Swans." *Toronto Life*, April 1978: 52–53, 124–25.

"Half a Grapefruit." *Redbook*, May 1978: 132–33, 176, 178, 180, 182, 183.

"The Moons of Jupiter." *New Yorker*, 22 May 1978: 32–39.

"Spelling" [excerpt]. *Weekend Magazine*, 17 June 1978: 24, 26–27.

"Characters." *Ploughshares* 4:3 (1978): 72–82.

"Emily." *Viva*, August 1978: 99–105.

"Honeyman's Granddaughter" [revision of "Privilege"]. *Ms*, October 1978: 56–57, 75–76, 79.

"Connection." *Chatelaine*, November 1978: 66–67, 97–98, 101, 104, 106.

Who Do You Think You Are? Toronto: Macmillan, 1978 [*The Beggar Maid: Stories of Flo and Rose* in the United States]. Includes "Royal Beatings" (revised), "Privilege" (revised), "Half a Grapefruit" (revised), "Wild Swans," "The Beggar Maid" (revised), "Mischief" (revised), "Providence" (revised), "Simon's Luck" (revision of "Emily"), "Spelling" (revised and expanded), and "Who Do You Think You Are?"

"A Better Place Than Home." In *The Newcomers: Inhabiting a New Land*, ed. Charles E. Israel, 113–24. Toronto: McClelland and Stewart, 1979.

"The Stone in the Field." *Saturday Night*, April 1979: 40–45.

"Dulse." *New Yorker*, 21 July 1980: 30–39.

"Wood." *New Yorker*, 24 November 1980: 46–54.

"The Turkey Season." *New Yorker*, 29 December 1980: 36–44.

"Prue." *New Yorker*, 30 March 1981: 34–35.

"Labor Day Dinner." *New Yorker*, 28 September 1981: 47–56, 59–60, 65–66, 70, 75–76.

"Mrs. Cross and Mrs. Kidd." *Tamarack Review* 83–84 (1982): 5–24.

"The Ferguson Girls Must Never Marry." *Grand Street* 1:3 (1982): 27–64.

"Visitors." *Atlantic Monthly*, April 1982: 90, 91–96.

The Moons of Jupiter. Toronto: Macmillan, 1982. Includes "Chaddeleys and Flemings, parts I ("Connection" [revised]) and II ("The Stone in the Field" [revised]), "Dulse" (revised), "The Turkey Season" (revised), "Accident," "Bardon Bus," "Prue," "Labor Day Dinner," "Mrs. Cross and Mrs. Kidd," "Hard-Luck Stories," "Visitors," and "The Moons of Jupiter" (revised).

"Miles City, Montana." *New Yorker*, 14 January 1985: 30–40.

"Monsieur les Deux Chapeaux." *Grand Street* 4:3 (1985): 7–33.

"Lichen." *New Yorker*, 15 July 1985: 26–36.

"The Progress of Love." *New Yorker*, 7 October 1985: 35–46, 49–50, 53–54, 57–58.

"Secrets Between Friends." *Mademoiselle*, November 1985: 116, 118, 120, 122, 124, 126, 128, 130, 228, 230.

"A Queer Streak. Part One: Anonymous Letters." *Granta* 17 (1985): 187–212.

"Eskimo." *Gentlemen's Quarterly*, December 1985: 262–66, 301–02, 304.

"Fits." *Grand Street* 5:2 (1986): 36–61.

"The Moon in the Orange Street Skating Rink." *New Yorker*, 31 March 1986: 26–36, 38–41, 44.

"A Queer Streak. Part Two: Possession." *Granta* 18 (1986): 201–19.

"White Dump." *New Yorker*, 28 July 1986: 25–39, 42–43.

"Circle of Prayer." *Paris Review* 100 (1986): 31–51.

The Progress of Love. Toronto: McClelland and Stewart, 1986. Includes "The Progress of Love" (revised), "Lichen," "Monsieur les Deux Chapeaux," "Miles City, Montana" (revised), "Fits" (revised, "The Moon in the Orange Street Skating Rink" (revised), "Jesse and Meribeth" (revision of "Secrets Between Friends"), "Eskimo," "A Queer Streak" (revised), "Circle of Prayer," and "White Dump" (revised).

"Oh, What Avails." *New Yorker*, 16 November 1987: 42–52, 55–56, 58–59, 62, 64–65, 67.

"Meneseteung." *New Yorker*, 11 January 1988: 28–38.

"Five Points." *New Yorker*, 14 March 1988: 34–43.

"Oranges and Apples." *New Yorker*, 24 October 1988: 36–48, 52, 54.

"Hold Me Fast, Don't Let Me Pass." *Atlantic Monthly*, December 1988: 58–66, 68–70.

"Differently." *New Yorker*, 2 January 1989: 23–36.

"Goodness and Mercy." *New Yorker*, 20 March 1989: 38–48.

"Wigtime." *New Yorker*, 4 September 1989: 34–50.

"Pictures of the Ice." *Atlantic*, January 1990: 64–73.

"Friend of My Youth." *New Yorker*, 22 January 1990: 36–48.

Friend of My Youth. New York: Knopf, 1990. Includes "Friend of My Youth," "Five Points," "Meneseteung," "Hold Me Fast, Don't Let Me Pass," "Oranges and Apples," "Pictures of the Ice," "Goodness and Mercy," "Oh, What Avails," "Differently," and "Wigtime."

"Carried Away." *New Yorker*, 21 October 1991: 34–61.
"A Real Life." *New Yorker*, 10 February 1992: 30–40.
"A Wilderness Station." *New Yorker*, 27 April 1992: 35–51.

ARTICLES AND LETTERS

"An Appreciation." *Room of One's Own: A Feminist Journal of Literature and Criticism*
9:2 (June 1984): 32–33.
"Author's Commentary." In *Sixteen by Twelve: Short Stories by Canadian Writers*, ed.
John Metcalf, 125–26. Toronto: Ryerson, 1970.
"The Colonel's Hash Resettled." In *The Narrative Voice: Short Stories and Reflections by
Canadian Authors*, ed. John Metcalf, 181–83. Toronto: McGraw-Hill Ryerson, 1972.
"Everything Here is Touchable and Mysterious." *Weekend Magazine*, 11 May 1974: 33.
"On John Metcalf: Taking Writing Seriously." *The Malahat Review* 70 (March 1985):
6–7.
"On Writing 'The Office.'" In *Transitions II: Short Fiction. A Source Book of Canadian
Literature*, ed. Edward Peck, 259–62. Vancouver: Commcept, 1978.
"An Open Letter." *Jubilee* 1 (1974): 5–7.
"What is Real?" *Canadian Forum*, September 1982: 5, 36. Reprinted in *Making It New:
Contemporary Canadian Stories*, ed. John Metcalf, 223–26. Toronto: Methuen, 1982.
"Working for a Living." *Grand Street* 1:1 (1981): 9–37.

INTERVIEWS

Frum, Barbara. "Great Dames." *Maclean's*, April 1973: 32, 38.
Gerson, Carole. "Who Do You Think You Are? Review-Interview with Alice Munro."
Room of One's Own 4:4 (1979): 2–7.
Gibson, Graeme. "Alice Munro." In *Eleven Canadian Novelists*, 237–64. Toronto: House
of Anansi, 1973.
Gzowski, Peter. "Interview with Alice Munro." *Morningside*. CBC Radio, 2 June 1987.
Hancock, Geoff. "An Interview with Alice Munro." *Canadian Fiction Magazine* 43
(1982): 74–114.
———. "Through the Jade Curtain." In *Chinada: Memoirs of the Gang of Seven*, 51–55.
Dunvegan, Ont.: Quadrant Editions, 1982.
Horwood, Harold. "Interview with Alice Munro." In *The Art of Alice Munro: Saying the
Unsayable*, ed. Judith Miller, 123–34. Waterloo, Ont.: Univ. of Waterloo Press, 1984.
Kroll, Jeri. "Interview with Alice Munro." *LiNQ: Literature in North Queenland* 8:1
(1980): 47–55.
Metcalf, John. "A Conversation with Alice Munro." *Journal of Canadian Fiction* 1:4
(Fall 1972): 54–62.
Murch, Ken. "Name: Alice Munro. Occupation: Writer." *Chatelaine*, August 1975: 42–
43, 69–72.
Sandor, Suzanne. "An Intimate Appeal." *Maclean's* 99:46 (17 November 1986): 12j–
121.
Scobie, Stephen. "A Visit with Alice Munro." *Monday Magazine* [Victoria], 19–25
November 1982: 12–13.
Slopen, Beverly. "Alice Munro." *Publishers Weekly*, 22 August 1986: 76–77.

Stainsby, Mari. "Alice Munro Talks with Mari Stainsby." *British Columbia Library Quarterly* 35:1 (July 1971): 27–30.

Struthers, J. R. (Tim). "The Real Material: An Interview with Alice Munro." In *Probable Fictions: Alice Munro's Narrative Acts*, ed. Louis K. MacKendrick, 5–36. Downsview, Ont.: ECW Press, 1983.

Twigg, Alan. "What Is: Alice Munro." In *For Openers: Conversations with 24 Canadian Writers*, 13–20. Madeira Park, B.C.: Harbour, 1981.

2. Remittance Men: Exile and Identity in the Short Stories of Mavis Gallant

In a semi-autobiographical series of stories in Mavis Gallant's *Home Truths*, the nineteen-year-old Linnet Muir returns to Montreal after a childhood spent, from the age of four, in a series of Canadian and American boarding schools. After probing various mysteries about her family and her past, such as the circumstances of her father's death, Linnet will, like Gallant, leave Canada permanently for France.

Linnet's investigations among her father's friends—she has broken with her mother—produce several versions of her father's death, and the girl soon decides that, whatever the actual events, "he had died of homesickness; sickness for England was the consumption, the gun, everything" (*Home Truths*, 235). Then, on a commuter train, she meets Frank Cairns, a remittance man, and in studying him, the young Linnet seems to find a key that unlocks the mystery of her father's life and her own.

The Remittance Man, Gallant writes, was a peculiarly British institution through which young people, usually sons, were sent away to live lives of puzzled exile, never quite understanding what had been their crime:

> Like all superfluous and marginal persons, remittance men were characters in a plot. The plot . . . described a powerful father's taking umbrage at his son's misconduct and ordering him out of the country. . . . Hordes of young men who had somehow offended their parents were shipped out. . . . Banished young, as a rule, the remittance man . . . drifted for the rest of his life, never quite sounding or looking like anyone around him, seldom raising a family or pursuing an occupation . . . remote, dreamy, bored. . . . They were like children waiting for the school vacation so they could go home, except that at home nobody wanted them: the nursery had been turned into a billiards room and Nanny dismissed. (266–68)

In characterizing the Remittance Man, Gallant describes not only Linnet's English-exiled father, lost to his child and himself, not only the child Linnet, exiled at an unusually young age to a particularly strict religious school by non-religious parents, but also something she sees in the Canadian personality. Here, everyone seems to feel a sense of loss; it is a country of children pushed from some all-but-forgotten nest: "I've never been in a country where there was so much gap between reality and dream," Gallant said of Canada in an interview. "The people's lives don't match up to what they seem to think they were and the people invent things or they invent backgrounds or they invent families. . . . In Europe, you can't invent because everyone knows too much" (quoted in *The Light of Imagination*, 8).

The Remittance Man also seems to provide a model for the array of characters, usually Canadian or English but sometimes Central European, who have been transplanted to the Paris or Riviera of Gallant's short stories. All are versions of the Remittance Man, for all, though we may not be shown the reasons, are adrift, not quite connecting with the life going on around them. All seem to have suffered some early loss, and, by choosing to live abroad, they are only acting out their inner sense of exile. Life abroad is Gallant's pervasive metaphor, not only for exile but also for the self-exile that inevitably follows. Paradoxically, life abroad also is seen by Gallant's characters as holding out the hope of a cure, at least for the symptoms of self-exile. In a foreign place, connection can be replaced by romance; identity can be replaced by a role that is necessarily simplified for foreign consumption. The unlucky among Gallant's characters are cured of their yearning for connection and identity; they find a role and disappear into it. The lucky may be forced, for a moment, to see themselves in their full infirmity; in this moment, though fleeting, they find home.

In Gallant's boarding-school story, "Thank-you for the Lovely Tea," included in the "At Home" section of *Home Truths*, Gallant goes even further than in the avowedly autobiographical Linnet Muir section to get to the source of self-exile. Here we see in its infancy the loss of the places and relationships that allow one to know oneself. In the story, three young girls leave school for a few hours to take tea with Mrs. Holland, the mistress of Ruth's father. The girls have suffered different types of loss: May has been separated from her identical twin, who has been sent to another school thousands of miles away; Helen has been torn from a large, warm, crude family by a relative who wants to make her a lady; Ruth's mother, for unknown reasons, has gone to live in another country and Ruth has been sent to school.

At tea, Mrs. Holland's tense insecurity rocks the girls' emotional boat, and their responses show how self-exile works at an early age. May, lost from her twin and mirror, is lost from herself. With no self to refer to, she imitates Ruth, whether in the choice of ice cream or her example of cruelty to Helen, even though it is much more painful to be the torturer than to be the victim. Helen, who has been trained to despise her crude family, desires only to stay in the controlled boarding-school world forever, even though her reverence for the school's stiff gentility makes her the butt of the other girls' jokes. She can't imagine facing life as an adult because she perceives the limbo into which she has been cast; she can never go back to being like her family, but also knows she will never really be a "lady" like the girls with more refined backgrounds. Ruth demonstrates the third and most chilling response. While the others, despite their defenses, blunder against their real feelings of loss during the tense tea, Ruth does not, for already she has learned to banish the suffering self by banishing all feeling. Afterwards she wonders if she would "ever care enough about anyone to make all the mistakes those around her had made" (*HT*, 16).

In "The Other Paris," the title piece of Gallant's first short-story collection, published in 1956, we see a young North American woman a few years older than the Ruth in "Thank-you for the Lovely Tea," but one who has not yet learned how to make herself invulnerable to the desire for some kind of feeling. At twenty-two, Carol Frazier is working in an American governmental agency in post–World War II Paris, and has just become engaged to marry her boss, Howard Mitchell. Carol is not in love with Howard and feels this to be a problem, but is certain she would be if only she could find the romantically picturesque Paris of films and songs. She believes that if she "spoke to the right person, or opened the right door, or turned down an unexpected street, the city would reveal itself and she would fall in love" (*The Other Paris*, 9).

Though she is young and "romantic," Carol has already unconsciously given up any claim to real connection or deep feeling, hoping only that charming scenes might allow her to manufacture a mood resembling love and happiness. But cold and dreary postwar Paris does not oblige. Rain obscures the sunrise from the steps of Sacré-Coeur, Christmas carols on the Place Vendôme are a crass media event, and a private concert to which Carol and Howard have been invited is a crashing failure as part of the ceiling comes loose, faulty wiring causes lights to flash off and on, and Carol is snubbed by her hosts, faded aristocratics who are not, after all, particularly picturesque.

Finally, and by accident, Carol does "turn down an unexpected street," finding herself in the impoverished and dirty room where her coworker, Odile, carries on an entirely uncharming affair with the refugee Felix, a boy much younger than Odile, closer in age to Carol herself. And suddenly Carol does feel something, moved by the love Felix and Odile have for one another, an emotion so authentic it does not need to be charming or even appropriate to survive. Suddenly, Carol imagines a powerful love, being loved herself, not by Felix, certainly not by Howard, but by "some other man, some wonderful person who did not exist." For a moment she feels as if she has "at last opened the right door," but quickly she retreats (*OP*, 28). A true Remittance Man, Carol cannot want love, she recognizes in this moment, only romance, and what she has just experienced must be scorned out of existence: "That such a vision could come from Felix and Odile was impossible. . . . she remembered in time what Felix was—a hopeless parasite. And Odile was silly and immoral and old enough to know better" (*OP*, 29). She decides to forget the real, troubling, fantasy-challenging Paris, to remember instead "the Paris of films." She will also, it is clear, forget her momentary "vision" of love and settle for a marriage that has, after all, begun in Paris and "would sound romantic and interesting, more and more so as time passed" (*OP*, 30).

In "The Remission," a story in Gallant's 1979 collection, *From the Fifteenth District*, Alec Webb, upon learning that he has an incurable disease, leaves England with his wife and children to die on the French Riviera. Here he goes into a three-year remission, and both illness and remission represent another "variety of exile."

Like the father in the Linnet Muir stories, Alec is a father who is there but not there, who can "see his children, but only barely." Cut off from adult responsibility by illness and exile, he had "left [them] behind" (*From the Fifteenth District*, 90). He cannot see his children because he has become a child again himself, aimless, of the moment, utterly unable to comprehend responsibility to others or self. Only romance moves him. For him, the momentary cure is not a romantic French scene, but a dream of lost England, as in the midst of a medical "crisis" he appears fully dressed—though having substituted a scarf for a tie—to watch the coronation of Elizabeth II on television.

Alec's condition is mirrored by the entire English colony; though they are not literally ill, all exist in a limbo similar to Alec's remission. Cut off from adult responsibility, they play at life, acting out parts. When they do have ailments, the local doctor notes, they are "nursery ailments; what his patients really wanted was to be tucked up next to a nursery fire and fed warm bread-and-milk" (*FD*, 82). They all have a story of themselves, a role they play, which, like Alec's illness, explains their existence in simple terms. The caricature of this is Wilkinson, who literally plays the role of an Englishman in films set on the Riviera. He plays "the chap with the strong blue eyes and ginger mustache . . . who flashed on for a second, just long enough to show there was an Englishman in the room," and who is good with a line such as "Don't underestimate Rommel" (*FD*, 95, 99).

The others, too, have invented roles for themselves, repeating their lines over and over. Mr. Cranefield is a writer of romance novels that repeat the story of the same imaginary blond couple. On his table are framed pictures of the young man and woman, actually illustrations cut from magazines, which are his models. "I keep them there," he says, "so that I never make a mistake" (*FD*, 87). There, too, is Mrs. Massie, who greets every newcomer with a gift of her *Flora's Gardening Encyclopaedia* (her name is not, of course, Flora) and the information, "It is by way of being a classic. Seventeen editions. I do all the typing myself" (*FD*, 107). And there is Major Lamprey, whose story is that he intends "to die fighting on my own doorstep" (*FD*, 112) no matter who invades the Riviera.

Alec's wife, Barbara, also finds release on the Riviera from adult responsibilities, as she ceases to function as a parent and takes on a new, simpler role as Wilkinson's lover. It is as if, having moved up in English society by marrying Alec, Barbara now sees that a pretend upper-class Englishman is even better than a real upper-class Englishman.

While characters in many of Gallant's stories are offered the chance to break out of their roles—though they seldom take that opportunity—that does not happen here. "The Remission" is not really about the adults, but about the children and how they are formed. Here we see both the hopeless end and the near-hopeless beginning of the life of exile that obsesses Gallant's work. The children are deserted not only by their parents, who are lost in their own childish dreams, but also by the other adults who are equally useless in their vague offers of help, possible typing jobs, pocket money from gardening, or advice: "You will grow up you know" (103). As exile produces adults who cannot act as adults, it also produces children who cannot act as children. As the adults slough off responsibility for fantasy, the children are crushed by the need to find something to tell them who they are. They cling to their one useful memory of their father, his warning that it is dangerous to smoke in bed. "'Death is empty without God,' one of the children shrills at the funeral. 'Where did that come from?' everyone asks. 'Had he heard it? Read it? Was he performing? No one knew'" (*FD*, 111). Their mother is only an embarrassment, and they study her "as if measuring everything she still had to mean in their lives" (*FD*, 102). As if aware that they have been stunted, the children now "talk as if they are still eleven or twelve when Alec had stopped seeing them grow," and to others they look like "imitations of English children—loud, humorless, dutiful, clear" (*FD*, 103). Slowly the children begin to lose identifying characteristics. They no longer look much alike, or like their parents. They stop fighting, stop speaking to each other, barely seem to know each other. Though the details of these children's exile are different from Ruth's in "Thank-you for the Lovely Tea," the result is the same. Banished young from adult concern, they are miniature versions of the Remittance Man. Until the children can invent roles for themselves, they are defined by nothing but loss, and the only way to banish the suffering is not to feel. At fourteen, Molly knows "there was no freedom but to cease to love" (103).

In her collection *Overhead in a Balloon*, 1979, Gallant no longer sees Europe through the eyes of romantic North Americans or British. The Paris of these stories is seen rather "through the imaginations of native or long-time Parisians [who] see Paris as the centre and the circumference of the universe." This is a Paris in which "old buildings are being demolished, trees cut down, whole blocks gutted to make way for parkades or shopping centres" (*LI* 140). The politics of the seventies and eighties also infuses the stories and, in "Speck's Idea," art dealer Sandor Speck loses one gallery to demolition when his block is replaced by a parking garage. Another gallery is bombed by Basque separatists who mistake his gallery for a travel agency exploiting their country.

But though we now have a more sophisticated and knowledgeable view of Paris, it is still the city of dreams, still holding out the promise of an answer, a cure. In Speck's Paris, there will always be an audience for lectures on such topics as "the secrets of Greenland," because "in no other capital city does the population wait more trustfully for the mystery to be solved, the conspiracy laid bare" (*Overhead in a Balloon*, 12). And even longtime residents like Sandor Speck cannot help glimpsing Paris as a movie set in a "French film designed for export . . . the lights . . . reflected, quivering, in European-looking puddles" (*OB*, 5).

Sandor Speck is both a native Parisian and another variety of exile, the second generation in France of a family coming from somewhere in central Europe. Even if he is on his native soil, we still recognize him as a

Remittance Man, a "character in a plot" he must work to invent. As Carol Frazier believes love will follow if she can contact romantic and picturesque Paris, Sandor Speck—whose failures in marriage have caused him to all but give up on love in its ordinary form—believes he will feel secure if he can connect himself to wealthy and powerful Paris. Thus, he moves his gallery to an exorbitantly expensive building and seeks out opportunities to rub elbows with the prominent. Though Speck is more sophisticated than Carol, he is not much more successful at inducing Paris to provide the settings he believes will allow him to manufacture the feelings he needs. The "upper class hush" of his expensive neighborhood is continually shattered by left-wing attacks on a right-wing bookstore, and the sirens of ambulance and police. And his exalted neighbors, counts and princes, are "spiteful, quarrelsome, and avaricious" (*OB*, 1), even more disappointing than the aristocrats who snub Carol.

Speck does not maneuver Paris into the proper settings much better than does Carol, yet he is more practiced at manipulating his love life, which, after the breakup of his last marriage, appears to be subsumed by art. He is in search of an unknown painter who will give the art industry the "revitalization" editorials are calling for, and will benefit his finances and reputation. Much as Mr. Cranefield of "The Remission" lovingly depicts the perfect blond couple in romance after romance, Speck sits down with a pencil and pad to draw up specifications for the perfect French artist:

> A French painter, circa 1864–1949, forgotten now except by a handful of devoted connoisseurs. Populist yet refined, local but universal, he would send rays, beacons, into the thickening night of the West, just as Speck's gallery shone bravely into the dark street. (*OB* 8)

The artist's politics must be drawn with painstaking precision. Should the artist have been a member of the Resistance? The Resistance is no longer chic; its youngest members are in their seventies. But what about state-subsidized museums, where Resistance work would be prized, possibly even required? Speck solves the problem by writing: "1941—Conversations with Albert Camus" (*OB*, 9). As Speck lists on his pad all the characteristics of the perfect artist, only one little thing is missing, a person who can be made to embody these characteristics, the artist himself, "the tiny, enduring wheel set deep in the clanking, churning machinery of the art trade" (*OB*, 14).

Speck happens to hear of an obscure, long-dead artist named Hubert Cruche ("Don't get rid of the Cruches," Speck advises the acquaintance who mentions his collection of the artist's work), and Speck sets out to the Paris suburbs to court the painter's widow. He approaches her, as he always approaches artists' widows, through a "subtle approximation of courtship" (*OB*, 18), winning her to his will by listening to her accounts of life with the great man and of her own vital importance to his work, as he pretends to eat the sickening sweets she adores. He plays his role, never forgetting his mission, to take possession of the Cruche paintings she owns and, most importantly, to appropriate the myth of the artist, which he will then rework into the myth he needs. Indeed, Speck's attempt to win the widow and her dead husband, his mixing of "courtship" and "bargain hunting," serves as a metaphor for the attempt to love, or find something resembling love, in much of Gallant's work. And while Carol Frazier and even Barbara Webb, the adulterous wife of "The Remission," are still romantics, Speck knows himself to be more advanced, a bit of a whore: "It was true that his feeling for art stopped short of love; it had to. The great cocottes of history had shown similar prudence." He is a whore for the obvious financial reasons but also, as probably is the case with most whores, as with remittance men, he does not dare feel: "For what if he were to allow passion for painting to set alight his common sense? How would he be able to live, then, knowing that the ultimate fate of art was to die of anemia in safe-deposit vaults?" (*OB*, 29). And how to love if love, too, is always locked away to die?

But Speck's manipulations crash to a halt as the artist's Saskatchewan-born widow, Lydia, not only fails to respond to Speck's "pseudo courtship" in the expected way but also seems to see through his manipulations with bewildering ease. Deprived of the role he relies on, Speck is suddenly naked and vulnerable. The ridiculous old widow in her shabby house now appears "as a tough little pagan figure, with a goddess's gift for reading men's lives." As Carol, exposed to the passionate Felix, has a sudden vision of being loved, Speck has "a quick vision of himself clasping her knees and sobbing out the betrayal of his marriage" (*OB*, 24), the last thing in the world he meant to include in his assault on the widow.

Indeed, Speck has met his match. Far from being charmed and manipulated, Lydia seems to take Speck's approach as an opportunity to arrange a contest between him and an Italian art dealer, the prize being Lydia, her paintings, and the myth of Hubert Cruche. Speck responds by "falling back on the most useless of all lover's arguments . . . 'I was there first'" (*OB*, 41).

In the end, after seeming to favor the Italian, Lydia comes back to Speck and allows him to mount the first Cruche show. The show will then proceed to Milan, where, hyped by the prestige of a Paris opening, Lydia's paintings will probably sell for a great deal of money. Speck sees that his choices had been arranged for him, either to go second and to seem to be taking crumbs, or to go first and set up the fortunes of his rival. He elects to go first.

Speck is thoroughly defeated by Lydia and knows it. Still he is granted a moment of uplift at the end of the story, an uncommon event in Gallant's work. The weather improves, there's a cab at the cab stand as he returns from Lydia's suburb by bus (having wrecked his Bentley upon hearing about his rival), and he "seemed to have passed a mysterious series of tests, and to have been admitted to some new society, the purpose of which he did not yet understand. He was a saner, stronger, wiser person" than he had been before (*OB*, 47). He decides to sign his own catalog introduction to the Cruche show, rather than ghosting it for some important person as he had intended.

The tests Speck has passed are similar to those undergone by many of Gallant's adult characters. He has been given the dangerous opportunity to see through his own pretenses to the real self beneath. When this danger presents itself to Carol Frazier she flees, preferring a life of empty illusion to catching a glimpse of her desire for and fear of connection. Speck emerges, however, as from the wreck of his Bentley, battered but alive, and feels an immense if fleeting sense of relief. He is, after all, unlike Carol, momentarily alive. And he has formed a real, if tawdry, connection, finding with Lydia "a patch of landscape they held in common—a domain reserved for the winning, collecting, and sharing out of profits, a territory where believer and skeptic, dupe and embezzler, the loving and the faithless could walk hand in hand" (*OB* 46). This is not much of a connection, and it is steeped in irony. But it is something, and more than Speck had before he met Lydia.

Lydia's secret weapon, that which allows her to wreck Speck's sophisticated and practiced charade, seems to be the bleak power she derives from her childhood in Saskatchewan. Speck, as he recognizes, has been both "defeated" and paradoxically, albeit briefly, saved by a "landscape," the "cold oblong" of a province (*OB*, 43). Similarly, in "The Ice Wagon Going Down the Street," a story collected in the "Canadians Abroad" section of *Home Truths*, the urbane, lost Peter Frazier is momentarily ripped out of his self- and life-denying pretenses by Agnes Brusen, a plain little woman, "poor quality really" from a small town in Saskatchewan (*HT*, 129). It is as if in Gallant's world pretense will spring up given the slightest nourishment of culture or sophistication. While it may be true, as Gallant says, that "in Europe you can't invent because everyone knows too much," this does not stop her characters from going to Europe and devoting themselves to the attempt. Integrity, ironically, seems to be nurtured in those cold and barren Canadian landscapes where buds of pretense, along with almost everything else, freeze on the vine.

In "The Ice Wagon Going Down the Street" Peter Frazier is doing the postwar "international thing," but not very successfully. He is a true Remittance Man, living on the crumbs of a fortune which was made by his great-grandfather, a Scottish immigrant to Canada, guarded by his grandfather, and used up by his father. Like the British abroad in "The Remission," Peter is cut off from the wealth and prominence that is the only birthright he can imagine, and he tries to reinvent himself by playing a role. He poses as the devil-may-care son of a wealthy and powerful family, entirely unable to take the ordinary struggles of life seriously, living as if his work were a "pastime, and his real life a secret so splendid he could share it with no one except himself" (*HT*, 115). He has married Sheilah, a flashy woman of a poor background, one who supports Peter's view of himself as "a peacock" and does what she must to lure opportunity their way as Peter dreams his life.

Banished from his birthright, Peter is banished again, this time from the Canadian society of Paris. Having made an ass of himself at an important wedding—he is only beginning to grasp that he must be a little careful—his connections fail him. He is shipped out to glamourless Geneva, where he makes a faint pretense of working at a clerk's job while he and Sheilah await their next opportunity. His superior in this job is a young Canadian woman, Agnes Brusen, whose education and career is the product of great sacrifice by her Norwegian immigrant family. Though Peter finds her unattractive, boring, even ridiculous—she cannot begin to function at one of Sheilah's mock-elegant little dinners—he is also afraid of her. In her, he recognizes his own proud, ambitious, fervent immigrant ancestors, feels the "charge of moral certainty round her, the belief in work, the faith in undertakings." And in her presence, he glimpses himself as the played-out end of the line. She is at the beginning, and she seems to say to him, "You can begin, but not begin again" (*HT*, 118).

Nothing much happens between Peter and Agnes. Unused to alcohol, she gets drunk at a party, and Peter is ordered by the hostess, a woman he now understands he must cultivate, to take her home. Lonely and frightened, sickened by the swinishness of the supposedly refined and educated world her family has sacrificed so much for her to reach, she clings to him briefly and tells him *her* story, how, as a child in a big family, she would get up early on a summer morning to watch the ice wagon going down the street. In such a moment, she tells him, "it's you, you, once in your life alone in the universe. You think you know everything that can happen. Nothing is ever like that again" (*HT*, 132). And that is really all. Peter returns home, where Sheilah is just coming in all aglow, having apparently seduced a man she met at the party and thereby secured Peter the promise of a job in Ceylon.

Nothing happens. But for the rest of Peter's life, as he and Sheilah knock around the world, "always on the fringe of disaster, the fringe of a fortune," still viewing themselves as "peacocks," he thinks of Agnes almost as if they had once been lovers. Like Peter, Agnes is also in exile, lonely and lost. Unlike Peter, she has a little shred of home to hold onto, a moment when the self was felt, that gives her an integrity Peter has never had. She shares this with him, and sometimes throughout the years he allows himself to use it, to feel how it would be to have a self:

> Nothing moves except the shadows and the ice wagon and the changing amber of the child's eyes. The child is Peter. He has seen the grain of the cement sidewalk and the grass in the cracks, and the dust, and the dandelions at the edge of the road. He is there. He has taken the morning that belongs to Agnes, he is up before the others, and he knows everything. There is nothing he doesn't know. (*HT*, 134)

This knowledge does not have much to do with the life Peter must live. In real life as he knows it, morning is all about "dimness and headache and remorse and regrets" (*HT*, 134). In real life, Peter doesn't know what he would do with Agnes's morning. Finally, self-knowledge and the integrity that comes with it is as bleak and barren as a slab of sidewalk in a dusty Saskatchewan town. Gallant's characters don't want it at this price. But in cherishing Agnes and her morning, Peter, one of the lucky in Gallant's world, is able at least to know what has been lost.

Writings by Mavis Gallant

NOVELS

Green Water. Green Sky. Boston: Houghton Mifflin, 1959; London: Andre Deutsch, 1960.
A Fairly Good Time. New York: Random House, 1970; London: Heinemann, 1970.

COLLECTED STORIES

The Other Paris. Cambridge, Mass.: Houghton Mifflin, 1956; London: André Deutsch,
1957; reprint, Freeport, N.Y.: Books for Libraries Press, 1970. Includes "The Other
Paris," "Autumn Day," "Poor Franzi," "Going Ashore," "The Picnic," "The Deceptions
of Marie-Blanche," "Wing's Chips," "The Legacy," "One Morning in June," "About
Geneva," "Señor Pinedo," and "A Day Like Any Other."

My Heart is Broken: Eight Stories and a Short Novel. New York: Random House, 1964;
London: Heinemann, 1965 (as *An Unmarried Man's Summer*); Toronto: PaperJacks,
1974. Includes "Acceptance of Their Ways," "Bernadette," "The Moabitess," "Its
Image on the Mirror" (short novel), "The Cost of Living," "My Heart is Broken,"
"Sunday Afternoon," "An Unmarried Man's Summer," and "The Ice Wagon Going Down
the Street."

The Peonitz Junction: A Novella and Five Short Stories. New York: Random House, 1973;
London: Jonathan Cape, 1974. Includes "The Peonitz Junction," "The Old Friends,"
"An Autobiography," "Ernst in Civilian Clothes," "O Lasting Peace," and "An Alien
Flower."

The End of the World and Other Stories. Toronto: McClelland and Stewart, 1974. Introduction by Robert Weaver. Includes "The Other Paris," "The Picnic," "About Geneva,"
"An Unmarried Man's Summer," "The End of the World," "The Accident," "Malcolm
and Bea," "The Prodigal Parent," "The Wedding Ring," "New Year's Eve," and "In the
Tunnel."

From the Fifteenth District: A Novella and Eight Short Stories. New York: Random House,
1979; London: Jonathan Cape, 1980. Includes "The Four Seasons," "The Moslem
Wife," "The Remission," "The Latehomecomer," "Baum, Gabriel, 1935–( )," "From
the Fifteenth District," "Potter," "His Mother," and "Irina."

Home Truths: Selected Canadian Stories. Toronto: Macmillan, 1981; New York: Random
House, 1985. Introduction by Mavis Gallant. Includes "Thank You for the Lovely Tea,"
"Jorinda and Jorindel," "Saturday," "Up North," "Orphan's Progress," "The Prodigal
Parent," "In the Tunnel," "The Ice Wagon Going Down the Street," "Bonaventure,"
"Virus X," "In Youth Is Pleasure," "Between Zero and One," "Varieties of Exile,"
"Voices Lost in Snow," "The Doctor," and "With a Capital T."

Overhead in a Balloon: Stories of Paris. Toronto: Macmillan, 1986; New York: W. W.
Norton, 1988. Includes "Speck's Idea," "Overhead in a Balloon," "Luc and His Father," "A Painful Affair," "Larry," "A Flying Start," "Grippes and Poche," "A Recollec-
tion," "Rue de Lille," "The Colonel's Child," "Lena," and "The Assembly."

In Transit. Markham, Ont.: Penguin Books, 1988; New York: Random House, 1989.
Includes "The Wedding Ring," "The End of the World," "An Emergency Case," "April
Fish," "The Statues Taken Down," "The Circus," "When We Were Nearly Young," "The
Hunter's Waking Thoughts," "The Captive Niece," "Malcolm and Bea," "Vacances
Pay," "In Transit," "By the Sea," "Careless Talk," "In Italy," "Better Times," "A
Question of Disposal," "Good Deed," "Questions and Answers," and "New Year's Eve."

COLLECTED ESSAYS

Paris Notebooks: Essays and Reviews. Toronto: Macmillan, 1986.

PLAYS

What Is To Be Done? Dunvegan, Ont.: Quadrant, 1983.

UNCOLLECTED STORIES

"Good Morning and Goodbye." *Preview* 22 (December 1944): 1–3.
"The Flowers of Spring." *Northern Review* 3 (June–July 1950): 31–39.
"Three Brick Walls." *Preview* 22 (December 1944): 4–6.
"Madeline's Birthday." *The New Yorker*, 1 September 1951: 20–24.
"Thieves and Rascals." *Esquire*, July 1956: 82, 85–86.
"A Short Love Story." *The Montrealer*, June 1957: 48–60, 62.
"The Old Place." *Texas Quarterly* 1 (Spring 1958): 66–80.
"Rose." *The New Yorker*, 17 December 1960: 34–37.
"Crossing France." *The Critic* 19 (December–January 1960–61): 15–18.
"Two Questions." *The New Yorker*, 10 June 1961: 30–36.
"Night and Day." *The New Yorker*, 17 March 1962: 48–50.
"One Aspect of a Rainy Day." *The New Yorker*, 14 April 1962: 38–39.
"Willi." *The New Yorker*, 5 January 1963: 29–31.
"Paola and Renata." *Southern Review* 1 (Winter 1965): 199–209.
"A Report." *The New Yorker*, 3 December 1966: 62–65.
"The Sunday after Christmas." *The New Yorker*, 30 December 1967: 35–36.
"The Rejection." *The New Yorker*, 12 April 1969: 42–44.
"The Burgundy Weekend." *The Tamarack Review* 76 (Winter 1979): 3–39.
"A Revised Guide to Paris." *The New Yorker*, 11 February 1980: 30–32.
"From Sunrise to Daybreak (A Year in the Life of an Émigré)." *The New Yorker*, 17 March 1980: 34–36.
"The Assembly." *Harper's*, May 1980: 75–78.
"Dido Flute, Spouse to Europe (Addenda to a Major Biography)." *The New Yorker*, 12 May 1980: 37.
"From Gamut to Yalta." *The New Yorker*, 15 September 1980: 40–41.
"Europe by Satellite." *The New Yorker*, 3 November 1980: 47.
"Mousse." *The New Yorker*, 22 December 1980: 31.
"French Crenellation." *The New Yorker*, 9 February 1981: 33.
"This Space." *The New Yorker*, 6 July 1981: 35.
"On With the New in France." *The New Yorker*, 10 August 1981: 31.
"La Vie Parisienne." *The New Yorker*, 19 October 1981: 41.
"Siegfried's Memoirs." *The New Yorker*, 5 April 1982: 42–43.
"Treading Water." *The New Yorker*, 24 May 1982: 33.

3. Anne Hébert: The Tragic Melodramas

Despite a writing career of over five decades and many prestigious awards[1]—including the Prix Femina for *Kamouraska*—Quebec author Anne Hébert is little known by general readers in the United States, although excellent translations of her works are available. And with the exception of specialists in French or Canadian studies, there appears to be limited American scholarly interest in her oeuvre.[2] This is unfortunate, not only because Hébert is an important figure in the development of French Canadian literature but also because her characteristic combination of dramatic intensity of plot and extraordinary delicacy of characterization has produced a distinguished body of fiction that explores complex themes of victimization by circumstance which should be of special interest to female readers and feminist critics.

With the exception of *The Silent Rooms* 1974 (*Les Chambres de bois* 1958) and *Héloïse* 1982 (*Heloise* 1980), which concentrate on inner psychic processes, Hébert's fiction conceives of space in terms of the effect of the restrictive mores of small, tightly knit communities on the options of her protagonists, both male and female. That influential space is further contracted because community influence conditions individuals through the miniaturized world of family relationship. The effect of this process is most frequently experienced as the inadequacy of gender roles to the fulfillment of human needs and to the completion of personal identity. In her finest works, *Kamouraska* 1973 (*Kamouraska* 1970), *Children of the Black Sabbath* 1977 (*Les Enfants du Sabbat* 1970), and *In the Shadow of the Wind* 1983 (*Les Fous de Bassan* 1982),[3] Hébert explores these preoccupations though the evocation of memory from the point of view of a later date, a perspective which clearly demonstrates an absence of progressive improvement.

In December of 1839, in the northern section of Canada known as Kamouraska, one Achille de Tachy, the hereditary *seigneur* of the region, was brutally murdered by the lover of his young wife.[4] The crime, as reconstructed in Anne Hébert's best-known novel,[5] has all the elements of popular melodrama—the damsel threatened with death at the hands of a depraved villain, the dramatic rescue by the virtuous hero, a lurid appeal to emotion, and cliff-hanging suspense[6]—but *Kamouraska* has something more: the dignity, heightened seriousness, and fatedness of classic tragedy. The paradoxical mingling of these high and low genres accounts for the extraordinary force combined with astute subtlety that is the distinguishing feature of Anne Hébert's fiction.

In addition to formulaic plots full of action and sentimental strife, melodramatic works share a fundamental pattern: John G. Cawelti argues that they are narratives which occur in a world full of the conflict and misfortune we associate with the "real world," but in melodrama that dangerous world seems, finally, "to be governed by some benevolent moral principle." A reader can be certain that, by the end of the melodrama, evil will be punished and good rewarded. It is precisely on the basis of this assertion of preponderant morality that Cawelti opposes melodrama to tragedy: "It is not a tragic or naturalistic world because no matter how violent or meaningless it seems on the surface, the right things will ultimately happen." Melodrama, then, is conservative literature that endorses the "essential 'rightness' of the world order."[7] But the "right things" do not happen in Hébert's narratives; it is precisely the moral conservatism of melodrama that is countered by the tragic dimension of her fiction.

Tragedy is similar to melodrama in presenting an exciting story, "a causally related series of events in the life of a person of significance," but differs meaningfully in that this chain of events culminates in "an unhappy catastrophe, the whole treated with great dignity and seriousness."[8] Tragedy, in contrast to melodrama, by withholding the reassurance of a happy ending that endorses the status quo, effects a revolutionary critique of the world order it represents.

While presenting the sensationalist events related to melodrama that humanize her best work, Anne Hébert refuses all sentimental resolution of the conflicts that generate her plots, thereby attaining for her fiction the critical effect of tragedy. While presenting an intriguing, story-like world, Hébert's work also anatomizes the social and psychological conditions which produce individual suffering.

This striking generic duality is generated and replicated in Hébert's oeuvre at the levels of both theme and style. For a thematic example we shall return to the novel *Kamouraska*. The antithesis notable in Hébert's literary technique is matched by motifs of unrelenting opposition throughout this novel, in which the central problem of the protagonist is the choice between virtue and passion, as expressed through her two marriages. Raised in strict Catholic conventionality by her three maiden aunts and her widowed mother, seventeen-year-old Elisabeth d'Aulnières is eager to experience the freedom of personal expression and barely apprehended passion she perceives in her young suitor, Antoine Tassy, and naively expects for herself in married life. She is unprepared, however, for the unrestrained freedom and destructive passion that is the exclusive prerogative of her husband. "My son is a good boy," her mother-in-law explains. "But he will go off on his little flings once in a while. . . . Simply ignore it. . . . Don't forget that, and you're sure to be happy. No matter how my son mistreats you..." (*Kamouraska*, 74).[9] Antoine's little flings include the accidental death of a fifteen-year-old paramour he has run off with, and his mistreatment includes an attempt to slip Elisabeth's head into a noose so that she can join her husband in a double suicide. Antoine is murderous and manic-depressive, and the privileges of his social and marital roles serve to authorize the full expression of his dangerous tendencies. The reader is sympathetic to Elisabeth's affair with a responsible American doctor, Antoine's converse, but the lovers' plot to murder Antoine plunges them into a depravity of passion comparable to his.

In her second marriage, to Monsieur Jerome Rolland, Elisabeth opts for the other alternative: strict virtue. When the story opens, she is the mother of eleven children and has been a proper wife for eighteen years, but during the deathwatch for her failing husband, Elisabeth must confront the inadequacy of the second option:

> This man can only protect me just so far. When the fright becomes too real, when it fills the night with the noise of a rattling old wagon, Jerome is caught up in it just like me. Caught in the trap, the two of us. That's what marriage is. (*K*, 18)

Elisabeth's apprehension of the unsolvable nature of her problem during the period of Rolland's moral illness plunges her into the hallucinations, reverie, and nightmares that retrace the course of her past life and form the substance of the novel. The figurative oppositions presented through her history—the innocence of young Elisabeth opposed to the sexual sorcery of her maid Aurélie, the license of the French North against the propriety of the Anglicized South, the erratic violence of Antoine and the niggling regularity of Jerome—can neither annul nor balance one another. The narrative of petty distrust in the second marriage frames in counterpoise the narrative of unsavory passion in the first. There is no resolution to the female dilemma of Elisabeth's life as a nineteenth-century French Catholic wife: her world allows no accommodation of passion to respectability. And the antithetical options of *Kamouraska* typify the irresolvable contradiction of psycho-social experience in all Hébert's novels.

Style also contributes to the effect of irreconcilable alternative. From her earliest *contes* collected in *The Torrent* 1973 (*Le Torrent* 1950, 1967) through the novels of later years, Hébert has skillfully combined sensational incident with a modified French symbolist aesthetic to produce an analysis, at the same time exquisite and naturalistic, of the moral predicament of women and men whose fates are determined by their environments.

To account for the literariness of Hébert's work one only has to look as far as her family background. As the daughter of noted literary critic Maurice Hébert,[10] she reports that she received a thorough grounding in syntax and grammar as well as encouragement as a poet.[11] And she was also greatly influenced by the artistic milieu and death of her cousin the poet Hector de Saint-Denys Garneau, an advocate of the French Christian revival movement. As a member of his literary set during her years of higher education in Quebec City, Anne Hébert, four years his junior, became acquainted with the work of the French avant-garde, especially that of Paul Élouard, Jules Supervielle, and René Char. After a bout with rheumatic fever in 1928, which damaged his heart, Garneau eventually withdrew into solitude to write poetry and journals that demonstrate obsessive concern with puritan conscience, death, and the symbolism of "complete absorption in the reality of an imaginary world."[12]

Garneau died in 1943. During the winter and spring of 1945, Hébert was working on her first important prose work, "The Torrent," a novella; like the later *Kamouraska* it was based on an actual and grisly incident.[13] She may have been denouncing Garneau's mental isolation, was probably rejecting the deep and traditional Catholic faith which she had shared with her influential cousin, and was certainly forecasting the themes and style of her future fiction.

The plot of this work concerns a young man whose utter seclusion, psychological confusion, and withdrawal into suicidal imagination is conditioned by his mother's renunciation of the world and her attempt to fashion for him a priest's vocation out of the same principle of bitter rejection. When François, the young man, tries to thwart the mother's domination, she manages to destroy his hearing, a symbolic loss which irrevocably separates him from any connection to normal existence. The mother's unmitigated cruelty first denies François an ordinary childhood and finally robs him of common language. Eventually, the protagonist's overpowering anger circuitously produces the death of the mother, and his unbearable loneliness generates an attachment to a young woman whose only motive for the relationship turns out to be robbery.

This stark and melodramatic tale acquires its psychological depth from the manner of its telling. Presented entirely from the point of view of the disturbed young man, the logic of the conventional narrative is shattered initially by his limited ability to comprehend his mother's inhumanity, and ultimately by his passionate rage. "As a child," he explains,

> I was dispossessed of the world. By the decree of a will higher than my own, I had to renounce all possession in this life. I related to the world by fragments, and only at those points that were immediately and strictly necessary, and which were removed from me as soon as their usefulness had ended. I was permitted the scribblers which I had to open, but not the table on which they lay; the corner of the stable which I was to clean, but not the hen perching on the windowsill; and never the countryside which beckoned through the window. I could see the large hand of my mother when it was raised towards me, but I could not perceive my mother as a whole from head to foot. I could only feel her terrible size, which chilled me. (*T*, 7)

Since François is "dispossessed" of any but the most truncated version of "the world" as it is customarily perceived, he must employ a means of presenting his story that conveys the fragmentary, but vivid, effect of his own experience. His style turns out to be similar to that of the French symbolist poets, whose project was defined for Americans by Edmund Wilson:

> Every feeling or sensation we have, every moment of consciousness, is different from every other; and it is, in consequence, impossible to render them through the conventional and universal language of ordinary literature. Each poet has his unique personality; each of his moments has its special tone, its special combination of elements. And it is the poet's task to find, to invent, the special language which will alone be capable of expressing his personality and feelings. Such a language must make use of symbols; what is so special cannot be conveyed by direct statement or description, but only by a succession of words, of images, which will serve to suggest it to its reader.[14]

In the last paragraphs of the story, the young man uses a waterfall, the torrent of the title, which has been employed throughout to objectify his intense inner reactions, to symbolize his plight:

> I am weary of watching the water and the fantastic images within it. I am hanging over the brink as far as I can. I am within the spray. My lips taste its flatness.
>
> The house, the long and dour house, born of the soil, is dissolving within me also. I can see it crumbling in the backwash. My mother's room is turned upside down. . . .
>
> I am leaning out as far as possible. I want to see down in the gulf as far as I can. I want to lose myself in my own adventure. My sole and fearful wealth. (*T*, 47)

François's response to his own desperate situation—the irresolvable conflict between a need to control his own destiny and intolerable isolation—is probably suicide, but the reader's sympathy for this melodramatic expedient must be a result of the symbolic rendering attained through word and image, exemplified here by the torrent. The waterfall is presented as an object of the young man's physical environment and also as a representation of the roaring that he has been aware of inside his head since the onset of his deafness, but it stands for much more. A symbol of dissolution of his old existence and the creative force necessary for any implementation of a new one, inhuman yet attractively mobile, awesome yet familiar, the torrent is a summarizing emblem for François's internal confusion and anger and his external submersion in the deterministic world of his mother's destructive religiosity.

But Hébert, while making use of the nuanced precision of symbolism, also striking in her own skillful poetry,[15] rejects, especially in her subsequent fiction, its characteristic solipsism[16] by putting it in the service of identifiable, if extreme, human passions. The divergence, as in this example, of melodramatic plot and the subtle psychology of verbal expression, the distinctive mark of the Hébertian text, serves also to effect a dialectic between the totalizing forces of family, society, and religion associated with the conventional morality invoked by melodrama and the fragmented individual psyche rendered in the sharp phenomenological detail Hébert adapts from the symbolist method.

But Anne Hébert characteristically refuses the new synthesis which is supposed to resolve any classic Hegalian dialectic. Instead, the needs and desires of her heroes and heroines relentlessly collide with larger pressures they cannot comprehend, contain, or disregard. The resulting collision is expressed in the murders and passionate confrontations of melodrama. In fact, Hébert has stated that violence "is certainly a will not to accept the world as it is, as one has made it. To wish to remake it is a violent gesture."[17] Thus, Hébert consciously strips melodrama of its ameliorating effect to employ violent incident as a form of resistance to determinant conditions. The very irresolvability of conflict, registered in the symbolic expression of her characters' dilemmas, of which the waterfall image is a good example, lends Hébert's work its tragic dimension.

This confrontation of the individual with the implacable demands of a dominating society produces three distinct but interrelated schools of strong readings of Hébert's work: analysis of Québeçois concerns, religious explication, and feminist interpretation, which this study will conclude by demonstrating.

Religion and patriotism have been the fundamental tenets of a traditional French Canadian culture trying to maintain its separate identity against the English majority. Apparent in all the arts, these precepts are particularly evident in literature. "Literature must be chaste and pure, religious in character, evangelistic in aim; it must reveal a people's devotion and faith, its noble aspiration and heroic traits"—Maurice Cagnon's description of the principles of the nineteenth-century movement known as the *École Patriotique de Québec* defines French Canadian literary tendencies well into the twentieth century.[18]

It is with reference to this dogma that we must understand Hébert's accomplishment as the deliberate creation of what is at once literature and anti-literature. The demands for positive presentation of French Canadian life were traditionally met in stories extolling the contentment of country life and the moral superiority of the French family.[19] It is obvious that the retreat of the mother in "The Torrent" to the acrimonious labor of the farm is a rejection of the idyll of traditional ideology.[20] Similarly, her brutal relationship with the son is a rejection of family solidarity, as is the dangerous perversion of married life in *Kamouraska*. It has been the special task of the twentieth-century Québeçois writer, according to Cagnon, to "search for a people's tangible identity" in place of "an outworn idealization of a collective self."[21]

Besides rejecting "outworn idealization" in her fiction, in her manifesto "Poetry Broken Solitude," Hébert appears to be calling for the artistic creation of "a people's tangible identity" by French Canadian writers: "Our country is at the age of the earth's first days. Life here is still to be discovered, still to be named . . . this obscure discourse of ours, as yet a murmur in the darkness."[22] And in addition to thematic reformation, Hébert is credited with enriching the realistic and psychologic repertoire of modern French Canadian fiction with a poetic prose previously unknown in Québeçois fiction.

If Hébert seems to be practicing the interrogation of the ideology of traditional literature, she has also been understood as an important antagonist of traditional religion. Much of the endeavor to retain a separatist identity has taken the form of a celebration of French Catholicism in the face of English Protestantism. But religion as portrayed by Hébert has also operated as a repressive force. Lorraine Weir sees the central issue of Hébert's writing as confrontation with the implications of Jansenist Catholicism[23]: she "perhaps more than any other modern Quebec writer analyzed the profound impact of the Jansenist cosmology upon a cross-section of human types representing its most thoroughly bound victims."[24] Certainly, analysis of religious restriction is the central project of *Children of the Black Sabbath*, a work in which the narrow observance of Catholic practice in the Quebec Convent of the Sisters of the Precious Blood is confounded by an outbreak of witchcraft.

The novel reflects church domination of everyday life in general society:

> The temperance society, directed by the priest, made us swear never to drink. Just as women swear obedience and submission to their husbands. While the children solemnly pledge, as soon as they are ten years old, to renounce Satan, his pomp and his works. . . . We are bound by promises and bans. We are subjected to the climate's hardships and the poverty of the soil. We are held in check by the fear of hell. (*Children of the Black Sabbath*, 124)

The antithesis of such restraint is embodied in the novel by Adélard and Philomène, moonshiners, devil-worshipers, and child rapists, who tempt the villagers away from the severity of their faith.

The ancient struggle between the two extremes of regulation and freedom is reenacted in the visions of Sister Julie, a novice in the convent and the abused child of these licentious parents. In the 1940s, she relives her childhood in the 1930s—a short history of isolation, incest, and degradation. The irony of *Children of the Black Sabbath* is that life in the convent—comprised of incidents of inflated jealousy and petty vengeance, culminating in the act of infanticide—is certainly no more deplorable than Julie's corruption outside its protective walls. The plot presents the results of Julie's choice of the control afforded by her mother's witchcraft over the constraint legislated by her Mother Superior's religion. When the Sisters of the Precious Blood, who probably establish Julie's occult powers through their superstitious belief in them, implore her to satisfy their secret wishes, they also express the religious theme of the novel: in an atmosphere of inhumane repression, "God or the devil. What's the difference?" (*C*, 130).

This melodramatic story, which draws on legendary accounts of witch-craft in Canada,[25] achieves its tragic impact from the particularity and poignancy of the presentation of Julie's double abasement and the ambiguity of the complex layers of the immorality of religious vocation, which it in no way resolves. Anne Hébert is, however, not a writer who has confined her interests to one religion, group, or location. *Heloise* is set in France, for example, and *The Shadow of the Wind* locates its study of social restriction in a settlement of American emigrés to Canada.

Griffin Creek, a fictive community located between Quebec and the Atlantic Ocean, was founded by British loyalists escaping the American revolution, and in 1986, the period in which the frame story is set, still retains its ethnic and religious isolation. The strict Protestantism and rigid insularity of this community of only four families and their descendants conditions the melodramatic-tragic events of the summer of 1936 which are the subject of the novel.

The emotional austerity of all aspects of life in Griffin Creek finds its fullest articulation in destructive gender roles conditioned by family experience. "Hairy and evil, rifles over their shoulders, the men around here always seem to want to kill some living creature," muses Nicholas Jones, whose own sense of male entitlement takes the form of bullying his eternally childlike female servants:

> Without ever having been women, now they are suffering the change of life with the same look of astonishment as their first periods. . . . I have taught them to live frugally, in the fear of my displeasure. I like to see them tremble when I reprimand them. (*The Shadow of the Wind*, 2)

This grotesque parody of patriarchal relation appears to be the result of the involuted family cycle of the community. Indisputable paternal privilege creates maternal resentment, which takes the form of the mothers' coldness towards sons. The sons, in turn, both deeply idealize and profoundly resent their distant mothers, a dichotomy which finds expression in the combination of attraction to women and brutal domination of women, through which the son replicates the violence characteristic of his father.

This destructive pattern is evident in the life of Stevens Brown, the protagonist of the novel. Having left Griffin Creek five years before, as the result of a fight that is the culmination of years of abuse by his father and a history of frigid relations with his mother ("It's surprising that she can even bring live babies into the world, from such a glacial belly you'd expect only corpses... [S, 62]), twenty-year-old Stevens has returned to try to confront the implications of his heritage: "to organize my memories, arrange images, quite simply to split myself in two and still remain myself. To be able to witness the life I have lived without danger" (S, 61).

But in such a life, danger is unavoidable. Two beautiful young cousins, fifteen and seventeen, on the flickering verge of womanhood, must bear his ingrained attraction-repulsion. On 31 August 1936, Stevens's love/hate comes to fruition in the rape of one of the girls and the murder of both, an overt expression of the inner dynamic of this community, which, according to its last patriarch, caused the dispersal of "the chosen people of Griffin Creek" (9). Characteristically, the Reverend Nicholas Jones, whose musings introduce the novel, blames a woman for this catastrophe. Nora Atkins, the fifteen-year-old cousin, whom her Uncle Nicholas has been trying to seduce throughout the fateful summer, recalls: "He seems to want to hit me. He says that through me, sin has entered Griffin Creek" (S, 93).

Unlike *Kamouraska*, which is recounted through the voice of Elisabeth, the female protagonist, *In the Shadow of the Wind* is related in separate sections from the perspectives of many of the participants and witnesses to the story. In an epigraph from Shakespeare to the book which includes the voice of Stevens's idiot brother, Hébert alludes to the evident influence of William Faulkner's *The Sound and the Fury* on the style of this novel. Her use of poetic symbolism throughout, and the particular poignancy of the voices of the two young women are also reminiscent of Faulkner's *As I Lay Dying*, which in monologues by both Dewey Dell and Addie Bundren connect female passion with death.

As in *Kamouraska*, the tragedy of *In the Shadow of the Wind* is that women's desire can lead only to death, not to mature female experience, for which there is no model and no hope in the world of Griffin Creek. The title is a reference to a maternal heritage which warns Olivia Atkins, the seventeen-year-old cousin, of the fated danger of her burgeoning attraction to Stevens: "You mustn't, they all say in the shadow of the wind, mothers and grandmothers on the alert." But Olivia, slain before she had the opportunity to experience the inevitable disappointments of her female predecessors, in her transmuted form of the foam on the waves of a feminine sea, is the voice speaking of the dream of something else: "Only love could turn me into a full-fledged woman, communicating as an equal with my mother and grandmothers in the shadow of the wind" (*S*, 63). In Griffin Creek, however, love appears to be impossible.

Because he has no future, Nicholas Jones decides to honor the past by constructing a "gallery of ancestors": "I beget my father, who begets my grandfather in his image . . . and so on to the first image. . . . In black suits and white linen my ancestors loom into sight like the flat figures on playing cards" (*S*, 10). The interchangeability of these figures represents the thorough determination of the patriarchal community they created.

Jones cannot even imagine his women forebears, a project he relegates to the twin servants, who themselves embody the collective restriction of women. But art allows even them the imagination of unrestrained alternatives:

> Set loose with brushes and paint . . . the twins have slathered the wall with cascades of lace, with flounces, checks and dots and multicolored stripes, with flowers, leaves, red birds, blue fish, crimson seaweed. A few heads of women emerge from it all wearing hats, quills, ribbons, some with only one eye or lacking a nose or mouth, and more alive than any dream creature who has haunted Griffin Creek since the mists of time. (*S*, 11)

In a like manner, Anne Hébert uses art to imagine, because it cannot yet record, the transformation of the narrow world of gender identity. She employs symbolist prose to transmute the perpetrators and victims of her melodramatic plots into tragic figures—memorable, serious, and complex—irrevocably at odds with the psycho-social structures of societies that their ultimate defeats serve to censure.

Writings by Anne Hébert in English Translation

NOVELS AND STORIES

Children of the Black Sabbath. Trans. Carol Dunlop-Hébert. Don Mills, Ontario: Musson, 1977.
Heloise. Trans. Sheila Fischman. Toronto: Stoddart, 1982.

Kamouraska. Trans. Norman Shapiro. New York: Crown, 1973.

In the Shadow of the Wind. Toronto: Stoddart, 1983.

The Silent Rooms. Don Mills, Ontario: Musson, 1974.

The Torrent: Novellas and Short Stories. Trans. Gwendolyn Moore. Montreal: Harvest House, 1973.

COLLECTED POETRY

Poems. Trans. Alan Brown. Don Mills, Ontario: Musson, 1975.

The Tomb of the Kings. Trans. Peter Miller (includes both French and English). Toronto: Contact, 1967.

4. Margaret Atwood: Reflections in a Convex Mirror

"This is how I got here," Rennie says at the opening of Margaret Atwood's fifth novel, *Bodily Harm*.[1] Six of Atwood's first seven novels are narrated by women who, even when cast into positions of victimization, respond creatively to life through rational self-understanding. Their memories, often presented in fully dramatized flashbacks, intertwine with present events, revealing the persistence and pressure of the past. The examined life, Atwood implies, is a necessary first step toward becoming a three-dimensional person in a world that continues to cast women into two-dimensional roles, offering flat mirror images. Atwood's protagonists narrate their struggles toward a sense of identity, which, in her recent novel *Cat's Eye*, is symbolized by a convex mirror, suggesting the power of an eye that sees things whole and a mind that comes to terms with the world through words or through art.

Endowed with Atwood's own high-spirited, cynical wit—wit which is omnipresent in her interviews and nonfictional writing—and her ability to cast a cold eye on social absurdities and the jests of fate, Atwood's women characters are clear-eyed and unromantic. Their wit and candor make these narrative voices appealing, so much so that Atwood has attained extraordinary popularity for a serious literary writer. And yet the common thread that ties together Atwood's novels, that they are women's confessional narratives on a theme as old as "Know thyself," is not immediately evident because her work is so diverse in tone and type. Although most of her novels are set in Toronto, a city she establishes on the map of world literature as Joyce did Dublin, Atwood never enters the same fictional world twice. Her work includes, for example, social satire (*The Edible Woman*), an "anti-gothic" novel (*Lady Oracle*), a dystopic future fiction (*A Handmaid's Tale*), and a richly developed portrait of the artist as a middle-aged woman (*Cat's Eye*).

Atwood makes use of a full palette of tones and effects, as though there were many empty spaces to be painted in—portraits of women whose stories are as yet untold and a national literature just beginning to discover itself. In her controversial 1972 handbook to Canadian literature, called *Survival*, Atwood urges her fellow writers to break free of a Canadian literary heritage that she describes as "undeniably sombre and negative," its grimness "a reflection and chosen definition of the national sensibility."[2] She characterizes earlier Canadian literature as a dreary record of victimization and struggle whose "true and only season" is winter (*S*, 49). Seeing herself as working against a literary tradition dismal as a continent of snow, Atwood writes novels filled with color, wit, transformation, and surprise while retaining that key theme of the national literature, the struggle to survive.

Atwood implies that women must pay a price for survival. She prefaces her first novel, *The Edible Woman*, with an epigraph taken from instructions for making puff pastry: "The surface on which you work (preferably marble) . . . should be chilled throughout the operation."[3] From her first novel on, Atwood's narrators speak in voices purged of sentiment. If a woman wants to become more than a walking two-dimensional reflection of social expectations, sentiment must be jettisoned, along with all pre-packaged romantic dreams, including—this is the hardest—the dream of love. In Atwood's novels male-female relations, mother-daughter relations, as well as friendships between women are portrayed as problematic at best, tyrannous at worst. Atwood's narrators are nearly always isolated figures, distanced from others, disturbingly, by their most admirable assets: their honesty, desire for autonomy, and need for self-expression.

Escape and metamorphosis are the dominant themes of Atwood's first three novels, which have to do with rescuing her women characters from the marriage plot—the one that makes marriage the prescribed end of every woman's story—and putting them in motion in stories of their own devising. The delightful satire *The Edible Woman* serves as a prelude to all the novels. Feeling consumed, eaten up by social expectation, Marian McAlpin flees like a hunted rabbit from her fiance Peter and his camera that will "fix" her. Her engagement deprives her of the ability to narrate her story in the first person. She experiences a Kafkaesque sense of entrapment, at one point even hiding terrified in the dust under a sofa like Gregor Samsa. Marian's less-than-indifferent affair with Duncan, a frail, emotionless graduate student who likes to iron blouses, leads to a doleful anti-wedding night with Duncan as an anti-Peter, exorcizing the dream of marriage. In *Surfacing*, a melodrama set in the Canadian wilderness, the anonymous narrator, having been forced by her married lover into a traumatizing abortion, undergoes a descent into madness and nearly drowns; human language having failed her, she reverts to a wordless animal state in which she meets the ghosts of her parents. Joan Foster in *Lady Oracle* runs away, "drowns" herself, and changes her name and appearance. A writer of "costume gothics," Joan is the most vibrant and independent of the first three narrators, and the escapes and metamorphoses of her picaresque life create high comedy.

After staging a fake drowning, Joan Foster hides out in Terremoto, Italy, where she narrates her whole story: her miserable childhood; her flight to England, where she lives with a Polish count, a closet writer of nurse novels; her marriage to the unimaginative Arthur, a leftist agitator; her separate careers as a writer of gothic novels and as a feminist poet; her affair with the Royal Porcupine, an avant-garde "artist" who displays frozen road kills; and her escape from blackmailer Fraser Buchannan via the staged drowning. Metamorphosis is Joan's guiding principle. An escape artist, she performs her disappearing act several times over, compartmentalizing her multiple identities and fleeing from one to another so as not to get stuck in any of them. She also writes escape fiction, providing absurdly romantic vicarious experiences to readers who are as disappointed in reality as she is. Joan deliberately casts things off—weight, clothes, hair, noms de plume, a husband, lovers—living her life in counterpoint to the stories of her gothic heroines, who by an ineluctable formula are destined to acquire things, husbands and rich estates, after undergoing *their* harrowing experiences.

Lady Oracle, like much modern comedy, tells a near-tragic story: a life of marginality and the burden of stealth are the price that Joan must pay for her radical need for freedom. On the first page of the novel she says that her life tends "to scroll and festoon like the frame of a baroque mirror."[4] That Joan chooses the frame rather than the mirror as a metaphor for her wayward life is indicative of the difficulty she has seeing herself as a whole person. Her longtime identification with the Lady of Shalott also indicates a marginal relation to reality. "I fabricated my life, time after time," Joan says: "the truth was not convincing" (*LO*, 167). The Lady's entrapment in a looking-glass world in Tennyson's poem and her death as a punishment for turning her gaze on the real world may be read as a metaphor for the confinement of women's psyches to a secondary, ready-made reality in Tennyson's century and our own. Joan escapes one such world only to enter others; she cannot get beyond the looking-glass.[5]

All through her early years, Joan wages war with her rigid, impossible mother, using her own body as a battleground and obesity as her weapon. Joan's mother's triple mirror, in which she performs frightening rituals with make-up, does not offer her three-dimensionality; rather, it reveals her to young Joan as a three-headed monster (*LO*, 70). When Joan's Aunt Lou leaves her a legacy contingent on losing weight, Joan does so and escapes to England, beginning to look into mirrors herself for the first time, though she possesses a meager sense of the boundaries of her own body. Later, Joan even acquires a triple mirror herself, and in the experiments with automatic writing which she performs to "act out" a scene for a costume gothic, she "goes into" the mirror by candlelight in search of spiritual enlightenment, even getting stuck there (*LO*, 247). But although she seeks identity beyond the mirror—"the thing, the truth or word or person that was mine, that was waiting for me"—Joan does not find it (*LO*, 247). All she fishes out from the mirror is the first of many second-rate poems about a Shalott-like goddess figure, poems which, humorously enough, launch Joan's career as a popular feminist poet, the author of *Lady Oracle*. At the end of the novel Joan comes to the realization that her detested mother, now dead and haunting her, is the dark face behind hers in the mirror, the enchanted Lady of Shalott (*LO*, 263). Forgiving her mother, Joan shatters a window through which she sees her mother's astral body and then cuts her feet dancing on the broken glass. This elaborate epiphany is meant to be humorous, not convincing; Joan makes it up to satisfy her romantic need to act out a colorful story.

Joan is a transitional figure among Atwood's narrators. Having mastered the art of escape, she seems destined to go on casting off identities without finding one she can live with. The comic futility of her never-ending metamorphoses is an ironic commentary on our modern propensity, men and women alike, to suppose we can make ourselves over, become a new and self-made person with a little effort, a change of clothing or a haircut—a watering down of an earlier Protestant ethos that dictated the necessity of killing off the old self and being made anew in the spirit. It is in church, albeit a bizarre spiritualist temple, that Joan hears the parable about the pessimistic caterpillar, who expects to crawl into a dark place and die, and the optimistic caterpillar, who expects to be reborn with gorgeous wings (*LO*, 117). Joan comments cynically, "So what if you turn into a butterfly? Butterflies die too" (*LO*, 125). Joan is remembering her humiliation in dancing school when, as a fat child rehearsing "Butterfly Frolic," she looks "more like a giant caterpillar than a butterfly" in her costume, and the teacher Miss Flegg cruelly makes her play the part of a big mothball instead (*LO*, 48). As a fat teenager Joan wears violently bright colors, mainly to torment her mother, and in her later slimmer phase she puts on and casts off butterfly clothes of velvet and silk just as she dresses and undresses the victim-heroines of her costume gothics. Despite, or because of, her early mortifications, Joan has learned to play at metamorphosis like a game.

The high comedy of *Lady Oracle* derives mostly from Joan's lively narrative voice. She offers seemingly rational explanations for all the mad things she does, and she presents herself as teary and distraught, like one of the heroines of her fictions, when it is perfectly evident that she is an immensely robust person who loves to take risks. Joan's narrative is delightful rather than tragic because, although Joan never knows herself, the reader sees that all her selves, her avatars, are projections of her own fertile, restless imagination, which finds outlet not in one self but in creating them all.

Atwood adheres to an anti-romantic tone in her next novel, *Life Before Man*, which follows the streams of consciousness of three characters associated with the Royal Ontario Museum. A work of grim psychological realism, *Life Before Man* traces the last stages of disintegration of the marriage of Nate and Elizabeth Schoenhof and Nate's joyless affair with the young paleontologist Lesje. Elizabeth, the most complex of the three characters, probably deserves a novel of her own, since the subplot of the intergenerational struggle between Elizabeth and her hated Aunty Muriel is the most dynamic material in the novel. Atwood wisely returns to the single woman narrator in *Bodily Harm*.

In *Bodily Harm* and *A Handmaid's Tale*, the prevalent theme of the first three novels, of escaping entrapments to find one's identity, takes a much darker turn. The narrators of both novels are literally imprisoned by corrupt, abusive political systems run by men who are abetted by women. Although Atwood's earlier work includes characters who are political activists, treated both lightly and seriously, *Bodily Harm* insists that one must bear witness to the brutal injustices of modern global politics; the examined life demands that one cultivate a political and moral conscience. Rennie Wilford's story traces the growth of such a conscience.

A freelance journalist who writes trendy trash on "lifestyles" for papers and magazines, Rennie thinks of herself as an "expert on surfaces" who never writes about serious issues.[6] "Other people make statements," she says; "I just write them down" (*BH*, 15). In a variation of a theme of *Lady*

Oracle, Rennie often writes about "make-overs," instant metamorphoses through change of costume and hair style. Her live-in boyfriend Jake, a designer of packages, wants to repackage her in glamorous clothes. "It's all there underneath," Jake says; "I just want to bring it out" (*BH*, 105). In *Bodily Harm*, the notion of being made over, of the inner self's being brought out, takes on serious implications as Rennie undergoes a journey which, unlike Joan's picaresque escapades, leads her into a heart of darkness that profoundly changes her.

Traumatized by a partial mastectomy, the subsequent defection of her lover Jake, a futile infatuation with her surgeon Daniel, and a break-in in her apartment, Rennie travels to the united islands of St. Antoine and St. Agathe in the Caribbean to escape reality, get some sun, and write a travel piece. The islands immediately seem menacing, with mysterious figures hidden behind mirrored sunglasses. Soon Rennie is drawn into the convoluted post-colonial politics of the country, implicating herself by unknowingly transporting a machine gun for the local communist party and by having a brief affair with Paul, a big-time drug dealer and gunrunner for the party. Dr. Minnow, an honest leftist reformist running for president, continually urges Rennie to report "what you see" on the island to newspapers in Canada (*BH*, 133). It is her duty, he insists, to witness what is happening before her eyes. When Rennie explains that her subject is only "lifestyles . . . what people wear, what they eat," Minnow beams, "That is all I wish," alluding to the conspicuous poverty of the island (*BH*, 136). Minnow is shot in the back during a premature leftist rebellion fomented by the local CIA agent solely for the purpose of ensuring that the right-wing Ellis, a corrupt Papa Doc figure, will win the election. Rennie is thrown into a cell in a fortress prison along with Lora, the white mistress of the duped communist candidate Prince, known as The Prince of Peace. (Both Prince and Minnow, whose campaign symbol is the fish, are martyred Christ figures.) After suffering wretched deprivations in the dungeon and witnessing the savage beating of Lora, Rennie is perhaps rescued by a Canadian diplomat and perhaps lives to tell her story; the reader cannot be certain because the ending is narrated in future tense.

Whether or not Rennie escapes, she tells her story in the novel as one who is deeply changed by her experiences. She has become three-dimensional, a person who pays attention: "she will pick her time; then she will report" (*BH*, 301). The novel begins with first-person narration but quickly switches to third, suggesting objectivity, and it is narrated in very short scenes, like a journalistic piece. Past-tense memories of Toronto life are interwoven with present-tense events on the island to highlight phases of Rennie's moral growth. First Rennie has to leave behind the cruel Calvinistic moral calculus of her hometown, Griswold, which insists that all misfortunes are deserved, brought upon oneself. Then she has to eschew the frivolous amorality of artsy, trendy Toronto in order to assume full stature as a responsible human being. Rennie could not undergo such a change, of course, were she not already a serious person, one hiding what she calls her "closet honesty" (*BH*, 64).

Rennie's heightened political awareness as a witness and victim of oppression causes her to make connections among all sorts of bodily harm: pornographic violation of women, Jake's sadistic love-talk, the torture she witnesses on St. Antoine, the humiliations she undergoes in the prison, and the abusive life story told by Lora. Even Rennie's mutilation by cancer surgery is a benevolent form of bodily harm, linking her with all who suffer loss. When Rennie grasps the hand of the bloodily beaten Lora, trying to will her back to consciousness, Rennie has learned the lesson that no one escapes bodily harm and that "there's no such thing as a faceless stranger" (*BH*, 299).[7] Although Rennie remains as solitary as Atwood's other narrators, she has opened to the necessity of human connectedness. Having come to full understanding that no woman is an island, Rennie leaves behind a lifestyle and gains a life.

Rennie is the first of Atwood's narrators to approach becoming a serious writer or artist: Marian in *The Edible Woman* is a market researcher, the narrator of *Surfacing* a commercial illustrator, Joan a writer of escape fiction. But what if Rennie were denied a pen to write with and what if blinders were put upon her so that she were perpetually islanded and unable to bear witness? This almost unthinkable situation takes the reader into the world of *The Handmaid's Tale*, where eyes and seeing have negative connotations. The handmaids are not allowed to look at the world, but they are constantly watched. Offred is allowed no mirror in her room at the Commander's house, because she could kill herself with a piece of it, but she can see her red-robed figure reflected and distorted in the convex mirror on the stairs. That menacing mirror, which "bulges outward like an eye under pressure" is a reminder of the constant watchfulness of the state, symbolized also by the tattoo of four digits and an eye branded upon each handmaid's ankle and the white-winged eyes on the police vans, vehicles of the death squads.[8] In a continuation of the Lady of Shalott theme, the handmaids are not allowed to look directly upon the world or at one another; the state owns all the mirrors. Offred meets the eyes of Ofglen looking straight at her in a plate-glass window only in that moment when Ofglen musters the courage to tell her about the resistance movement. Offred finally gets a full look at herself in the mirror when the Commander takes her to the illicit nightclub and she sees herself as a "travesty" of a woman, almost like a female impersonator, in the garish feather-fringed costume and cheap make-up in which he has dressed her (*THT*, 330). This reflection is important because, of course, women's gender is travestied in every part of the color-coded society of Gilead, where Offred has been reduced to a "sacred vessel," a walking womb.

One of the pleasures of reading this haunting dystopic novel is the gradual realization that the book provides a satiric vision of the past history of women. Indeed, Atwood has frequently made the point in interviews that there is no detail in this novel that does not correspond to real conditions past or present. The deprivation of jobs and property and one's own name; the denial of rights under the state; the social isolation of women and their separation into rigid, subservient roles of wives, wombs, workers, and whores—these things have all happened and in some places are still happening. The enforced whispers of the handmaids, their boredom and their lack of reading materials, of pens, of ways of telling their stories, add up to a familiar aspect of the history of women, their silences. Thus, though mirrors are forbidden to Offred, her world is itself a mirror in which anyone can see reflected large parts of our history, along with the caveat that there is no guarantee that history will not repeat itself.

Speaking illicitly into thirty tape cassettes, Offred tells her story despite the great odds against her telling it. For one thing, she has constantly to fight against the internalized voice of her instructor Aunt Lydia, a mouthpiece of the state who blames women for their own victimization. Moreover, memory is a minefield for Offred because of her grief for her husband and child, although the recollections of their normal family life throw Gilead's horrors into sharper relief. Memory brings out forbidden connections, and so does metaphor. Offred cannot allow herself to make a connection, for example, between the blood of the hanged political martyrs, her own red robe, and the red tulips in Serena Joy's garden because metaphors, by carrying meaning from one thing to another, force us to look at life steadily and entire. Offred must stay literal in order to stay sane: "Each thing is valid and really there. It is through a field of such valid objects that I must pick my way" (*THT*, 44–45). Nonetheless, such metaphors linger in her mind in repressed form, so that later she thinks of

Serena's flower garden as "subversive." The flowers, naturally sexual, burst forth like the organic life that Gilead distorts and perverts. Looking at the garden, Offred thinks, "Whatever is silenced will clamor to be heard, though silently," and those words resonate through the novel (*THT*, 196).

Offred, speaking in first person and present tense, is Atwood's first self-conscious narrator. She constantly speaks to the imagined "you," the audience in her head, commenting on the pain of narrating her own story and the impossibility of shaping it—how can she, with so little chance of controlling her destiny? Offred draws the reader into the dangerous enterprise of her narrative:

> A story is like a letter. *Dear You*, I'll say. Just, *you*, without a name. Attaching a name attaches *you* to the world of fact, which is riskier, more hazardous: who knows what the chances are out there of survival, yours? I will say *you*, *you*, like an old love song. (*THT*, 53)

Offred has a sophisticated understanding of the nature of narration. She knows that every story is a "reconstruction" that cannot get at life itself with perfect exactitude (*THT*, 173). In contrast to the many-colored, lyrical narrative style of the artist Elaine in Atwood's next novel, *Cat's Eye*, Atwood creates for Offred a prose style so poignantly plain that the occasional flashes of color or sharply observed images—a flower, an egg—stand out in austere beauty. And the reader is invited to share with Offred her sensuous delight in words as palpable, tactile things when the Commander absurdly invites her to an illicit game of Scrabble: "I hold the glossy counters with their smooth edges, finger the letters. The feeling is voluptuous. This is freedom. . . . *Limp*, I spell. *Gorge*. What a luxury. The counters are like candies, made of peppermint, cool like that" (*THT*, 180). Amusingly, these particular words, *limp* and *gorge*, subconsciously give Offred a sense of power over her sexual tormentor, the Commander, but Atwood has a serious point. Nowhere else has she stated it so clearly: words are precious, they are freedom, and they are not to be taken for granted.

Atwood turns from the life of buried, smothered women to examine the other side of the coin, the woman who has fought her way to freedom as an artist. Elaine Risley in *Cat's Eye*, Atwood's semi-autobiographical novel, can escape the situations that entrap her, like Joan Foster, and like Rennie and Offred she is driven to bear witness to what she knows and feels.

Again, memory is the key to identity. But unlike any of the previous narrators, Elaine finds the means to shape her most painful memories into works of art, although she too pays the price of isolation.

Cat's Eye has been justly praised for its faithful re-creation of the sights, sounds, smells, and tactile sensations of a childhood in Toronto in the 1940s and 1950s and for its dramatic portrayal of the schoolyard victimization of young Elaine Risley. But critics like Judith Thurman, who thinks that *Cat's Eye* should have ended "on page 206," at the moment when Elaine turns her back on her chief tormenter, Cordelia, and walks away, disregard the fact that Elaine's seemingly self-contained narrative of her early triumph over victimization bears a causal relationship to a larger confessional narrative which ratifies her career as an artist.[9] There is a direct line of cause and effect between Elaine's experience of cruelty at the hands of Cordelia and her career as an artist who is driven to arrest, transfix, and freeze the people and scenes of her life that have given the most pain.

Middle-aged, fading, sounding tougher, more sardonic than her true nature warrants, Elaine confides in the reader with such candor and forthcoming specificity that no lacunae seem to exist in her re-creation of her memories. Yet her paintings reveal the existence of gaps and silences in her narrative by alluding to what has been left unspoken. Because her art reveals what she cannot otherwise say, Elaine refuses to theorize about her work or proclaim its redemptive value. She calls herself a painter, not an artist. She paints women, she insists, because that's what painters do. Atwood thus invites her readers to piece together Elaine's words and her pictures to arrive at an understanding of her artistic motives and her true nature. The cat's eye marble that Elaine treasures as a talisman in her childhood offers a clue in the form of an expanding symbol of the power of vision which Elaine struggles toward in her life and art. That vision is a mixed blessing: to see through the cat's eye is to make yourself remote from other people, to freeze them out of your heart, for the sake of survival. Indeed, the novel ends with Elaine alone on an airplane wistfully observing the happy camaraderie of some elderly women passengers. But cat's eye vision also guides Elaine toward the creation of paintings which, luminous, often textureless, and laced with antic wit, offer a second version, a revision of her memories. The art has an air of forgiveness about it, retrieving and transforming what previously has been frozen out.

Returning from Vancouver to Toronto, the city of her youth, to attend a retrospective showing of her work, Elaine also holds an inner retrospective in which she recalls long sequences of her life in Toronto from early childhood through art school, a disastrous love affair with her drawing teacher, and her failed first marriage. The memories of her life down to the present moment culminate in the exhibition of her paintings. As at the end of Virginia Woolf's *To the Lighthouse*, the artistic effort of the novelist converges with that of the artist in the novel, so that both may rightly say, "I have had my vision."[10] Only in this case, Elaine's words are, "I have said, *Look*. I have said, *I see*."[11] Elaine cannot work her way progressively through grief and loss to artistic vision in the conscious, internally articulate manner of Lily Briscoe; her art bears witness to aspects of her life she cannot otherwise express.

In *Picoseconds*, for example, Elaine paints a landscape depicting her parents picnicking above an iconic band of old gas pump logos, emblems of their traveling days. The parents are tiny and painted in the position of Breughel's disappearing Icarus. These are parents who have twice abandoned her, most obviously by dying—she cannot bring them back for a trillionth of a second—and less obviously by her father's obliviousness and her mother's mute bafflement in the face of Elaine's torment at the hands of her supposed friends in childhood. Another work has a series of panels showing Elaine's mother dematerializing. More conspicuously, an old searing hatred is made to bear fruit in Elaine's repeated transformations of the detested Mrs. Smeath, mother of her second tormentor, Grace, who, with her dowdy apron, sagging underwear, and rubber plant represents middle-class Canadian Protestant hypocrisy at its deadliest. It takes a long time for Elaine to exorcise Mrs. Smeath, because unlike Elaine's own sympathetic but ineffectual mother, Mrs. Smeath is a mother figure who openly countenances the other children's cruelty to "heathenish" Elaine. Elaine exorcises Mrs. Smeath by painting her half-undressed in various absurd postures of apotheosis appropriate to someone who has a monopoly on God.

Painting from memory rather than from life means that all of Elaine's art is extremely personal, even when it seems objective; moreover, the unconscious has already played a role in selecting and shaping the images that offer themselves to the artist. And the very events which make art a necessary means of expression for Elaine are also the subjects of her art. As the novel begins, Elaine sees herself in the middle of life's journey, like Dante on his pilgrimage, a position she images as "the middle of a river, the middle of a bridge" (*CE*, 14). The bridge is a literal one; it crosses a river in a ravine in Toronto, the scene of Elaine's most extreme duress, when she nearly freezes to death following a command of Cordelia. Cordelia and the cat's eye marble which Elaine uses as a talisman against her are inextricably involved in Elaine's psychological, moral, and artistic growth. And both Cordelia and the marble symbol are internalized, Cordelia as Elaine's inner demon, embodiment of all her self-doubts, and the marble as the inner energy source which protects her and urges her to more acute vision.

The transformations of the marble from child's toy, to talisman, to symbol of radiant art parallel Elaine's own transformations as she grows up and learns how to evade victimization. A transparent crystal with a flowerlike shape of opaque blue inside, the luminous cat's eye marble hints at possibilities of vision, energy, and beauty—an instrument to capture the light. Later, it merges with a convex mirror as a symbol of a world caught and transformed in the mind and reflected back in art. Finally, its blue globular shape suggests a reconciling of macrocosm and microcosm: the eye, the world, and the stars. Inside it, Elaine says at one point, she can "see my life entire" though such an insight is necessarily fleeting (*CE*, 420).

Having lived in the wilderness (like Atwood herself) while her father did field research on insects, Elaine is innocent even for her young age when her family moves to the city, and she is unprepared when games of jump rope, ball, and marbles yield to a far crueler game of psychological sadism in which Cordelia and the two others systematically dominate and brutalize her for a period of almost two years. Elaine first saves the cat's eye marble, so like and unlike an eye in its crystalline transparency, because it seems beautiful and mysteriously alien, perhaps the first object she has ever looked at aesthetically. The marble's purity and its gelid look suggest to her the power of disembodiment, of resisting torment by seeing without feeling, a way of freezing out those who have frozen her out.

In the respite of an unconfined summer camping out with her parents, Elaine dreams of the marble as a sun or planet falling from the sky into her sleeping body and making her cold, a dream which suggests that unconsciously she is maturing, acquiring new strength (*CE*, 155). In the next school year, as the torment increases, she holds on to the marble as though it were a magic third eye with an "impartial gaze" that allows her to "retreat back into my eyes" (*CE*, 166). As an objective correlative for her own eye and her ego (her "I"), the marble enables her to hold on to a core of herself and to cast a cold eye on her tormentors. When the situation reaches a crisis in the freezing river in the ravine, Elaine has already gathered the strength to pull herself out and go on living, although she imagines that she is saved by a vision of the black Virgin floating above the bridge. Now she can deny the other girls' power over her and walk away: "There's something hard in me," she thinks, "crystalline, a kernel of glass" (*CE*, 208).

The first half of *Cat's Eye* builds suspensefully to that moment when Elaine turns her back on Cordelia. The second half of the novel covers Elaine's life up to the present, a life that she herself views as the aftermath of her ordeal with Cordelia. Recognition of the Cordelia within, a voice which urges both cruelties and self-doubts, takes Elaine a very long time; she is still wrestling with that dark angel at the end of the novel. Her bitter experience with Cordelia prepares the adult Elaine, however, to extricate herself from an absurdly constraining and pseudo-romantic affair with her art teacher Josef and gives her strength to walk away from her unsuitable and exhausting first marriage, to the irresponsible artist Jon, although not until after a theatrical suicide attempt with an Exacto knife, with the internal voice of Cordelia urging her on (*CE*, 395). The only relationship in her adult life which is not tainted by the victor-victim struggle of wills is her peaceful second marriage, to Ben. Significantly, Ben, who is by far the most attractive male in any of Atwood's novels, runs a travel business, is off in Mexico, and never appears in the novel.

Elaine's adult life centers upon her art, about which she refuses to theorize, even privately; for all her retrospection, Elaine is not introspective. In contrast to the career of Jon, who slavishly follows every trend from abstract expressionism to op art to pop art, and who ends up doing special effects for chain-saw-massacre films, Elaine follows the more difficult path of painstakingly crafting her own style. The first significant stage in her artistic development occurs in college when, after all the art history and life-drawing classes, she becomes fascinated with painting reflective surfaces, "pearls, crystals, mirrors" and such domestic items as ginger-ale bottles, ice cubes, and frying pans (*CE*, 347). Turning away from impasto or even the use of textured brush strokes in favor of pure color and reflectivity, Elaine teaches herself the ancient art of mixing tempera, colors suspended in a water and egg emulsion. It is evident that the vision of the cat's eye marble, the "kernel of glass," has been absorbed into a painterly eye which leads her to depict "objects that breathe out light" (*CE*, 346). This is the first stage of Elaine's artistic growth, the rejection of "viscous," textured, self-expressive art in favor of a highly skilled and optically precise art of painting the light as it strikes the world. The next and more difficult task is to bring the vision of a world of radiance to bear upon her own emotions and memories. Her rejection of impasto, indeed of any textured brush strokes that betray the artist's hand, leads to a cold, dispassionate presentation of subject matter drenched in passions, her own most memorable moments of being.

And yet Elaine becomes fascinated with Van Eyck's well-known painting, *The Arnolfini Marriage*, not so much for its pellucid rendering of the wedding couple as for the framed convex mirror in the background, which reflects the figures of two people who exist in a different world outside the picture. "This round mirror," she thinks, "is like an eye, a single eye that sees more than anyone else looking" (*CE*, 347). The surrogate eye fascinates her because it shows the outside of the painting's inside, peeling back its reality and revealing the figure of the artist. By trickery, the artist is both concealed and revealed. For Elaine, I believe, that mirror, which, art historians tell us, symbolizes the spotlessness of the virgin, externalizes the artist's vision, the eye and the ego, cleansed and made spotless by the will of the artist. At Elaine's retrospective, the last two paintings described, *Cat's Eye* and *Unified Field Theory*, allude to their own making and contain the artist's presence through images of the mirror and the cat's eye marble.

Both paintings refer to the crisis at the ravine, and both represent objects suspended against the sky without visible support, suggesting a precariousness, an uneasy balance. *Cat's Eye* depicts not the marble but the convex mirror, ornately framed and hung against a blue field. Facing forward in front of the mirror is the upper half of Elaine's middle-aged wrinkled face, while the convex mirror shows the back of her head at a younger age, and beyond it, the reflection of her three childhood tormenters advancing through the snow. This painting is ambiguous. It may be read as witnessing a triumph: since Elaine's back is turned to the image of the girls, she may be said to have put the childhood crisis behind her by capturing it in her art. On the other hand, the mirror reflection in the painting indicates that the tormentors are actually in front of her, a forever-approaching reminder of their false friendship and her lonely pain.

Unified Field Theory is ironically titled. Elaine is well aware that she is far from having a unified, comprehensive theory of space and time as she has experienced them. Rather, this long, vertical painting is like a map of Elaine's psychic and intellectual world, holding in delicate balance several of the emotionally significant elements of her life and bracketing them in a single vision. The background of the painting shows the sky and stars blended together with the earth and roots in Escher-like fashion. This interpenetration of galaxies and stones is a poetic conceit suggesting the unity of existence and, perhaps, the fragility of the eco-system. Stretching laterally across the painting is the familiar bridge over the ravine, under which runs the stream that flows from the cemetery, the world of the dead. Since the opening of the novel, the bridge has repre-sented Elaine's life span, the structure that holds her up above the icy river. The sky and the bridge thus create space-time coordinates, the field of life. Floating over the bridge is the Black Virgin, Elaine's self-generated hallucination, who saved her from freezing. The Black Virgin who, as Elaine learns in Mexico, restores lost things, levitates over the bridge bearing in her hands an oversize cat's eye marble. In part, she is a figure for memory, proffering the marble of luminous vision, now en-larged to suggest a globe.

What *Unified Field Theory* may tell us about Atwood's own art of the novel is problematic. It suggests the necessity of transforming those events which are most wounding, to turn them to some account in works of art, as Atwood evidently does in this semi-autobiographical novel. At the same time, Atwood's own opinions and feelings are only hinted at in the novel: the device of a narrator who addresses us in brisk staccato rhythms, usually assuming an ironic stance, effectively removes the brush strokes that betray the artist's hand. *Unified Field Theory* also conveys the precariousness of one woman's modern existence as a fragile bridge across the void, unsustained by institutions or external props. Elaine goes it alone. Her Black Virgin, detached from Christianity, is projected from Elaine's own heart and mind like a photographic nega-tive, back-lit against the sky, not only a symbol of memory but also a dark portrait of the artist. That artist is a woman, and she brings a world and the light to see it by.

Writings by Margaret Atwood

NOVELS

The Edible Woman. Boston: Little, Brown, 1969.
Surfacing. New York: Simon & Schuster, 1973.

Lady Oracle. New York: Simon & Schuster, 1976.
Life Before Man. New York: Simon & Schuster, 1979.
Bodily Harm. New York: Simon & Schuster, 1982.
The Handmaid's Tale. Boston: Houghton Mifflin, 1986.
Cat's Eye. New York: Doubleday, 1989.

COLLECTED SHORT STORIES

"Dancing Girls" and Other Stories. New York: Simon & Schuster, 1982.
Murder in the Dark: Short Fictions and Prose Poems. Toronto: Coach House Press, 1983.
Bluebeard's Egg. Boston: Houghton Mifflin, 1986.
Wilderness Tips. New York: Doubleday, 1991.

COLLECTED POETRY

Double Persephone. Toronto: Hawkshead Press, 1961. [self-published chapbook]
The Circle Game. Toronto: House of Anansi Press, 1967, 1978.
The Animals in that Country. Boston: Little, Brown, 1968.
The Journals of Susanna Moodie. Toronto: Oxford University Press, 1970.
Procedures for Underground. Boston: Little, Brown, 1970.
Power Politics. New York: Harper & Row, 1973.
You Are Happy. New York: Harper & Row, 1974.
Selected Poems. New York: Simon & Schuster, 1978.
Two-Headed Poems. New York: Simon & Schuster, 1980.
True Stories. New York: Simon & Schuster, 1981.
Interlunar. Toronto: Oxford University Press, 1984.
Selected Poems II: Poems Selected and New, 1976–86. Boston: Houghton Mifflin, 1987.

COLLECTED NONFICTION

Survival: A Thematic Guide to Canadian Literature. Toronto: House of Anansi Press, 1972.
Second Words: Selected Critical Prose. Boston: Beacon Press, 1984.
Conversations. Ed. Earl G. Ingersoll. Princeton: Ontario Review Press, 1990; Firefly Books, 1990. [selected interviews]

SELECTED ARTICLES, REVIEWS

"An End to and Audience (A Lecture on Being a Writer in a Free Society)." *Dalhousie Review.* 60:3 (1980): 415–33.
"Midnight Birds—Stories of Contemporary Black-Women Writers" [review]. *Harvard Educational Review.* 5:1 (1981): 221–23.
Review of *Circles on the Water*, by Marge Piercy. *New York Times Book Review* 87:32 (1982): 10+.
Review of *The Burning House*, by Ann Beattie. *New York Times Book Review* 87:39 (1982): 1+.
"Significant Moments in the Life of my Mother." *Queens Quarterly* 90:3 (1983): 663–75.

"The Pleasures of Rereading." *New York Times Book Review* 88:24 (1983).

"That Certain Thing Called the Girlfriend (Women's Friendships in Literature)." *New York Times Book Review*, May 1986: 1+.

"Summers on Canada Rideau Canal." *Architectural Digest* 45:6 (1988): 84+.

"Bowering Pie, Some Recollections." *Essays on Canadian Writing* 38 (1989): 3–6.

"Scrooge-McDuck vs. The Trickster (Native Indian Writing in Canada)." *TLS* 4537 (1990): 282.

"Nine Beginnings." In Vol. 2 of *The Writer on Her Work: New Essays in New Territory*, ed. Janet Sternburg. New York: W. W. Norton, 1991.

"Northrup Frye Remembered" (reprinted from the Toronto *Globe and Mail*, 24 January 1991). *Michigan Quarterly Review* 30:4 (1991): 647–49.

5. Ties That Bind in Marie-Claire Blais's *Deaf to the City*

In the novel *Deaf to the City*,[1] Marie-Claire Blais uses stream-of-consciousness as a technique to intrigue her readers. In a surreal landscape, the characters realize that their greatest struggle is against fate. Salvation comes from understanding one's fate while living a fully realized human life in spite of it.

Ironically named, the Hôtel des Voyageurs rises out of the cold, a million miles from nowhere. Within this primary setting, the bleakness is reminiscent of a moonscape, each character like an isolated Latin-named crater unconnected to the others. As unwilling travelers, the characters feel that destiny, not choice, led them to this place, although the major characters do possess credos by which they live and define themselves.

If this novel has a general theme, an umbrella under which to gather all other ideas, it would be the idea of life in flux. Human beings drift in and out of this motion, this drama played out in nature which is seemingly indifferent to human presence. What perdures is art rather than individual lives, whether good or ill.

The characters exist in a world buffered by music, painting, sculpture, architecture. Against this framework, a theme of returning to the primal Garden elicits religious fervor, which expresses itself through a symbolic restructuring of nature through the arts. The biblical story, "The Song of Songs," the search for the ideal lover, is analogous to the development of this novel. In both stories, each character seeks the elusive lover who is at once beautiful and ugly, desirable and frightening.

Images of both death and life exist as parallels in *Deaf to the City*. Blais fully actualizes her skill in her depiction of Florence Gray, who comes to the hotel to commit suicide because her husband, a doctor, has left her. The reader shares her point of view completely, and the novel ends as Gray closes her eyes for the last time. By contrast, Gloria's son, Mike, is dying of a cancerous brain tumor. He accepts his death as inevitable, but regrettable.

Styles of mothering evolve. Because Gloria, the resident-proprietor of the hotel, is not above "turning tricks" to earn money to support her family, her son Mike interacts with unsavory people. Gloria's goal is to take Mike on a motorcycle ride out west while he is still relatively healthy. On the other hand, Madame Langenais, matriarch of a well-to-do family, protects her children from people whose speech patterns suggest a working-class background. Each mother seeks what is best for her child, with differing opinions about what is desirable.

The narrative centers on the Kafkaesque hotel inhabitants, who are seemingly drawn there to live out their lives even though they are trapped by each other. The story focuses on life as a waiting process. Some, like Florence and Mike, wait for death. Others wait for their version of a better life. Lucia, one of Gloria's other children, prostitutes herself to buy drugs for her lover, John. There are also Berthe Agneli, a student; Luigi, named for the absent father, and Jojo, for whom Mike babysits.

The Langenais family stands in contrast to Gloria's family. While her family is poor and wretched, the Langenaises are upper class, and their undoing comes not so much from impending physical death as from the personal experiences of their daughter, Judith, who is a counselor to people who have been identified as suicidal. Judith's involvement with these people diminishes the primary importance of class distinctions, but to the hotel guest named Florence, Judith remains the angel of death. Florence even shortens her name from Langenais, to Lange. L'ange: the angel.

Judith understands that death is the great leveler and that realization affects her personal interactions: because death is democratic, Judith cannot maintain the customary distance between herself, as upper class, and the servants. She even suggests to her mother that Gilbert, the gardener, lunch with the family. Both Gilbert and Madame Langenais reject that idea.

In this psychological novel, people interact with each other, then privately reflect on the nature of that interaction and its ultimate meaning. Blais stylistically constructs bridges between one person's thoughts and another's, as if the hotel itself were a nervous system, with the inhabitants as limbs connected by a central electronic impulse. Gloria provides the physical, earthy center of the universe; deeply troubled Florence probes that universe, allowing art and religion to confront death in nature.

Florence wonders about the twist of fate that brought her to live in a place where free-floating fear is a common constant. For her, life is bearable only when art keeps alive the illusions which people cherish. She depends on the stories that people tell themselves and each other to explain complexities. Violence, however, is the rule which governs her world. Her divorce proves to her that life is impossible in a world where violence is psychological as well as physical. The only way to gain control, therefore, is to empty herself of all hope, all expectations: to actively court death, rather than passively letting it happen.

Florence prefers solitude and the empty spaces where she broods on her troubles. There she decides on the proper time of her death. Everything seems lost—her husband, family, and her reason for being. An indifferent nature becomes the constant which will succeed her. Believing that humans reach for each other only for gratification, an embittered Florence loses herself.

Judith Langenais, Florence's angel of death, teaches philosophy. She is steeped in existentialism. She even hangs Kierkegaard's picture on her wall. Obsessed with the question of why a just, loving God would allow the Holocaust to occur, she keeps memories of it alive, lecturing about it to young students.

Judith is preoccupied with constructing an aesthetic of pain which would help to explain such suffering. In spite of all she knows about horror, Judith passionately loves the world, although she is well aware of its dangers. As a counselor, she helps suicidal clients maintain a balance between life and death, and she helps to provide the psychological support for her patients' decisions. Judith foresees that she will lose Florence, who believes that everything is lost, when Florence assumes the control over her own destiny. Judith, who believes that nothing is lost, is an idealist and Florence begins to accept her as an angel of death who brings merciful release.

Gloria's son Mike adores Judith and watches her as she walks to school everyday. Blais suggests, however, that Mike's death will be horrific because he experiences severe headaches which his medication does not alleviate. By the end of the novel, his condition has deteriorated. His longing for Judith symbolizes the release from suffering which the angel of death could bring him.

Blais balances the bleak portrait of an ill-starred life by positing the possibility of hope. In spite of life's inexplicable cruelties, Judith believes in life after death. Life, even painful life, is worth living. Her engagement with life's questions, however, is on a philosophical level. Judith, fully possessed of the will to effect people's lives, lacks familiarity with the consequences of life's choices. She herself has not suffered from the Holocaust or experienced Mike's pain, nor has she felt firsthand the intensity of passion which drives Gloria to pose her ultimate question, which is rooted in the earth. She asks Judith:

> What d'you teach? Philosophy! Well, then, you ought to be able to answer my question: what's the role of sex in life? (*DC*, 8)

The manner of Florence's suicide leaves uncertain whether or not Judith is present during Florence's last moments, although Florence thinks she hears Mike happily exclaim that Judith, as the angel of death, has come. But Florence no longer accepts that as desirable, even during her last moments. As the angel of death, Judith would guide Florence to a life in which she placed no trust—neither here nor in the hereafter.

In Mike's world, Judith represents heaven. His mother, Gloria, represents earth. These powerful women engage in a cosmic war over who would win the souls of the hotel guests. They are especially interested in Florence's soul. Mike's world deceives him, however. A young man should plan for life, not for an early death. As powerful as Gloria is, she cannot forestall his eventual painful death. Even the motorcycle trip with her is contingent upon his state of health. Because Gloria is not the chaste mother he wants, Mike believes that there is no salvation, since there is nothing in which he can ultimately trust.

Judith awakens Mike's sexuality with her youth and beauty. Her sexual nature is somehow purer than his mother's, which he experiences through watching her dance. As the angel of death, Judith would introduce him to the sensual world which he has never fully experienced. Does his angel of death, therefore, bring death or new life? Does she close doors or open them? Both Gloria and Judith represent life which is ultimately destructive for him. As a character, Mike struggles with that idea throughout the novel.

Judith and Gloria are complex contradictions. A prostitute herself, Gloria does not want her daughters to become prostitutes. Her question to Judith is sincere, summarizing her three main requirements of human existence—life, sex, and death, although later she revises the order—sex, death, and life.

Mike loves Gloria, but her inconsistencies confuse him. He has often seen Tim, her lover, pinch her hips. He has also seen her perform as a nude dancer at the Infini du Sexe, where she works part time. In spite of this, Mike considers Gloria to be like the classical Madonna figure, a suffering mother who is condemned to watch her son die an agonizing death. He even explains Gloria in religious terms: she becomes Mary, the Mother of Sorrows, at the foot of the Cross on Golgotha. Mike knows that she dances and prostitutes herself for him, just as his sister, Lucia, prostitutes herself for her lover, John. But while Lucia buys drugs for John, which could ultimately kill him, Gloria saves her earnings to take Mike out to San Francisco, where the restorative powers of nature might heal him.

Gloria named her son Michel Agneli, and calls him her angel. While Judith is a proactive angel, Mike functions both as a receptor and an enabler. His gentleness enables Gloria to express her maternal feelings. As Jojo's babysitter, he receives the unbridled affection of which young children are capable. He loves Judith, although she does not love him, and he intuitively understands Florence's plan of suicide.

Since various characters thematically have religious connotations, religious ideas act as an underpinning for the novel. Like the "Song of Songs," a richly imagistic long poem in the Old Testament, this novel describes a lover's search for the idealized beloved, the lover's longing, eventual return, and the subsequent loss of the beloved. *Deaf to the City* presents several characters who long for an ideal lover and for sanctity. Gloria's daughter, Berthe Agneli, questions the logic of dreaming of sainthood in a world which is so absurd. To achieve their desires, the characters transform real life into a more acceptable experience by using the imagination. The arts provide neutral ground, an avenue of escape, with the imagination as the vehicle.

The biblical idea of returning to the Garden of Eden suggests the ideal which each character seeks. For Gloria, Eden is west through deserts of clean air, where living close to nature is possible. For Mike, Eden is the park where he takes his baby sister, Jojo, to play. There, the class distinctions that divide their town should not intrude. Jojo smells of earth, of life itself, when she plays with Madame Langenais's son, Stephane. Although Stephane finds Jojo fascinating, his mother takes him out of the park to avoid contact with working-class children and to avoid social contamination. For Madame Langenais, the park, as Eden, is too ideal and too democratic.

Old Gilbert, the gardener, acts as gatekeeper; he is an angel with a flaming sword. Having served the Langenais family for many years, he becomes the guardian of family secrets. His refusal to eat with the family, at Judith's invitation, is more a refusal to leave Eden than a desire to maintain proper class distinctions.

Blais surrounds Gloria with garden images, comparing the garden of life with the garden of death. After Mike is diagnosed, he spends some time in a hospital which treats children with cancer. Calling it a poisoned garden lacking fresh air and sunshine, Gloria takes Mike to Florida, where he can feel refreshed by nature and by Gloria's cool hand on his forehead.

Because the reader sees life primarily through the thoughts of each character, the reader also experiences their dreams. The idea of imagination as it functions in the waking and sleeping person is discussed by Gaston Bachelard (1960) in *The Poetics of Reverie*.[2] For him, daydreams (rêverie) and night dreams (rêve) function differently for the dreamer. Reverie, dominated by the anima, brings tranquility. Even when the dreamer is melancholy, reverie brings repose, detached from the pressure to produce results. Images are loved for themselves alone (*PR*, 31).

Mike's daydreams (reverie) are filled with images of San Francisco, with the healing plants—the cactus, the indigo bush, desert lavender, honey—which Gloria will use to cure him. The paradise of his daydreams has neither God nor angels, only people and animals who survive great suffering. He dislikes most music because music negates his daydreams, where he constructs the perfect, pain-free world.

Images of fear dominate night dreams (rêve). Dreaming that wild dogs are attacking him, Mike sees his mother's smile drive off the dogs. But then she herself changes into a monster, only human in shape, a nightmare that alludes to her dual nature: Madonna and whore. In another dream, Mike is imprisoned on an island, forced as a slave to crush stones. Judith, as the angel of death, comes to free him, but that dream is erased by another. He awakens, realizing that he is trapped.

For Florence as well, night dreams (rêve) offer little solace. Hers are dominated by images of the life she knew with her husband. One dream begins as she recalls the paintings which she collects, particularly the one with a Mediterranean sky. But as the dream continues, born of fever and drowsiness, she experiences those days as tainted.

In one dream (rêve) Florence enters an Oriental garden, similar to a Chinese painting with which she is familiar. The plants comfort her— the strawberries, hedges, flowers. But white, in this painting, is an image of death, of mourning garments as it is in the Oriental culture where the painting was created.

Only in her controlled daydreams (reverie) does Florence find the peace she desires. Images of nature and the fine arts surface to provide an environment free of anger and betrayal. She wants to share with Mike her dream of the Himalayas, sacred mountains with mystical powers, but feels that death will claim him as long as he accepts Gloria's dream of the desert. Toward the end of her life, daydreams will absorb Florence, closing her off from the others. Mike wants to reach across her dreams but is unable to do so. Florence's night dreams supplant the images of her daydreams, with disquieting results.

While daydreaming (reverie), Florence and Mike achieve the solitude which their own waking lives do not provide. The nature of Florence's reverie is fed by her acquaintance with the arts, because of the great power of the anima to incorporate artistic images that use such symbolic language. She has amassed a ready supply of images from which to draw; Mike, for his part, only has Gloria's dreams of the desert and the sound of her voice as she sings lullabies.

The anima dreams and sings, producing the fruit of its dreams in art (*PR*, 67). While Florence persists in her desire to shoot herself, she also comes to terms with that decision. As Mike gradually loses his belief in the healing power of Gloria's desert, he loses also the calm acceptance of his fate which had been his from the beginning. When the reader first encounters Mike, his mien is compared to that of the androgynous figure in Munch's "The Scream," whose silent cry is a portrait of pain.

The arts provide the vehicle to enable Florence's suicide, and it is clear that Blais intends to use the arts as a fictive element in the novel. Blais, in fact, portrays Mike as an impoverished figure precisely because of his lack of artistic involvement. The only dance he experiences is his mother's nude dancing. The movies he sees are pornographic. Except for Gloria's songs, he dislikes music. But Mike's inexperience with the fine arts stems from Gloria's inability to provide it. Considering the fine arts as basically useless, Gloria sees Mike's salvation as a response to his visit to the desert, his return to nature. Likewise she disparages her daughter, Berthe, since she is a university student who writes poetry.

The fine arts function as a scrim which blocks out irrelevant or distracting material, while highlighting the obsessions of individual characters. From this locus of discourse, troublesome events or topics can be safely viewed when artificially rendered.

Characters who make the best use of the arts as a medium of exploration and discovery pass through three stages of development, as if the development of survival skills hinges on how well the characters relate to the arts and learn from them. Louise Wetherbee Phelps[3] describes similar stages as she considers the teacher's mediation of disciplinary theory and personal practice. The stages are (1) attunement, (2) critical examination, and (3) practical experimentation. Attunement connotes a readiness to entertain pertinent ideas. Critical examination involves an analysis of legitimate premises. Practical experimentation involves placing these ideas within the space of one's life in order to measure the fit. The major characters—Gloria, Mike, Florence, and Judith—pass through these stages, with different results.

Florence revels in the arts. Because she has money, she has traveled the world, visited museums, and, with her husband's help, assembled a collection. Munch's torturous paintings, in which the painter meditates on death and illness figure prominently in her reveries.

Florence remembers a visit with her husband to the ruins of an abbey. The abbey, surrounded by meadows under a stormy sky, illustrates her need to live her own life, to make her own decisions, in spite of the consequences. In Florence's imagination, Egyptian pyramids and Greek temples house the voices of the slaves who built them, and of the blood they spilled. She realizes that Judith Lange, in spite of her studies, knows nothing about Egyptian art, and nothing about the dark memories with which Florence is familiar because of the pain of her own life.

Music, too, stimulates Florence's reverie. As she listens to Mozart or Strauss, she imagines frightening thoughts of flowing blood and wild cries. In reverie, she imagines that Mozart listened to his *Magic Flute* as he lay terminally ill; that, buoyed on its strains, he willingly moved into the hands of death. This is the attitude toward death which she comes to espouse. Florence's reveries also define her husband negatively as a procurer of sculpture, maintaining his collection, rather than as a producer of art, like Mozart.

Ultimately the fine arts do not provide a solution to the problems that torment her. Rather, as Bachelard suggests, the arts provide an environment of solitude, a place of tranquility in which she pursues her thoughts. As she approaches her decision to commit suicide, she spends more and more time in reverie, focusing especially on life with her husband. Reverie makes the past available to the dreamer as a non-threatening, non-demanding construct. Florence is free to decide for herself.

That Blais chooses not to give Judith Lange the range of reverie or rêve that she does for Florence is important. That omission underscores Florence's disdain for Judith, who is too young and unformed to understand the forces which drive suicidal clients to kill themselves. Because Judith's life has been spared many of life's agonies, pain and death occur on a monumental, but distant, scale.

Judith's lack of personal involvement is revealed by her understanding of the arts. A medieval cathedral reminds her of the blood shed on its steps, of rebellion on a grand scale, but not of the individual lives which were lost. Egyptian art does not touch Judith in the same way it moves Florence. Florence rejects Judith because Florence perceives her as lacking a humanizing intimacy with pain. Even as an angel of death, Judith is completely dispassionate.

As the characters attempt to make meaning of the chaos of their lives, they illustrate the dichotomy between formal knowledge and wisdom, which are traditional sources of meaning. The university training which both Florence and Judith received does not provide strategies with which they can organize their major life events. Judith cannot muster enough counseling skills to help Florence find an option other than suicide. In Florence's case, she does not learn to see her life as anything other than a failure, for which she alone is responsible.

Phelps's discussion of the stages through which characters pass as they use the arts illustrates what options the characters had. Having decided to commit suicide, Florence accepts as relevant only that part of reality which supports a decision which, once carried out, cannot be reversed. In so doing, she severely constricts the boundaries within which she operates. The expansive nature of the arts is of little help. Her self-analysis separates her from Judith and the potential wisdom of a trained counselor. Experimentation is incomplete, as Florence's suicide becomes the final act.

Although she is younger than Florence, Judith has the openness to life which Florence lacks. While Florence sees Judith's lack of direct experience with suffering as a liability, that very innocence leaves Judith more receptive to relevant ideas; Florence is more cynical. Judith trusts her ability to rescue, even when she functions as the angel of death. Her work with clients involves the formulation of hypotheses to explain their problems, then the testing of theories through her interaction with clients. This scientific mind-set is what Florence perceives when she experiences the protective distance which Judith maintains between herself and her clients.

Thus, to find meaning in their lives, the characters must merge three different threads: lore, art, and local knowledge. The community these people form within the hotel becomes the background against which their theories are formulated and tested. Ideally, the community provides the space for change, should theories prove inadequate. The possibility of change implies a greater openness to the future than the characters demonstrate.

In Phelps's analysis, lore constitutes cultural accretions—traditions, practices, and beliefs which are communally produced and owned. General expression in symbolic form, equivalent to practitioner knowledge, results from communal sharing (*PWGKC*, 869). Judith's knowledge of counseling most illustrates the notion of lore. She is drawn to what she does, as if it were a religious calling. Her practice reflects insights gained during the course of working, rather than through her specific training. She knows *that* something is effective but can hardly articulate *why*. Thus, she impresses Florence as being too young and too inexperienced to be effective. By reasoning through analogous situations, Judith is able to help people. Florence, however, is a different person from Judith's other clients. Judith's analogical imagination will not help her save Florence. As Judith continues to explore the range of feelings and possibilities inherent in such relationships, she discovers that the very essence of practical wisdom is judgment.

While Judith knows how to act in situations by extrapolating from analogical experiences, Gloria's path to knowledge is through direct experience. She does not proceed (as Phelps's theories explain) to enlightenment through quiet consideration; rather, her way represents reflection-in-action, knowing-in-action. Gloria focuses intensely on her hotel guests, adjusting her way of living as she sees her concerns reflected in people's approving or disapproving responses. She monitors others for signs, feedback which she uses to become self-corrective. She lacks high-level critical skills, however. Consequently, she blindly drives herself to provide for Mike's trip west, with its ephemeral cure. Were she more objective, she would consider the deleterious effect her prostitution has on him, engendering his conflictual feelings about his Madonna/whore.

Gloria functions as an experimental artist. She reflects on her activities, as she practices her ideas. Gloria experiments with prostitution and finds that it suits her needs for money, although it is unacceptable as a legacy for her daughters. Therefore, Gloria's acceptance of her lot is not blind. She evaluates her situation and finds it fulfilling within a narrow range.

The lore that Judith practices circulates within the specific community among which she practices. Her lack of human experiences lessens the effectiveness which she could have were she more worldly-wise. Gloria's art is refined over time, as she is older and more experienced. Gloria's prejudgment of possible cures for Mike, however, precludes the full effectiveness of her art.

Florence manages to synthesize these two ways of knowing into a third, more personal knowledge base. By turning to the fine arts, Florence uses Judith's path of analogical knowledge. The arts reflect on the nature of life within the shadow of death. Florence extracts principles which she then applies to her situation. Judith could provide a systematic process of inquiry which would allow Florence to step beyond self-destruction. By dismissing Judith, Florence limits her options.

Gloria's process of testing hypotheses within the community could also provide Florence with a way out. Initially, Florence considers reaching out to Mike, who is dying. For him, death is not a hypothetical construct. However, she decides against this idea. Having decided to kill herself, she is not open to any other possibility.

The lost world of the hotel is the ultimate context in which these characters assess their options. Ideally, a community should provide a haven in which open-ended experimentation could occur in a non-judgmental atmosphere (*PWGKC*, 879). The hotel community is hampered, however, by its inability to embrace self-reflection as a communal norm, implying the sharing of wisdom gained. While personal knowledge results from the intersection of inner experience and external reality, shared knowledge becomes primarily a social concept that links awareness within the context of community (*PWGKC*, 880). Because the hotel community is not self-critical, its knowledge too tightly bound to individuals who dare not risk sharing, it becomes a closed system. In spite of the arts and the religious fervor which drive her characters, Blais depicts a claustrophobic community totally unable to heal its members.

Mike is sacrificed to his community's stagnation. Less abstract than Judith, less cynical than Florence, less desperate than Gloria, he has enough inner resources to reach beyond his pain and care for his younger sister, even trying to protect her from the sting of class snobbery. He will die, however, because no one around him formulates a more humane set of options for him, which would combine reason and desire with wisdom.

The tragedy in this novel is implicit in its title. The characters are deaf, unresponsive to qualities in each other which might alleviate the dreadful sense of suffering which they share. The characters manage to ignore or deny any possibility of healing if its source is unexpected. Consequently, although Florence's suicide is an obvious, overt act, other characters like Mike also gradually die of disease, or, like Gloria or Lucia, of dissipation, another form of suicide.

Fate closes in around the characters. Mike seeks an emotional involvement with Judith, even if that exists only on the level of fantasy. Blais suggests that just as the Mike-Judith liaison will not yield meaning or lasting results, neither will Gloria's trip prove efficacious.

The novel ends when Florence dies. The reader feels relief that she is no longer depressed, yet sorry that so reflective a person has chosen so irreversible a solution. Suggested in her death is the end of this unsettling world. The choices that characters make stem from good motives; the problem is that they make bad choices for good reasons.

Writings by Marie-Claire Blais

NOVELS

La Belle Bête. Montreal: Cercle du Livre de France, 1958; Quebec: Institut Litteraire du Québec, 1959; Paris: Flammarion, 1961. Translation: *Mad Shadows* (Merloyd Lawrence, trans.). Toronto: McClelland & Stewart, 1960; Boston: Little, Brown, 1960; London: Cape, 1960; Toronto: New Canadian Library, 1981.

Tête Blanche. Quebec: Institut Littéraire du Québec, 1960. Translation: *Tête Blanche* (Charles Fullman, trans.). Toronto: McClelland & Stewart, 1961, London: Cape, 1960; Boston: Little, Brown, 1960.

Les Voyageurs Sacrés. Ecrits du Canada Français, 14 (1962): 193–257. Translation: *Three Travelers* (Derek Coltman, trans.), published with *The Day Is Dark*. New York: Farrar, Straus & Giroux, 1967; Toronto: Penguin, 1985; Montreal: Editions NMH, 1969.

Le Jour Est Noir. Montreal: Editions du Jour, 1962; Paris: Grasset, 1970; Montreal: Livre de Poche (Stanké), 1981. Translation: with *Les Voyageurs Sacrés* in *The Day Is Dark and Three Travelers: Two Novellas*. (Derek Coltman, trans.). New York: Farrar, Straus & Giroux, 1967.

Une Saison dans la Vie d'Emmanuel. Montreal: Editions de Jour, 1965; Paris: Grasset, 1966. Translation: *A Season in the Life of Emmanuel* (Derek Coltman, trans.). New York: Farrar, Straus & Giroux, 1966; London, Cape, 1967; Toronto: Bantam, 1976.

L'Insoumise. Montreal: Editions du Jour, 1966; Paris: Grasset, 1970. Translation: *The Fugituve* (David Lobdell, trans.). Ottawa: Oberon Press, 1978.

Les Manuscrits de Pauline Archange. Montreal: Editions du Jour, 1968; Paris: Grasset, 1968; Montreal: Livre de Poche, 1983. Translation: *The Manuscripts of Pauline Arch-*

ange (Derek Coltman, trans.). New York: Farrar, Straus & Giroux, 1969; Toronto: New Canadian Library, 1982.

Vivre! Virve! Montreal: Editions du Jour, 1969; Montreal: Livre de Poche, 1983. Translation: Included as Part II of *The Manuscripts of Pauline Archange*. New York: Farrar, Straus & Giroux, 1969; Toronto: New Canadian Library, 1982.

Les Apparences (Tome III des *Manuscrits de Pauline Archange*). Montreal: Editions du Jour, 1970; Montreal: Livre de Poche, 1983. Translation: *Durer's Angel* (David Lobdell, trans.). Toronto: McClelland & Stewart, 1974; Vancouver: Talonbooks, 1976.

L'Insoumise, Suivi de Le Jour Est Noir. Paris: Grasset, 1971.

Le Loup. Montreal: Editions du Jour, 1972; Paris: Laffont, 1973; Montreal: Livre de Poche, 1980. Translation: *The Wolf* (Sheila Fischman, trans.). Toronto: McClelland & Stewart, 1974.

Un Joualonais, Sa Joualonie. Montreal: Editions du Jour, 1973; as *A Coeur Joual*, Paris: Laffort; Montreal: Livre de Poche, 1981. Translation: *St. Lawrence Blues* (Ralph Manheim, trans.). New York: Farrar, Straus & Giroux, 1974; Toronto: Bantam, 1976; London: Harrap, 1976; Translation: *David Sterne* (David Lobdell, trans.). Toronto: McClelland & Stewart, 1973.

Une Liaison Parisienne. Montreal: Stanké, Quinze, 1975; Paris: Laffont, 1976. Translation: *A Literary Affair* (Sheila Fischman, trans.). Toronto: McClelland & Stewart, 1979.

Les Nuits de l'Underground. Montreal: Stanké, 1978; Paris: Diffusion Hachette. Translation: *Nights in the Underground* (Ray Ellenwood, trans.). Toronto: Musson, 1979; Toronto: New Press Canadian Classics, 1982.

Le Sourd dans la Ville. Montreal: Stanké, 1979; Paris: Gallimard, 1980. Translation: *Deaf to the City* (Carol Dunlop, trans.). Toronto: Lester & Orpen Dennys, 1981.

Visions d'Anna ou le Vertige. Montreal: Stanké, 1982; Paris: Gallimard, 1982. Translation: *Anna's World* (Sheila Fischman, trans.). Toronto: Lester & Orpen Dennys, 1983.

Pierre ou la Guerre du Printemps. Montreal: Editions Primeur, 1984.

SHORT STORIES AND ARTICLES

"Her Beautiful Beast." In *The Oxford Anthology of Canadian Literature*, ed. Robert Weaver and William Toye. Toronto: Oxford University Press, 1973.

"La Fin d'une Enfance." Appendix in *Le Monde Perturbe de Jeunes dans l'Oeuvre de Marie-Claire Blais: Sa Vie, Son Oeuvre, la Critique: Essai*, ed. T. Fabi. Montreal: Editions Agence d'Arc, 1973.

"L'Exil, Liberté." 23 (January–February 1981): 31–51.

"The Forsaken." In *Stories by Canadian Women*, ed. Rosemary Sullivan. Toronto: Oxford University Press, 1984.

"Réponse à 'Figurez-vous' de Louise Cotnoir in *La Nouvelle Barre de Jour. Forum des Femmes* 172 (March 1986), 21–24.

POETRY

Pays Voilés. Quebec: Garneau, 1963. Translation: *Veiled Countries/Lives* (Michael Harris, trans.). Montreal: Vehicule, 1984; Garneau, 1964.

PLAYS

L'Exécution. Pièce en deux actes. Montreal: Editions du Jour, 1968. Translation: *The Execution* (David Lobdell, trans.). Vancouver: Talon Books, 1976.

Fievre et Autres Textes Dramatiques. Théâtre Radiophonique (Collection Le Théatre du Jour, K–6). Montreal: Editions du Jour, 1974.

La Nef des Sorcières. With Nicole Brossard, Marthe Blackburn, Luce Guilbeault, France Théoret, Odette Gagnon, and Pol Pelletier. Montreal: Quinze, 1976.

L'Océan, suivi de Murmures. Montreal: Editions Quinze, 1977. Translation: *The Ocean* (Ray Chamberland, trans.). Toronto: Exile, 1977; *Murmures* (Margaret Rose, trans.) Canadian Drama/L'Art Dramatique Canadien 5 (Fall 1979): 281–93.

"Sommeil d'Hiver." Montreal: Editions Pleine Lune, 1984.

PLAY PRODUCTIONS

La Roulotte aux Poupées. Quebec, Summer 1960.

Eléonor. Quebec, Théâtre de l'Estoc, November, 1960.

L'Exécution. Montreal, Théâtre de Rideau Vert, 1968.

La Nef des Sorcières. With Nicole Brossard, Marthe Blackburn, Luce Guilbeault, France Théoret, Odette Gagnon, and Pol Pelletier, Montreal, Théâtre du Noveau Monde, 1976.

L'Ocean. Radio Canada, 1976.

Journal en images froides. Scenario, Radio Canada, 1978.

L'Exil, L'Escale. Radio Canada, 30 April 1979.

6. Identity and the Family in the Novels of Janette Turner Hospital

In an autobiographical essay, "After Long Absence," Janette Turner Hospital writes, "Something there is that doesn't love a boundary line,"[1] and her life and novels attest to this. Born in Melbourne, she lives in Canada one-third of each year but teaches at an Australian university during the summer and in Boston during the fall. Her characters tend to be nomads like herself, and she writes about crossing boundaries rather than about Canadian settings. In her life, her values, and her themes, Hospital is, in the words of Mickey Pearlman, "a multi-national writer."[2] The internationalism in Hospital's fiction is, however, distinctively Canadian, for it reflects what Coral Ann Howells calls "that mixture of cultures which is characteristic of Canadian social geography."[3] Even the nomadic lives of Hospital's protagonists are typically Canadian, for, according to Robert Kroetsch, "Canadians are supremely at home when they travel. . . . The urban figures in Canadian literature are, typically, travelling."[4]

Hospital's fiction has garnered critical acclaim on three continents—Europe, her native Australia, and North America. Reviewers praise her novels for their lushness and "beautifully crafted phrases,"[5] and critics discuss her recurrent concern with the alienated and dislocated. But scant attention has been paid to the issues of identity that pervade her novels. Hospital repeatedly undermines the notion of a unified, knowable self, instead presenting the self as fragmented and enigmatic. The desire for self-knowledge becomes problematic for her characters since the boundaries between themselves and others are often blurred.

In Hospital's early novels, the family forms the context in which characters seek to define themselves. She reminds us that the family is where we first acquire our sense of self, as several of her characters turn to their original families to resolve issues from the past. Hospital's first two novels center on traditional, though troubled, families, but her more recent novels portray the family as fragmented, with a physically or emotionally absent father the object of the protagonist's quest. In *The Tiger in the Tiger Pit*, *Borderline*, and *Charades*, characters are obsessed with fathers whose absence creates in them feelings of loss and dislocation.

To overcome their personal sense of dislocation, Hospital's protagonists seek meaning and continuity through storytelling. They create narratives in which they use metaphors from art, literature, science, or nature either to gain self-knowledge or to insulate themselves from it, and for some of Hospital's characters, storytelling becomes a vehicle for reexamining and understanding past events that have shaped their identities. In her first two novels, characters must allow their repressed memories to surface before they can achieve self-knowledge. The narrators in her later novels—*Borderline*, *Charades*, and *The Last Magician*—gain insights into themselves by constructing narratives that center on characters who function as doubles or who seem in other ways an integral part of themselves.

Another way in which Hospital's characters achieve self-knowledge is through recognizing their accountability for others, particularly for a double. In *The Ivory Swing*, *Borderline*, *Charades*, and *The Last Magician*, major characters feel deeply responsible for women who exist on the margins of society and are victims of violence. This pattern reflects Hospital's abiding concern with "individual, moral and political accountability for things that are, in most senses, beyond our power to do much about." But, she insists, our powerlessness "doesn't let us off the hook."[6]

In her first novel, *The Ivory Swing* (1982), Hospital presents characters who are locked in internal conflicts until a redemptive character, in the form of a double, awakens their sense of responsibility. The novel takes place in southern India, where a family from Winston, Ontario, has been transplanted, much as Hospital herself was when she and her husband, Clifford Hospital, lived in southern India in 1977.[7] The protagonist, Juliet, manages a household that includes two children, an Indian houseboy named Prabhakaran, and her husband, who is doing research for a book on Hinduism. By crossing the borders between East and West, Juliet and her husband David are led to critically examine themselves and their relationship. Juliet's immersion in domesticity in a rigidly patriarchal culture causes her to sift through her memories, to question her choices, and to admit her frustration in wanting "to have it all." For her, "all" means living in a city, with its stimulation and career opportunities, but not giving up her family. In India Juliet finds an artifact that she interprets as a metaphor for her own vacillation between small-town family life and urban freedom. It is an exquisite carving of the Hindu goddess Radha embracing the god Krishna on an ivory swing. The suggestion that the figures are in ceaseless motion, constantly swinging, makes the carving a mirror for Juliet's own inability either to accept her life in Kingston or to move to Montreal.

India offers her no easy solutions. Instead it comes to symbolize that problematic linkage between knowledge and the self. India, writes Hospital, is "the lotus land . . . where things which existed in the mind had more substance than the blurred mirage of the external world" (140).[8] In India, "nonentity is contagious" (167). The ambiguity of India is embodied in a widow named Yashoda, a woman who fascinates both Juliet and David. To them she appears more apparition than living person, more artifact than human being, for both recognize her uncanny resemblance to the carved figure of Radha on the ivory swing, and both see her as a projection of their contradictory impulses.

Like Juliet, Yashoda "wants it all," but for her that means enjoying the independence and freedom of a Western woman as well as the approval of the Indian patriarchal family. Hospital has said "I am always bifurcating my women; I always have pairs."[9] She has also pointed out that "the shadow self" is her "constant theme."[10] In *The Ivory Swing*, Yashoda becomes Juliet's shadow self, the double who acts out desires that Juliet represses. Yashoda transgresses the boundaries for widows established by Indian patriarchy, while Juliet cannot break out of the role of traditional wife prescribed by Western patriarchy. Juliet's metaphorical imagination creates from Yashoda her double, a "figment of need, a reflection in a well, a transposed identity on an ivory swing" (104). As Juliet's double, Yashoda challenges her to face her own dilemma honestly and to question her choices.

Yashoda and the ivory swing also function as metaphors for the internal conflict of Juliet's husband, David. He is struggling with his sexuality and his "moral control" (153) and uses Yashoda as a scapegoat for his own frustrations. Attracted to her sensual beauty, he regards Yashoda as a *yakshi*, a Hindu demon-lover who threatens to free the "pterodactyl" that he imagines lurking within "the fen of . . . [his] libido" (153). Yashoda revives in David the memory of "the night of the pterodactyl" (80) when he let himself be seduced by a desperate undergraduate who climbed into his university office through a window.

When Yashoda and the houseboy Prabhakaran are murdered for violating the Indian patriarchal laws governing widows, David and Juliet ask themselves the question that Hospital poses in her later novel *Borderline*: "Just how accountable *are* we? You and me?" (*B*, 34). Since the Indian men who killed Yashoda used her as their scapegoat, blaming her transgressions for the monsoon that ruined their harvest, David feels complicitous in their crime. Juliet, too, feels responsible for Yashoda's death, because she tacitly encouraged Yashoda, as her shadow self, to rebel against patriarchal laws that she herself resents.

As often happens in Hospital's novels, taking responsibility for the plight of another character (particularly a double), becomes a means of redemption. When Juliet and David feel guilty about the deaths of Yashoda and Prabhakaran, they engage in self-questioning that leads them to decide to move to Montreal. The decision to move suggests that their encounter with a double in India has been a catalyst for growth in self-knowledge, though the novel ends on a note of uncertainty about the future of their marriage.

David and Juliet have both learned to accept "the terrible limits of knowledge and understanding" (252). This is another dominant theme in Hospital's work, particularly in her second novel, *The Tiger in the Tiger Pit* (1983). This novels' narrative structure resembles those in two novels by Virginia Woolf: *To the Lighthouse* and *Mrs. Dalloway*, where past events are narrated in the interior monologues of characters who often describe the same scene from various perspectives. These multiple viewpoints underscore the theme that "nothing could be clear" (*TTP*, 106). As in Woolf's novels, Hospital's characters, seeking order and meaning, explore their individual and shared memories. To free themselves from delusions and unresolved guilt, they must do what a British schoolteacher admonishes his class to do during a field trip to Roman ruins: "Look for the present in the past, and for the past in the present" (*TTP*, 57).

The Tiger in the Tiger Pit also focuses on a traditional family, though one fractured by deep, unresolved resentments of the patriarchal father: Edward Carpenter, a seventy-three-year-old retired school principal, who lives with his wife, Elizabeth, in Ashville, Massachusetts. Edward is estranged from his three adult children: Emily, a concert violinist; Jason, a therapist; and Victoria, a patient in a mental institution. Edward sits "caged" in his bedroom because of a heart condition, which is symptomatic of his repressed emotions. As in *To the Lighthouse*, it is the father who stands outside the family circle, wanting love but lacking the mother's gift for expressing it. He spends his days narrating to himself the story of his past, "pacing through a litter of memories like an unquiet ghost" (45), and raging over a lifetime spent conforming to "the laws of moral propriety" (13). Most of all he resents his choice of "renunciation and responsibility" (13) instead of resenting the consummation of his illicit love for Marta Wilson, the wife of his assistant principal, Joe Wilson. Like David in *The Ivory Swing*, Edward cannot resolve the tension between his sexual passion and his "moral rectitude" (8). The struggles of David and Edward may reflect the tensions Hospital herself experienced growing up "in such a lush physically hedonistic place as a sub-tropical rainforest" and being "brought up a rigid puritan" in a Pentecostal family. [11] Hospital's portrait of Edward Carpenter also reflects her interest in "tyrannical fathers," the impact they have on their adult daughters, and their own vulnerability. [12]

Though Edward has the perspicacity to know "how selective the memory gets, coddling and pandering" (115), he never recognizes that his selective memory blinds him to signs of his wife's long-term affair with Joe Wilson. He never realizes that Marta had not loved him but felt connected to him only because of their spouses' affair. Rather than face disturbing truths about his past, Edward reconstructs his own life in metaphor, and retreats into a fictive world. He reinvents himself and Marta as "Paolo and Francesca, Antony and Cleopatra, Anna Karenina and Vronsky" (83); he imagines himself ending his life as a tragic hero—like Milton's Samson Agonistes or Marlow's Faustus. By fictionalizing his past and future, he bars himself both from self-knowledge and love. Unlike Juliet in *The Ivory Swing*, he never recognizes his double—Joe Wilson—who experienced the same inner conflict but made choices that Edward can only imagine. Nor does he ever understand how his puritanical attitude toward his wife and daughter Victoria ruined his relationships with them.

Finally, in an attempt to express his love for Marta Wilson before he dies, Edward contrives to meet her in the family gazebo, a space that combines both enclosure and openness and that reflects Edward's contrary impulses toward restraint and freedom. But as Edward is about to declare his love to Marta, a scene from his past intrudes: his mad daughter, Victoria, attacks him with a garden hose just as he had assaulted her, naked with her lover, thirty years earlier, when he interrupted their lovemaking in the gazebo. Victoria's revenge triggers Edward's second heart attack, which nearly kills him. At the end of the novel, Edward asks Elizabeth for forgiveness, a request she fails to understand, since he has told no one, least of all her, about his obsessive love for Marta. Though Edward's anger is temporarily dispelled, he is back where he started—

locked in illusions and suffering from symbolic and real heart disease, both produced by his frustrated emotions. He never faces his past honestly or takes responsibility for contributing to Victoria's derangement. As the novel ends, he lovingly touches Elizabeth's face, a gesture so uncharacteristic of him that it moves her to tears.

At first Elizabeth is no better at dealing with the past than Edward is: "She is afraid of dislodging another slag heap of memory. This is the problem: nothing is settled in the past, it is a shifting region of fault lines and instability" (249). She insulates herself from painful memories through metaphors from music. She imagines herself Prospero in an Elizabethan opera, restoring harmony to her family. And she plays the part of a composer orchestrating the last movement of her family symphony—the family reunion to celebrate her and Edward's fiftieth anniversary. She composes "an adagio for Victoria," "an allegro for Jason," and "a scherzo life" for Emily (21). These metaphors give her an illusion of control over her life and the lives of her children, and keep the past, including Victoria's traumas, at bay. But Elizabeth's memories lie in her brain like "a hand grenade, waiting" (247). Her most threatening memory is of the time when she and Joe Wilson, making love on the living-room couch, were interrupted by the child Victoria, who soon afterward suffered a mental breakdown. It is only after Elizabeth relives this painful memory, through the intervention of her double, Marta Wilson, that she can accept and return Edward's love in the moment of reconciliation that ends the novel. Unlike Edward, she succeeds in moving beyond an aesthetic retreat from life to self-honesty. Because of her growth and Edward's gesture of tenderness, Hospital's novel closes with a traditional, if contrived, resolution, the only one like it in her first five novels.

Hospital departs further from the conventional, realistic plot and ventures into postmodernism in her third novel, *Borderline* (1985), which she says is "*meant* to be muddled, self-conscious and intrusive."[13] *Borderline* combines the suspense and intrigue of a mystery thriller with the lyricism and eloquence of a meditation on the eliding of borders between the self and the double, art and life, fact and fiction. Though these ideas are present in Hospital's earlier novels, here she explores them in more depth. Critics greeted *Borderline* as the work that established Hospital "as a significant novelist."[14] It was hailed as her "Borgesian" novel, a novel in which "nothing ever *is* until it is imagined; once imagined, it can become something else."[15] (At one point Jean-Marc tells Jorge Luis Borges's *Circular Ruins*.) It is her first novel to include the postmodernist element of absent subjects—two characters who have disappeared and are called Los Desparecidos, "the missing ones." *Borderline* also emphasizes the postmodern ideas that the self is unknowable and that uncertainty is an inescapable fact of life.

An atmosphere of Borgesian phantasmagoria is established in the first scene at the U.S.-Canadian border, which turns out to be the borderline between dreams and reality. Here two strangers meet—Gus Kelly, a Canadian insurance salesman, and Felicity, an art historian and the curator at a private gallery. Felicity is the former lover of Jean-Marc's father, who is called simply "Seymour." Gus and Felicity witness the apprehension of illegal El Salvadorean aliens, who are hidden in animal carcasses in a refrigerated van. The police overlook one alien, an unconscious woman whom Felicity immediately recognizes as the artist's model in the fifteenth-century Florentine painting *Magdalena* by Perugino, a painting that Felicity has been trying to procure for her gallery in Cambridge, Massachusetts. The border between art and life dissolves, and the fusion of the two permeates the novel.

Both Gus and Felicity doubt the reality of Dolores Marquez's existence. As Yashoda in *The Ivory Swing* seems a fiction created by Juliet and David to reflect their internal conflicts, Dolores seems a metaphor that Gus and Felicity have invented to fill a void in themselves. Her several names underscore the ambiguity of her identity: "Dolores Marquez," "La Desconocida," "La Salvadora" (The Savior), and "La Magdalena." "La Desconocida" translates as "the unknown or unknowable one" (1). She is rumored to be "a guerilla commando" or "an army informer" (207), and Jean-Marc believes that she must be a dangerous criminal. Moving beyond her initial reaction to Dolores as a work of art, Felicity suspects that Dolores has been raped, a suspicion supported by Dolores's fearfulness and her muteness. Feminist concerns that are evident in Hospital's earlier novels become central in *Borderline*, in particular, women's victimization, marginality, and silencing.

Both Felicity and Gus become obsessed with finding Dolores, for she compels them to ask themselves the question posed in each of Hospital's novels: "Just how accountable *are* we? You and me?" (34). How much are those with power and privilege responsible for the marginalized and disempowered? Having asked herself this question, Felicity, a Hospital nomad, takes responsibility for Dolores Marquez's welfare and departs from her usual habit of traveling light and avoiding commitment. Felicity's fear of commitment is reflected in her nightmares of being "trapped in one painting" (9). This resistance to being locked into one space began in childhood when she felt abandoned by her missionary father, who, according to reports, "'went native'" (5). In an epiphanic moment, Felicity recognizes in Dolores a double, herself at the moment when she "knew she would never see her father . . . again" (37). Dolores's sense of loss and dislocation mirrors Felicity's, for Dolores reflects the absence that Felicity felt as a child and that still haunts her. The absence compels her "to be on the road, on the move, defying another border" (13), searching for something to fill the vacancy within herself but afraid of the commitment that entails. The narrator, Jean-Marc, observes that "there has always been a quality of absence about her" (8). By devoting herself to finding Dolores, Felicity finally overcomes her longing for her father and forgives him, because she learns, from the unexpected detours in her own quest, that her father "never meant to leave" but "got caught in a rip tide, there was nothing he could do" (214).

Jean-Marc is also obsessed with his absent father. In his case, emotional, not physical, distance produces his feeling of loss. This common loss causes Jean-Marc to identify with Felicity and to claim her past as his own: "Her stories bombard me, they seem to become my own memories" (159). By telling Felicity's story, Jean-Marc develops the capacity to forgive his own father.

The third absent father in *Borderline* is Gus Kelly, whose disappearance allows Jean-Marc to become a surrogate father to Gus's daughter, Kathleen. Jean-Marc's preoccupation with Gus also arises from the reflexive nature of Jean-Marc's storytelling: in seeking the truth about Gus, he seeks self-knowledge, for he realizes that Gus, his double, mirrors his own Dantean desire for an ideal woman. When Jean-Marc relates Gus's Dantean vision of Dolores, Jean-Marc knows that he is actually writing about himself and Felicity when he was ten years old and she became his Beatrice. According to Hospital, both Gus and Jean-Marc are searching for "elusive and idealized love objects."[16] Both have visions of perfect love, Gus when he sees Dolores with "a ring of light around her head" (165) and Jean-Marc when he sees a painting in which his father, Seymour, "has painted the mind of the sun, the concept of light, the idea of God" (288). Jean-Marc's illumination allows him to forgive his father, Seymour, which their embrace at the novel's end suggests. Hospital says that although her editor urged her to cut Gus's Dantean vision, she refused because she wanted to stress the similarities between Gus's quest for Dolores and Jean-Marc's for Felicity. Hospital notes that her "moral and literary purpose"[17] in *Borderline* was to tell about those on the margins, through the perspective of a narrator, Jean-Marc Seymour, who "is working out his salvation."[18] He achieves salvation through recognizing his responsibility for Felicity and Gus and, indirectly, for Dolores Marquez. In *Borderline*, the parallels and doubling among characters questing for some form of redemption illustrate Gerry Turcotte's comment that Hospital "refracts reality through an infinity of spinning mirrors."[19]

Hospital's use of mirrors becomes even more complex in her fourth novel, *Charades* (1989), where she explores themes of identity and accountability in the context of physics and cosmology. She creates another protagonist, Charade Ryan, on a nomadic quest for a missing father. Hospital again expresses the idea that crossing familial, social, and national boundaries can be a key to self-knowledge. Charade leaves her native Australia to seek her father, Nicholas Truman, in Canada, England, and finally in Cambridge, Massachusetts. There, in the office and apartment of her lover, an MIT physics professor named Koenig—who resembles her father—Charade narrates the story of Nicholas and the three women who loved him and whose lives shaped hers: her adoptive mother, Bea Ryan; her mother's foster sister, Aunt Kay (Katherine Sussex); and her biological mother, Verity Ashkenazy. In order to know herself, Charade must re-create the lives of these three women. Like Jean-Marc, Charade learns about herself and works out her salvation through identifying with the subjects of her narrative. She emphasizes the fluidity of the self and its multiple identities when she observes, "I've thought and thought, and I don't understand where one life ends and another begins" (87). Because diverse and sometimes contradictory stories have formed Charade, her identity is fragmented and ambiguous. Its elusiveness is underscored by her nickname, "Enigma," which she adopts when visiting her British aunts in search of her father.

Charade was brought up by Bea Ryan, the "Slut of the Tamborine Rainforest" (13), an earth-mother who raised ten children. (Some were not hers, and all had different fathers.) Bea understands life only through her senses, and "knowledge comes to her like heat through the pores of her skin" (171). Bea understands instinctively what Koenig, Charade's lover, knows through Heisenberg's physics theories—that two contradictory statements can both be true. For example, Bea insists that though another woman, Verity, is Charade's biological mother, Bea and Truman "made" Charade (295). Bea devalues the importance of the intellect; instead she mirrors the sensual side of Charade. This is emphasized when Bea asks

Charade, "'Why can't you let things be? Why can't you let sleeping dogs lie? Why do you want to know everything? You think *knowing* is so great?'" (294). Only after Charade appreciates Bea's wisdom and realizes that she can never know the truth about Nicholas, much less find him, can she return home to Bea—"to be."

In *Charades*, Hospital's theme of the quest for a missing father can be read as an allegory in which the protagonist, Charade, needs to integrate the sensual, intellectual, and unconscious dimensions of herself in order to become whole. She achieves this through telling the story of the women who love her father, Nicholas, and who represent three sides of herself— Bea the sensual, Kay the intellectual, and Verity the unconscious. Conse- quently, Charade leaves Bea's sensual world to learn about Truman from Bea's estranged foster-sister, Kay Sussex. A Canadian scholar of medieval English and French literature, Kay is an intellectual who articulates concepts of uncertainty that are central to the novel. "'Do time and space really exist?' Katherine [Kay] asks Charade. Or are they, she wonders, like soul and eternity, just clever ideas? Metaphors of explanation. A way of holding things apart in our minds?" (166). Kay's questions introduce Charade to the ideas that she will hear in Koenig's lectures—postmodern ideas about the lack of objectivity and truth in scientific theories. From such theories, Charade concludes that she can never know the truth about her father and that human identity itself is only a useful fiction.

Another character who teaches Charade about the enigmatic nature of identity is Verity Ashkenazy. Charade will never be certain whether Verity was indeed the daughter of French Jewish victims of the Holocaust or simply the daughter of Mick and Thelma Delancy, as Verity's classmate, Myra, claims. Only at the novel's end does Charade learn that Verity is both her biological mother and Sleeping Beauty, the silent woman whom she and Bea used to visit in a mental institution. This knowledge comes to Charade in a dream, in which Verity speaks through Charade's lips the words that express the paradox of Nicholas's simultaneous absence and presence in their lives: "'He is coming, but not getting closer'" (289). Verity's associations with sleep and dreams, her muteness, and the ambi- guity of her origins suggest that she reflects Charade's unconscious, which provides the insight she needs to achieve wholeness and to go home.

Before that can happen, however, Charade must learn about account- ability from the negative example Koenig provides in the tale of his mar- riage. Like Nicholas, Koenig married a Holocaust survivor who never overcomes her fear that she is the next "to be carried off, to be arrested, to be mugged, to be stabbed, to be raped, to be committed to an asylum, to be burned at the stake" (218). Although Koenig could not stay married to his wife, he will always feel responsible for her victimization. Because of the parallels between Koenig and Nicholas, Charade realizes that Nicholas, too, may never overcome his guilt for Verity's suffering. By understanding this, Charade can forgive him for leaving both herself and Verity, and she can end her quest.

In this ending *Charades* parallels *The Arabian Nights*, for both celebrate women's strengths through storytelling. Charade, like Scheherazade (their names rhyme), wins her freedom from her male lover and becomes more powerful than he. Unlike Koenig, Charade has conquered her past by accepting the uncertainty of it and by acting on her sense of responsibility for those she loves. She persuades Bea, for instance, to call Kay and renew their sisterhood after years of estrangement. Charade's quest for her absent father ends in the discovery of her mother and of her own identity as a strong woman.

In *The Last Magician* (1992), Hospital continues to examine issues from her past novels—identity, uncertainty, the double, and accountability. But her approach to these issues in *The Last Magician* is significantly different. Now she focuses on five characters who are representative of various layers of Australian society: Lucy, the narrator, a "hooker" turned filmmaker; Catherine, Lucy's collaborator and the former lover of Charlie Chang; Gabriel Gray, "a renegade law student, a troublemaker" (266), Lucy's former lover, and the son of Judge Robbie Gray; Charlie Chang, a postmodern photographer and filmmaker, the son of Chinese Australian greengrocers; Cat Reilly, a farm laborer's daughter and twice the victim of Robbie Gray's violent jealousy. *The Last Magician* is about the distance that separates these characters from each other, and the spaces that unite them.

Hospital deconstructs the borderlines between these characters as they themselves repeatedly express a feeling of oneness with each other. Lucy says that both Gabriel and Charlie are part of her. She even claims that she has acquired "the habit of thinking Charlie's thoughts" (11). Catherine, Cat, and Charlie mysteriously blend in their childhood swimming hole at Cedar Creek: "that fluid place where shapes undid themselves" (189) and "where everything connects with everything else" (192). Cedar Creek becomes a metaphor for the communal identity shared by the main characters in this novel. Charlie says that in the pool he "couldn't tell where Cat ended and Catherine began" (189). Reunited after twenty-five years apart, Charlie thinks of Catherine as his twin and self, and realizes that she holds "the missing parts of himself" (285). But the relationship of Charlie and Catherine is doomed without Cat, who makes them whole because they both take responsibility for her victimization. Lucy believes that Charlie, Catherine, and Cat are all a part of herself and that Cedar Creek is always with her. This fusing of individuals problematizes identity, as Lucy recognizes when she says, "What a riddle that is. Where, in the grab bag of costumes and masks does the self hide out?" (49).

Identity is further complicated in *The Last Magician* by Hospital's tendency to bifurcate her characters. This is underscored by their double names: Lucia becomes Lucy; Gabriel Gray is Gabriel Brennan; Robbie Gray poses as Sonny Blue; Charlie is really Fu Hsi. Hospital suggests that no one is just one person, a concept which is illustrated by Charlie's photographs and films, for in them characters acquire double or multiple identities. Examining Charlie's photographs and her memories, Lucy, like Charade and Jean-Marc, reconstructs the stories of other characters in order to learn about herself. She, too, becomes the product of her narratives, as she identifies with her missing subjects—Charlie, Gabriel, and Cat. Self-knowledge is also problematic for Lucy because of the multiple identities she acquires by crossing national and class borders. Her nomadic career as filmmaker takes her from London to New York to Australia, "living on the move half the time and treating the world as an office" (6). She says, "As for me, I go back and forth, above and under. I cross borders. That world, this world, they coexist all the time and I move between them. It's a greedy curiosity I have, a voraciousness, I was born with it, a hunger to live all my possible lives" (19). Lucy's lives have ranged from being a model student at a private school to becoming an intellectual prostitute and then a documentary filmmaker.

Lucy has crisscrossed the borders between the upper-class world of power and privilege and the "quarry," Hospital's term for the "nether world" of Sydney, inhabited by the poor and homeless. According to Lucy, no one knows how this underground world began: "It's anybody's guess if this was once a subway, or an underground parking lot, or the remnants of warehouse storage cellars" (17). Whatever its origins, the quarry, like Cedar Creek, is a metaphor for oneness. It allows characters to transcend their individual identities and to merge with each other, though Lucy admits that drugs aid quarry dwellers in their ability to "dolphin about for hours in the ocean of I-am-you, you-are-me" (18).

As the quarry spreads, the Australian upper classes deny its existence, since it threatens to undermine the class structure on which their privilege rests. The character most representative of this attitude, Judge Robbie Gray, Gabriel's father, refuses to cross class borders to marry Cat, the woman he loves. Instead, consumed with jealousy, he murders her. Hospital implies that because Gabriel and Charlie are on the brink of discovering this fact, Robbie has them killed. In refusing to be accountable or to cross borders, Robbie becomes "a caricature of himself" (345). As accountability in Hospital's novels is an avenue to self-knowledge, its absence causes self-alienation. This is illustrated by Robbie's behavior when he murders Cat and then abuses his wife. She says, "'It was someone else in his body, it wasn't him, it was horrible'" (345).

In contrast to Robbie's self-alienation, Hospital ends *The Last Magician* with Lucy, her protagonist, defining her identity as a woman whose art is grounded in accountability and connectedness. She persuades Catherine that their next documentary will focus on "Aboriginal land rights in northern Queensland" (351) and that then they will make a film on the quarry. They choose these subjects to affirm their oneness with Gabriel, Charlie, and Cat in the face of their apparent deaths.

This ending celebrates the power of the woman artist to overcome silencing and marginality. It is an ending that reflects Hospital's own moral aesthetic, her commitment to breaking down the borders separating nationalities, classes, and individuals. Janette Turner Hospital writes novels that invite her readers to share her sense of "individual, moral and political accountability."[20] In her recent novels she achieves this through combining the politics of feminism with the strategies of postmodernism: absent subjects, open endings, and critiques of traditional concepts of identity and truth. The adroit blending of these two divergent literary movements in her novels comes as no surprise, since Hospital has devoted her life and her writing to crossing boundaries.

Writings by Janette Turner Hospital

NOVELS

The Ivory Swing. Toronto: McClelland & Stewart, 1982; Seal, 1983; Dutton, 1983; Bantam, 1984.

The Tiger in the Tiger Pit. Toronto: McClelland & Stewart, 1983. Seal, 1984; Dutton, 1984; Bantam, 1985; Virago, 1991.

Borderline. Sydney: Hodder & Stoughton, 1985; Toronto: McClelland & Stewart, 1985; Dutton, 1985; Seal, 1986; Bantam, 1987; Virago, 1990.

Charades. St. Lucia, Australia: University of Queensland Press, 1988.

A Very Proper Death (mystery published under pseudonym Alex Juniper). Melbourne: Penguin, 1990; Toronto: Random House, 1990, 1991; Scribners, 1991; Virago, 1992.

The Last Magician. Australia: University of Queensland Press, 1992; New York: Henry Holt, 1992.

COLLECTED SHORT STORIES

Dislocations. Toronto: McClelland & Stewart, 1986; Norton, 1990.

Isobars. Toronto: McClelland & Stewart, 1991; Baton Rouge: Louisiana State University Press, 1991; Virago, 1992.

ARTICLES, REVIEWS, STORIES

"Some Have Called Thee Mighty and Dreadful" (story). *North American Review* 264 (Summer 1979): 33–36.

"Golden Girl" (story). *Mademoiselle*, October 1981: 104+.

"Ashes to Ashes" (story). *Encounter* 60 (May 1983): 3–8.

"Amazing Grace" (story). *Ladies' Home Journal*, June 1986, 114+.

"The Mango Tree" (story). *The Yale Review* 75 (Summer 1986): 601–09.

"Happy Diwali" (story). *North American Review* 271 (September 1986): 26–30.

Review of *The Beet Queen*, by Louise Erdrich. *Toronto Globe and Mail*, 11 October 1986: 7.

"Letter to a New York Editor." *Meanjin* 47 (Spring 1988): 560–64.

Review of *A Time to Dance, No Time to Weep*, by Rumer Godden. *New York Times Book Review*, 3 January 1988: 13.

Review of *The Late Mattia Pascal*, by Luigi Pirandello (trans. William Weaver). *New York Times Book Review*, 17 April 1988: 32.

Review of *The Satanic Verses*, by Salman Rushdie. *Toronto Globe and Mail*, 22 October 1988: 17.

Review of *My Place*, by Sally Morgan. *New York Times Book Review*, 19 February 1989: 13.

Review of *For Love and Money: A Writing Life, 1969–1989*, by Jonathan Raban. *New York Times Book Review*, 1 October 1989: 20.

"*Dislocations, Borderline, Charades*" (transcription of lecture and questions). In *Writers in Action: The Writer's Choice Evenings*, ed. Gerry Turcotte, 63–85. Sydney: Currency Press, 1990.

Letter to the Editors. In *Language in Her Eye: Views on Writing and Gender by Canadian Women Writing in English*, ed. Libby Scheier, Sarah Sheard, and Eleanor Wachtel, 146–47. Toronto: Coach House Press, 1990.

Review of *Chekhov's Sister*, by W. D. Wetherell. *New York Times Book Review*, 25 March 1990: 12.

Review of *India: A Million Mutinies Now*, by V. S. Naipaul. *New York Times Book Review*, 30 December 1990: 1.

"The Last of the Hapsburgs" (story). *LiNQ: Literature in Northern Queensland* 17 (1990): 1–13.

"Janette Turner Hospital" (autobiographical essay). In *Homeland*, ed. George Papaellinas, 14–25. Sydney: Allen & Unwin, 1991.

"Books in the Hand, Books in the Bush." *The Women's Review of Books* 9 (October 1991): 22–23.

7. Isabel Huggan and Jane Urquhart: Feminine in This?

It's been frequently observed that women who wish to assume control of their own identities or even to assume power won't seem feminine—that is, they won't seem attractive to men. In fiction as in life, therefore, even in novels written by women, women tend to be portrayed not as heroes but as heroines—that is, "Women must be depicted not in 'actual independence but [in] action despite dependence.'"[1] Often they are situated in confining spaces that ensure dependency, a sense of their being "feminine." As we have recently witnessed, the Thelmas and Louises who hit the road remain the recipients of intense (primarily masculine) critical concern. In first novels by Canadian writers Isabel Huggan and Jane Urquhart (both in their forties and both mothers of daughters), we find that trying to be "in action despite dependence" becomes an integral concern. Huggan and Urquhart are very different writers, but in their fiction the familiar difficulties arise: while placed in spaces determined and controlled by others, women struggle to shape or at least to understand their identities. They seek to increase and shape the space available in which to conduct their lives.

"What did it *mean* to be a girl or a boy, and why did I feel like such a failure?"[2] Elizabeth Kessler's cry rings through Isabel Huggan's *The Elizabeth Stories*. Elizabeth, narrator of the eight loosely connected stories,[3] knows she is a girl; she is sexual from the age of three, when she uses her teddy bear to "greet" the tingling in her "plump little crotch" and to allay her loneliness. Family, however, and the predominantly German Canadian community of Garten work against rather than with Elizabeth in her effort to understand what it means to be a girl; their contributions primarily make her feel like a failure. In her review of her childhood, Elizabeth identifies with only one woman—an outsider. Eventually she will manage to leave "Garten," her garden for growing up, the confining space in which she is insistently informed that she is sinful and nothing else. Elizabeth is trapped in her body as she is in Garten, and she is trapped in the misunderstanding between her parents and herself, trapped in the roles and the spaces into which they drive her. Her goal is to be different from her parents, and specifically different from her mother. She wishes to escape whatever Garten represents, and to find freedom in unknown spaces. As Huggan has said, "The 50's formed character in very specific ways. Either you became what you were 'meant' to become or you fought against it. Elizabeth is the prototype for young women who looked at their mothers and said, 'I don't want to become that.'"[4] Of course, it is not just the fifties that tried to form character: the power of the book lies in the timelessness of the childhood it describes. Girls such as Elizabeth have always been destined to suffer.

Nancy Chodorow has shown that girls develop a positive gender identity by identifying with their mothers, thus developing the qualities necessary to one day become mothers themselves.[5] But Mavis, Elizabeth's mother, is not good at motherhood. Elizabeth herself points out that "there was always a darkness under us, as if we were floating on a deep river of distrust and suspicion, pretending to each other that our little raft was safe and sure" ("Queen Esther," 87). Mavis assumes that if anything is wrong, Elizabeth is responsible for its being so. She is incapable of knowing anything about Elizabeth's real experiences, although she is sure that she can "read [Elizabeth] like a book" ("Secrets," 158). Her mother's lack of faith helps to destroy a loving relationship between Elizabeth and a retarded cousin and leaves Elizabeth realizing that "I was more frightened of the people in the house behind me than of anything in the woods" ("Into the Green Stillness," 80). Elizabeth lacks the emotional and physical space in which to develop the feminine identity that a mother should attempt to provide. At eleven, Elizabeth has to take the part of a boy in the annual ballet recital. *And*, at her mother's insistence, she must wear her first bra in order to look like a boy—she won't "jiggle."[6] Trudy, the daughter of her mother's best friend and supposedly Elizabeth's friend, is everything feminine that chunky, tall Elizabeth is not, and she gloats over the fact. In the performance of the ballet she humiliates Elizabeth by sitting on her knee during the final bow, as if Elizabeth were actually a boy. Desperate at being so confined in the wrong role, Elizabeth protests from the stage: "I'm really a girl!" ("Jack of Hearts," 51).

A woman from whom Elizabeth derives better help than from her mother and her childhood friends is "Aunt" Eadie, a close friend of her mother. Aunt Eadie is not actually a member of the family or community. From her, however, Elizabeth finds her first means of escape from the confusion of Garten and "the dark abyss" of sex ("Jack of Hearts," 51). Aunt Eadie teaches Elizabeth poker, a game she will continue to play by herself in the privacy of her closet whenever she needs to escape. Flamboyant Aunt Eadie fascinates Elizabeth: Aunt Eadie is safe because she doesn't care and is therefore protected from society. She is clearly an outsider to Garten and its notions of what it means to be a girl. Elizabeth's father, Frank, solid citizen of Garten and arbiter of standards for women, emphatically does not approve of her, and Elizabeth's mother can only envy her. Elizabeth *does* care about what a girl should do, and so although Aunt Eadie offers a new perspective from which to see Garten and her family, she provides only a means of temporary escape, not a cure—and Aunt Eadie herself, we note, also turns to alcohol.

Help for Elizabeth, then, does not come from other women, who are either beyond the pale, or, conversely, are themselves too confined within Garten's male structures to be useful. Men are certainly no better at helping her, with the partial exception of a six-foot-five American teacher at Elizabeth's school named Mr. Wheeling. He provides substantial assistance to adolescent Elizabeth in her quest to be happily herself, and naturally she falls in love with him. Mr. Wheeling looks with fresh eyes at Elizabeth, who, as girls are taught too often to do, judges herself and her abilities by her appearance: is she "feminine"?[7] Mr. Wheeling enables her to change how she sees herself during this teenage growing period—to see her height, for instance, not as a horrible flaw but as an asset, especially for basketball. With his help, both she and the basketball team triumph. Success "transforms" her view of her height: she is the perfect height to dance with equally tall Mr. Wheeling at the basketball victory dance; and other male teachers now refer to her as one of the "pretty girls"; if men see her as feminine, she can do so, too.

But Mr. Wheeling's lessons about what it means to be a woman are mixed. He has beaten his wife so often and so severely that he receives a jail sentence. Mr. Wheeling loves his wife, but she is dependent on him— shut in her house, isolated in caring for a hopelessly malformed baby. During the time that we learn about Mr. Wheeling we also learn that Elizabeth's father gives his wife, Mavis, the look of purest hate that Elizabeth has ever seen during a crisis in which he has had to rely on Mavis for love and trust. Mavis, too—at Frank's insistence—is housebound and dependent on him. Elizabeth herself, she tells us, had relied on a caged pet bunny for love and trust—and ended up wanting to strangle it because it was so passive and so dependent. What are we to make of this? Elizabeth's father concludes that "violence had always been part of the American character" ("Sorrows of the Flesh," 136)—a conclusion that does not keep him from leaving Canada and retiring to the States with Mavis as soon as he has enough money to do so from his new career. Is violence attractive, perhaps part of his own character, so that in America he can go home to what is natural?[8] Elizabeth must choose for herself what to remember about her teacher, and she "choose[s] to remember . . . [Mr. Wheeling's] courage, his compassion, his concern for our ignorant fears" ("Sorrows of the Flesh," 124). But memory is selective, and Elizabeth has also learned once again the danger of love and specifically of being a woman: "The formation of female identity is . . . fraught with conflicting views of the female self, with ambivalence and humiliation."[9] Be feminine, be beaten. Enter a cage at your own risk.

What does it mean to be a girl? Elizabeth's experiences with the men and boys she meets in "Garten" develop her fear of the feminine cage rather than encouraging a healthy open blossoming of female sexuality. As has so often been the plan for women, sexual development means increasing repression, means being silenced and controlled by men—means feeling a failure at being feminine and becoming secretive about real feelings. For instance, when Elizabeth is ten, a little boy with whom she had played innocent exploratory games changes his approach: "There was an urgency to his squirming on top of me that had never been part of the game before. I felt the first shreddings of female dread, the coming apart of the dream. . . . But he wouldn't stop, he kept moving rhythmically on top of me, saying, 'Shut up, Elizabeth, shut up'" ("Sawdust," 25). Needless to say, her parents blame her for this "sinful" episode, and she must lie about it. She discovers that one of her cousins regularly sexually abuses his sister; again, Elizabeth must be silent, and to escape punishment she must sacrifice an important friendship with another female cousin ("Into the Green Stillness"). Her father's view of her is disastrous. She realizes that her father "had wanted me to be a son. And what he had was a daughter who wasn't even very good at being a girl" ("Jack of Hearts," 42). But her father also makes it clear that to be unfeminine (e.g., to smoke cigarettes) is worse than being filthy ("Getting Out of Garten," 163). Physically, she resembles her father, but he is a pillar of the community— and if he is a pillar, "What does that make me?" ("Queen Esther," 89). With whom can she identify? Elizabeth has no name or label for herself. Men silence you, and her mother, so open and free with her female friends, is secretive and repressed with Frank. When Frank gives Elizabeth an order that insults Mavis's best friend, Eadie, Mavis "purse[s] her lips tightly and sa[ys], 'Be a good girl, Elizabeth. Do as you're told'" ("Jack of Hearts," 56).[10]

Mavis joins Frank (in an unverbalized sexual unity) to form a space that excludes and silences Elizabeth. Her parents, we understand, will get along just fine when free of Elizabeth, as she will without them, a revelation both share when Elizabeth takes her first weekend away from home ("Queen Esther," 98).[11] Elizabeth habitually eavesdrops on their conversation and on her mother's telephone conversations by lying alone in the dark at the top of the stairs; she escapes from their misunderstanding by hiding in dark spaces—a bathroom, her closet. They believe her to have "an amazing capacity for sins that ha[s] the ability to bring on disaster" ("Sawdust," 26). In Elizabeth's experience, then, men separate you from yourself, and they separate you from other women, even from your mother.

Nevertheless, as part of her growing up Elizabeth does learn something from her mother and therefore forms a stronger bond with her: she learns that her mother, like herself, is not happy with the feminine role Garten assigns and that she too has sought to escape to wider spaces. Mavis has always wanted to move out of Garten. She has seemed content in the confines of her kitchen, since Frank has forbidden her to have a job. Actually, however, she has a secret life involving another man and another religion in a neighboring city. Elizabeth, who has known nothing of this other life, must face the fact that her mother lies. Even her mother's friends and (especially) her father know nothing of Mavis's secret, and so Elizabeth becomes the unwilling and lonely sharer. Through keeping this secret Elizabeth takes on an ironic womanly identity: all women keep secrets about who they truly are, most especially from men, who can therefore continue to see women as they wish them to be. Elizabeth loves science because in this (typically masculine) field words openly, concretely label and organize the world. Her woman's world lacks language and words. Her relationship with her mother is defined, finally, by secrecy, by silently understood mis-understanding.

Elizabeth seems to succeed finally in independently constructing a view of herself as a girl with which she is at least comfortable, although it is limited. She finds a platonic boyfriend who also wishes to leave Garten. At a social outing with other friends, she notes coolly that "as often happened, I felt somewhere in between [the boys and the girls], in neither camp and both" ("Getting Out," 174)—she has no clearly defined sexual situation. Tellingly, Elizabeth and her boyfriend Dieter do not develop a sexual relationship—they primarily share the goal of leaving Garten. They do not make love, as do Trudy and Glen, remaining "prisoners in [their] bodies" ("Getting Out," 181). However, this means that Elizabeth does not become pregnant (as does Trudy), and she and Dieter therefore do not have to get married. Trudy, she realizes, is content to stay in Garten. Although wounded, Elizabeth will finally leave Garten "intact" ("Getting Out," 184). She seeks, and we hope will find, space in which to grow, space in which to find out what it means to be a woman. In the meantime, escape is her primary success, including escape from active sexuality which would compel her into a limited feminine role.

Isabel Huggan sets *The Elizabeth Stories* in the Canadian fifties, a time when men firmly placed women in the enclosed "landscape" of the kitchen; the spaces are those realized by fully realized plot and character, by Elizabeth and her struggle with her father, her mother, and Garten. In Huggan's fiction unornamented prose serves the development of plot and character. Jane Urquhart, however, is recognized for creating richly poetic prose in which plot and character development matter less than do pervasive symbolic landscapes. Characters tend to be static, dominated by the inner landscapes of their obsessions. Urquhart sets her first novel, *The Whirlpool*, in 1889 Niagara Falls, Ontario, with the whirlpool as its focus. In her second novel, *Changing Heaven*, Urquhart creates two intertwined stories, one beginning in nineteenth-century England's West Yorkshire moors, one in twentieth-century Toronto and the twentieth-century Yorkshire moors. In both novels, women linger within omnipresent landscapes. As in *The Elizabeth Stories*, the landscapes offered by men often conflict with those sought by women, for men tend to see women (to borrow Susan Gubar's terms) as "the blank page," "a tabula rasa, a lack, a negation, an absence," the surface for the male pen;[12] men can inscribe women into the landscapes of their choice. Not surprisingly, Urquhart's female characters (like Huggan's Elizabeth) spend considerable time trying to understand, change, or escape the visions or theories imposed on them. Once again they receive little help in their attempts.

"Lord," thinks Fleda, a central character in *The Whirlpool*, "these theories . . . no humans there at all. No actual people in these landscapes. What about the pain?"[13] Fleda has just been listening to the two men in her life speak of matters intensely important, to them. But the matters are only theoretical, and at this moment Fleda decides to abandon both men. For her friend Patrick and her husband Major David McDougal,

Fleda herself has been present primarily as a constructed part of the landscape in their minds; she has received their attention only as they have included her in their mental landscapes.

Patrick is an ailing nature-loving poet who has "hated the cold, but clung to the concept of landscape" [*W*, 59].) While prowling the woods, he accidentally and secretly discovers Fleda in her clearing above the whirlpool, and at once turns her into his obsession, wishing only to spy on her day after day as a silent object which will remain "completely still while everything move[s] around her, towards her and away from her, while he control[s] the distance" (114). Meeting her spoils his "idea" of her; he rejects the reality that she presents and refuses to talk to her. "Alone, with his imagination set free, he disregarded all he had seen and heard, and allowed the woman and the whirlpool to combine." He "completely reinvented her . . . [so that] once again, he could watch her in the pure and uncorrupted state he had carefully constructed for her" (*W*, 115). He will eventually refuse to look at Fleda herself but will look only at her shadow or her reflection. By clinging to his obsession with himself as poet, and with Fleda as whirlpool, Patrick ensures his continuing loneliness. When he discovers that Fleda knows that he has been spying on her, he never looks at her again: "She had now pulled his fantasy into the mundane architecture of fact" (*W*, 162); she becomes for him an ordinary housewife even as she is envisioning herself as his "legend in the forest" (*W*, 161). Patrick wants distance; finally, he prefers to find meaning by swimming in the whirlpool itself, a pure landscape with no figures, the whirlpool itself, but the whirlpool brings only death. He gets nowhere.

Fleda exists for her husband, Major David McDougal, a military historian, because he believes her to resemble the Canadian historical figure, Laura Secord. Secord was involved in the Seige of Fort Erie, a Canadian/American battle which obsesses David (the Americans won). A kind of Canadian Paul Revere, Laura Secord took a long hike to deliver some critical military news. We discover that David married Fleda primarily because she resembles Laura (as she appeared to him in his one and only sleeping dream), and he even occasionally has Fleda dress up in a Laura Secord outfit; this invariably arouses his sexual passion. But not Fleda's passion, for still she remains part of a theory: David makes love to her as if he is fighting a battle; she is the passive enemy (*W*, 44). Not surprisingly, it is Fleda, the woman, not David, who understands that battles bring real pain and death—she is the one to "read" and accept the message of an 1813 quilt they examine in a museum: it has coffins ready to be placed in the central cemetary each time a soldier dies. Quilts are, of course, one of the texts society has allowed women to create; it takes a woman to read this quilt.

In general, David pays little attention to what Fleda reads, writes, or thinks—he is too busy talking, refighting the battle against America.[14] He is tolerant of Fleda's passion for Browning, although he wishes she preferred Canadian poetry (for instance, that written by Patrick) and he wishes she had Canadian dreams (*W*, 88): that would integrate her into his obsession with Canada and Secord. Like Patrick, and because of his obsession with a concept, David ensures his loneliness: "Thinking Canadian is a very lonely business, my boy, and don't forget it" (*W*, 62), he tells Patrick. His lonely business will finally lose him his wife.

Fleda, dis-placed in her husband's and Patrick's landscapes, creates her own obsessive and dreamlike world with other men—her British poets. Their language and fantasies are her constant companions, and are "at times, more real to her" (*W*, 125) than is her own husband, who is absent in his own fantasy world. Fleda refuses to live in their town apartment when the weather warms; instead she camps in a tent above the whirlpool, and she prefers that the planned house for the site remain imaginary, "a dream, an illusion" (*W*, 125), rejecting the clutter of belongings that usually accumulate with a marriage. She wants walls you can walk through. She wants an "organic" life in a landscape of changing weather—no walls, no corners, no villas such as those even poets live in. Her idea of Patrick, the poet, resides in her mind (*W*, 126). Her existence consists of looking at or playing with the whirlpool. She sends out on it toy boats with symbolic names such as "Warrior" "Adonais," "Angel," and "Dreamhouse"—the four illusive inhabitants of the clearing. And it consists of reading Browning. Ironically, the framework of the novel consists of an account of Browning's death in the same year, 1889: in this framework story, Browning realizes he had lived in the midst of wondrous landscapes "with the regularity of a copy clerk" (*W*, 4), that his words have been too many—they have been fabrications rather than responses to life (*W*, 212).[15]

Fleda has little interaction with other living people. She has no female friends, no family. Patrick's arrival does not alleviate the situation but moves her further into a fabricated world. When she realizes that Patrick has been spying on her, she thinks of Patrick himself as if he were a gift from her husband like the books of poetry, and becomes obsessed with "a fixed idea of the poet" (*W*, 154). Because of him she feels more whole, feels "a part of the whirlpool, a part of the art of poetry" (*W*, 128); she sees herself as Patrick's legend in the forest. Patrick's poetry itself she will not read (until he rejects her), because through him she reads herself. Patrick's watching her helps her to envision herself: she wishes to become an artifact of the artist. For as Gubar has pointed out, many women can create an identity for themselves, can exist, only when their own persons become the art work through which they attain reality by being viewed.[16] Fleda gains substance and identity through Patrick's constructing gaze. As Fleda becomes preoccupied with Patrick, she finds that he creates "a curtain of memory" (*W*, 141) around her and her present situation; things acquire new names and she finds that "everything means something else" (*W*, 150). She uses her "idea" of Patrick "to protect her from the sordid, the ordinary, the real" (*W*, 154).

At the end of the novel, having recognized long ago that contact with her husband is impossible because he is locked into his obsession with the military, and now similarly rejected by Patrick, who is obsessed with his own illusive world, Fleda lets Patrick go. For sustenance, she mourns instead the Patrick of her dreams. No longer able to respond to either man, she disappears, leaving behind the Laura Secord costume, her husband, and the dead Patrick; she leaves behind "the dream house of this grey, obsessive landscape" (*W*, 196). She takes her books and her journal. (Like the quilt, the journal is an accepted form in which women may write and from which we have read excerpts throughout the novel.) Fleda has understood something about Laura Secord (how, we do not know)[17] that no one else has: "*It wasn't the message that was important. It was the walk. The journey. Setting forth*" (*W*, 197). Fleda sets forth, first also setting forth her four little boats on the whirlpool for the last time and then abandoning them. Unlike Laura Secord, she carries no military message; she does still carry Browning. But Browning himself, as we shortly learn, dies knowing that he did not himself set forth. It seems likely that Fleda will continue to wander in the landscape, lacking someone or something to give her the reality she does not create for herself.

In a separate line of action, Maud Grady[18] is not the object of any living man's obsessions, but she does live with memories of her dead husband and has taken his place as the town's undertaker. Like aspects of the whirlpool, hers is a circular, death-centered world. Her husband was obsessed with spiders, creators of those circular whirlpool-like webs that trap, circular spaces that bring death: he would not allow Maud to disturb the webs of spiders or to kill them. In fact, during their marriage, they themselves lived like spiders, for "emotion [was] held in suspense, so that the rest of the world could live and love and, more importantly, die" (*W*, 34). After her husband's death, Maud is confined in unwanted black widow's weeds which stain even her skin; her attention is focused on the bodies the whirlpool randomly brings forth.

As is true in the case of Isabel Huggan's Elizabeth and for Fleda in this novel, other women are not a source of knowledge and support for Maud; in fact, connections with women may be damaging. In the past Maud has loved, not her son, but only her "little friends" (*W*, 122), the bodies of dead little girls, more than she has loved her son. Every time a girl child died, she ignored her son for days afterward "as if he had never been born. And he, mimicking her, would behave as if his mother had never given birth to him" (*W*, 123). We are led to believe that Maud's fixation on girl children occurred because of her mother: as a child Maud broke all her china dolls, and her mother, "furious, would not from that time on allow her to own a doll" (*W*, 122). We saw earlier that Elizabeth's mother, like her father, contributed confusion and pain rather than clarity in the matter of what it might mean to be a girl. Here Maud's mother seems to have contributed to Maud's maternal inability: Maud makes space only for death; she does not give her son space even to exist.

But for Maud, Urquhart promises growth. Maud is a widow and has contact only with males who work for her in the undertaking business. She must therefore start to conduct her own life without depending on men. She also receives help from her son, who is abstractly and neutrally known only as "the child" throughout the novel; he helps her to emerge from the seemingly endless cycle of memory and death. "The child" is at first completely withdrawn and unable to speak at all; he seems autistic. As a toddler he had received no comfort from his mother while he watched his father and grandparents die during the flu epidemic. When Maud later begins to pay attention to him, he begins to speak, but only in words seemingly unrelated to any visible reality. He then begins to repeat verbatim all conversations he hears: "He had drawn the world that circled him inwards, had hoarded snippets of discourse" (*W*, 180). The child's fractured language, in other words, emerges from the life that circles whirlpool-like around him. [19]

With his fractured language, the child makes those who hear him stop to rethink words and their connection with reality. Patrick, who encounters the child, notes that "by virtue of its very randomness, the child's speech became profound" (*W*, 98). Maud has known the disconnective power of words. Her life, she sees, is being determined and circumscribed by the word *widow*, as so many women's lives are determined by the words *bride* and *wife* (*W*, 132). Finally the child reorganizes objects as well as language, when he raids Maud's "reliquary," the belongings she carefully catalogues and preserves for each unidentified body pulled from the whirlpool. He rearranges everything into his own categories, turning the relics into "merely objects." "Dreaming," he says, when his mother discovers the new piles of objects (*W*, 193) and Maud realizes she has been doing just that with her relics. Gradually the child breaks Maud's fixation on the dead and their memories. When she finally makes the child speak his first word, "sun," and at the same time shed his first tears (*W*, 57), she must see the sun herself. At last she fully offers warmth to her son, dressing herself in yellow, and pulling him back from Patrick's body when he reaches out to it. The whirlpool loosens its grasp on them. For Maud, then, Urquhart suggests growth into a life not dominated by dreams and death.

In her second novel, *Changing Heaven*, Urquhart continues to explore her intensely poetic interest in landscape and weather: "She wants to write a book about the wind, about the weather"[20]: so begins *Changing Heaven*. Several characters are ghosts who inhabit the landscape and weather, namely the ghost of the novelist Emily Brontë (we are informed several times that Brontë means "thunder") and of Arianna Ether (née Molly Smith). The weather dominates their ghostly lives and conversation, as it does that of the living twentieth-century Ann Frear.

Ann is obsessed with Arthur, a man for whom she wants to be a "curtain responding to a storm" (*CH*, 91). This is, of course, an image drawn from *Wuthering Heights*, a novel which also obsesses her—she is writing a book about it and the weather; its weather and moors dominate her imaginative life (just as Browning dominates Fleda's life).[21] For Ann, Arthur is the storm. To him, however, she is "a river of flesh, . . . a river whose source is the room. . . . The room's borders are the limits of her existence" (*CH*, 98). He does not love her. He does not want her to be part of his life, since he is a husband and father, and he does not want to share a landscape with Ann (*CH*, 106). Arthur likes imaginary rooms in which he can control the lighting; he is an art historian with a passion for the painted landscapes of Tintoretto. But like all the other men in this novel (Jeremy holds off Arianna, Brontë's brother Branwell distances his loved one, Brontë's Heathcliff closes out Catherine's ghost), Arthur shuts Ann out; he will not let in the weather beating at the windows. He will rendezvous with Ann only in curtained hotel rooms which are weatherless and anonymous. And so Ann tries in vain to introduce him to the stormy weather she constructs for her life, a life where real details disappear and where two lives are fused into one. She has constructed a romantic image of a man to which he will not accommodate himself. She wants to live within her fictional conceptions of reality; he will accept only the anonymous space of the hotel room. Finally acknowledging who Arthur really is, Ann returns from her constructed "heaven" to the real joys and pains of earth, and thus to the Yorkshire moors' John, who can control the moor. A mooredger, he pushes it back and walls it out (*CH*, 135); he takes care of Ann and tells her the stories she needs to hear about landscape, earth and sky. She has escaped her self-entrapment with Arthur, regaining a landscape much bigger than a hotel room. She still, however, needs this other man, John, in order to be a controlled part of the world and weather, to speak for her. "The landscape belongs to John, and through his attentions to Ann, to her as well" (*CH*, 178).

Ann's moors are occupied by two ghosts who are whiling away the century after their deaths by conversing with each other: these are the ghosts of Emily Brontë and of Arianna Ether, both of whom died in the nineteenth century. Arianna is obsessed with memories of her obsession for Jeremy, who, equally obsessed with her, wanted her to be an unchanging blank, white, featureless landscape (recall Ann's Arthur). While she was alive, he kept her in a featureless white room from which only he emerged. He changed her name from the homely Molly Smith to Arianna Ether to make her a thing of the air (eventually, and literally, a balloonist). She wished for "detail" in the featureless landscape of the white room in which he kept her and therefore secretly created an imaginary elaborately furnished home, which she finally described to him. Doing so broke his love for her, for "he could love her only if she were utterly absent from him" (*CH*, 253). To achieve this absence and regain the Arianna he loved, he caused her death by air: she fell to earth from her balloon when he ensured that her parachute would not open. After a century as a ghost, Arianna finally learns how she died by eavesdropping when John tells Arianna's story to Ann (Ann also fell to earth, from her obsession with Arthur). Released at last from obsession, Arianna and Emily's ghosts dissipate. They become part of the landscape.

Kathryn Chittick worries that "in the 1980s . . . the contemporary Canadian heroine . . . gives a sense of being completely encompassed by her own impotence."[22] Huggan and Urquhart are two very different Canadian voices. But they are similar in having created female characters who find it difficult if not impossible to create their own identities and to assume power over their own lives; the female characters in their works find themselves placed in constricting and silencing spaces; they receive little support in their difficulty, male or female. Urquhart's Arianna and Ann both construct elaborate fictional landscapes with which to resist or supplant the actual landscapes in which their lovers have placed them; they are alike in realizing that Arthur and Jeremy will never share these fictional landscapes. Arthur and Jeremy, alike across the centuries, refuse to change how they see Ann and Arianna. They do not displace Arianna and Ann from the featureless rooms in which they have enclosed them. If any change is to occur, it will occur for Arianna and Ann only through their own efforts. In this matter, *The Whirlpool* resembles *Changing Heaven*. Fleda successfully escapes a house and an apartment for the spaciousness of camping, but then David and Patrick begin constructing a house at the Whirlpool Heights tenting site that she no longer wants. Fleda cannot change the way Patrick and David perceive her or get them to share her own dreams. Patrick and David will not listen to her no matter how loudly she raises her voice, and so for her their words become "nothing." Isabel Huggan's Elizabeth never dreams of changing her father or her community, and the only spaces she can find for herself are a closet or bathroom stall; a game, poker, forms her only imaginative space—it is a game she can play by herself, and it depends on chance. She cannot construct a space or identity for herself in Garten, and she gets too big for the closets. Her father and the community will not change. Her mother will not discuss the problem with her; she and Elizabeth share only silence.

The fictional "solution" provided for these difficulties seems to be not resolution but avoidance, or at best re-vision rather than re-construction. Elizabeth will escape Garten for further education, presumably in the (masculine) sciences, where she has found that language effectively organizes and identifies reality (contrast the silence which forms her deepest tie with her mother). She will also try to avoid sexual entanglements with men since in the fifties, the time of *The Elizabeth Stories*, such entanglements lead inevitably to marriage. The only future action we are sure of for her is that she will write the reflective collection of stories we are reading. In these, as Liza Potvin points out, she tells her own stories in response to the stories her culture told about her; eventually, "she breaks women's silence."[23] Urquhart's Fleda hangs on to her overorderly Browning and disappears into the landscape; if she takes action, it will be to write in her journal, where she too has tried to represent her life.[24] Arianna spends her ghosthood trying to understand life and love; that done, she likewise disappears into the landscape with Emily Brontë, their voices disappearing into the voice of the wind. Brontë, her co-conversationalist, has tried to help Arianna come to her senses on these matters, matters which she has herself avoided experiencing other than vicariously. Ann, come to her senses and the earth, turns immediately to another man, one who cares for her when she is sick and who tells her instructive stories about the landscape—herself a writer, she still seems unable to write her own stories. As reviewer Pat Bolger noted, "Most young women would be disappointed that Arthur's second rejection of Ann freed her only to return to John; like the ghostly Emily and Arianna, she seems unable to exist for her own self."[25]

Of the female characters we have examined, only Urquhart's Maud successfully remains in a house of her own, emerging from it into the sun, a garden. For her, the spider webs are gone. Why is this so? With Maud, Urquhart has created a woman who, unlike Elizabeth or Fleda or Ann, does not depend on men directly or even vicariously (through their books or their opinions) for her existence or for her view of herself. The only men important in her life, other than dead ones, are two employees. Her very young son is neutralized into "the child"; her experience with him is also reciprocal rather than one-sided—she helps him learn language and feel the sun's warmth, while he in turn helps her to change the old organization of her house, and her life. Maud does not have to leave her home and town to gain space and identity. Why? Because with her husband dead, she claims his space—his job (usually a man's) and his house—and makes that space her own; she enlarges the landscape of her house and garden, dusts out the cobwebs, leaves family memories behind. Maud does not need to escape. Her life moves on and she has power over it; she has rejected the closure of the label, "widow."

Carolyn Heilbrun claims that "we women have lived too much with closure: 'If he notices me, if I marry him, if I get into college, if I get this work accepted, if I get that job'—there always seems to loom the possibility of something being over, settled, sweeping clear the way for contentment"; she notes, too, that the "acceptance of a new challenge . . . marks the end of fantasy. . . . It marks also the end of the dream of closure."[26] Space opens up for Urquhart's Fleda, Arianna, Emily, and Ann; male enclosure ends. But does this new space now bring growth, or simplyidance of the old enclosures? In escaping Garten, Huggan's Elizabeth may actually set forth to new challenges. She may one day be able to exist for herself; we know, through reading her book, that she will speak for herself—that at least she will re-structure her past from a woman's point of view. For Maud the world seems to have opened into continuing vitality; her vision of herself and her life does not depend on spaces and visions constructed by others.

In one respect, Urquhart's and Huggan's visions of women are alike. (En)closure cannot bring contentment. If to be feminine means we must be "content with much space in little room,"[27] a room determined by others, then we must be unfeminine, for self-understanding can often require much space in much room. We must be unfeminine in the hope that one day we will find out not just what it means to be women but what it means to act on that knowledge.

Writings by Isabel Huggan and Jane Urquhart

Huggan

COLLECTED SHORT STORIES

Isabel Huggan. *The Elizabeth Stories*. Ottawa: Oberon Press, 1984; New York: Viking, 1987; New York: Penguin, 1988; Toronto: Harper Collins, 1990. Includes "Celia Behind Me" (also published in *Grain* 4 [Fall 1976]: 3–8; *Best of Grain*, ed. Caroline Heath, Don Kerr, and Anne Sznmigalski, 39–44; Regina: Saskatchewan Writers Guild, 1980; *First Impressions*, ed. John Metcalf, 54–63 [Ottawa: Oberon Press, 1980]); "Sawdust" (also published in *First Impressions*, ed. John Metcalf, 64–81 [Ottawa: Oberon Press, 1980]); "Jack of Hearts" (also published in *First Impressions*, ed. John Metcalf, 82–105 [Ottawa: Oberon Press, 1980]; adapted for CBC-TV by Jack Blum and Sharon Corder); "Into the Green Stillness"; "Queen Esther"; "Sorrows of the Flesh" (also published in *83: Best Canadian Stories*, eds. David Helwig and Sandra Martin, 186–214 [Ottawa: Oberon Press, 1983]); "Secrets"; and "Getting Out of Garten."

UNCOLLECTED SHORT STORIES, REVIEWS, ESSAYS, POEMS

"Up and Down, Round and Round" (story). *Quarry* 26 (Summer 1977): 38–43.
"Bridges" (story). *Event* 7:2 (1978): 102–09.

"The Violation" (story) Hrrowsmith 4 (December 1979): 99–100, 102–03.
"Bus 7" (story). *Quarry* 29 (Autumn 1980): 4–7.
"The End of August" (poem). *Quarry* 35 (Autumn 1986): 8.
"Orpha Knitting" (story). *Western Living*, August 1987: 60j–60v.
Review of *Lulu Incognito*, by Raymond Kennedy. *New York Times Book Review*, 17 April 1988: 35.
"Mirror and World" (personal essay). *Books in Canada* 18 (August–September 1989): 1–2.
"Losing Face" (story). *Saturday Night* 105 (June 1990): 50–55.
"Skin the Colour of Money" (story). *Books in Canada* 20 (April 1991): 24–28.

URQUHART

NOVELS

The Whirlpool. Toronto: McClelland & Stewart, 1986; 1989 (paper); London: Simon and Schuster, 1989; Boston: David R. Godine, 1990 (first U.S. edition); London: Sceptre, 1991 (paper). (A selection from work-in-progress, then titled *The Whirlpool Dream House*, published in *Canadian Fiction Magazine* 55 [1986]: 8–22.)

Changing Heaven. Toronto: McClelland & Stewart, 1990 and 1991 (paper); London: Sceptre, 1990 (paper); London: Hodder and Stoughton, 1990; Boston: David R. Godine, 1993 (first U.S. edition). (Excerpts published in *Magic Realism and Canadian Literature: Essays and Stories*, eds. Peter Hinchcliffe and Ed Jewinski [Waterloo, Ont.: University of Waterloo Press, 1986]; in *The Malahat Review* 90 [Spring 1990]: 5–15); and in *Exile*, Vol. 13, No. 3, 1989, pps. 114–34 and in Vol. 16, No. 4, 1992: 453–57.

COLLECTED SHORT STORIES

The Storm Glass. Erin, Ont.: The Porcupine's Quill, 1987 (paper). Includes "Five Wheelchairs" (also published in *Canadian Fiction Magazine* 39 [1981]: 55–71; and in *Illusion One/Illusion Two: Fables, Fantasies and Metafictions*, ed. Geoff Hancock, *Illusion One*, 127–45 [Toronto: Aya Press, 1983]); "Storm Glass" (also published in *Metavisions*, ed. Geoff Hancock, 97–102 [Dunvegan: Quadrant Editions, 1983]; and in *Malahat Review* 64 [February 1983]: 106–12); "The Death of Robert Browning" (also published in *Descant* 15: [Spring–Summer 1984]: 67–77; and in *Views from the North: An Anthology of Travel Writing*, ed. Karen Mulhallen, 67–77 [Ontario: Descant/Porcupine's Quill, 1984]); "Forbidden Dances" (also published in *Family Fictions in Canadian Literature*, ed. Peter Hinchcliffe, 107–15 [Waterloo, Ont.: University of Waterloo Press, 1988]); "Seven Confessions" (also published in *Canadian Fiction Magazine* 44 [1982]: 57–84]); "John's Cottage"; and "Italian Postcards" (also published in *Descant* 16 [Fall 1985]: 124–35; *86: Best Canadian Stories*, ed. David Helwig and Sandra Martin, 64–80 [Canada: Oberon Press, 1986]; *More Stories by Canadian Women*, ed. Rosemary Sullivan, 155–67 [Canada: Oxford University Press Canada, 1987]).

POETRY BOOKS

False Shuffles. Victoria, B.C.: Press Porcépic, 1982 (paper); Toronto: Beach Home, 1982; *False Shuffles and the Disappearing Ace*. Providence, R.I.: Paradise Press, 1989.

I Am Walking in the Garden of His Imaginary Palace. Toronto: Aya Press, 1982.

The Little Flowers of Madame de Montespan. Erin, Ont.: Porcupine's Quill, 1983.

UNCOLLECTED SHORT STORIES, ARTICLES, POEMS, REVIEWS

"Bridges" (story). *Event* 7:2 (1978): 102–09.

"Mr. Bloombury" (poem). *Fiddlehead* 121 (Spring 1979): 49.

"Paul" (poem). *Fiddlehead* 121 (Spring 1979): 50.

"Location of Anthony's Dreams" (poem). *Antigonish Review* 10:38 (Summer 1979): 6.

"Return to Nova Scotia" (poem). *Antigonish Review* 10:38 (Summer 1979): 5.

"Between Brothers" (poem). *Antigonish Review* 110 (Winter 1980): 75.

"Grandmother Crosses the Suspension Bridge" (poem). *Prism International* 18 (Winter 1980): 43.

"Grandmother Keeps Score" (poem). *Prism International* 18 (Winter 1980): 44.

"The Limit of Suspension" (poem). *Prism International* 18 (Winter 1980): 47.

"The Train to South Dakota" (poem). *Prism International* 18 (Winter 1980): 45–46.

Four Square Garden: A Poetry Anthology, ed. Virgil Burnett, Stuart MacKinnon, and W. K. Thomas. Waterloo, Ontario: Pasdeloup Press, 1981. Includes "The Cleaning Ladies' Rag," 9–10; "The Boss," 11; "Santa Regina's Reliquary," 14; "Burnt Grass," 35; "Leave Taking," 36–37; "Fireman," 38–39; and "The Awkward Bow," 40–41.

"Other" (poem). *Malahat Review* 58 (April 1981): 117.

"Time After" (poem). *Malahat Review* 58 (April 1981): 116.

Review of *A History of Hereford Cattle and Their Breeders*, by E. Heath Agnew. *Times Educational Supplement*, June 14, 1983: 38.

"Night Walk" (article on Ken Adachi). *Brick* 35 (Spring 1989): 37–38.

"Notes on Fiction." *Event* 18 (Spring 1989): 56.

8. The I as Sight and Site: Memory and Space in Audrey Thomas's Fiction

> I'm not sure I want to transform us all into characters. And
> perhaps I am still hoping for, oh so unacceptable in
> literature, a happy ending?
>
> Audrey Thomas[1]

> I have memories preserved intact, like men in peat to be
> found by a later me.
>
> Audrey Thomas[2]

Novelist of memory, Audrey Thomas has hewn from autobiographical momenta both stable and unstable narrative foundations for her houses of fiction. That fiction, thematically and structurally, is recognizable by its continuous delight in repetitions. Also characteristic of Audrey Thomas is her successful delivery of and flair for what I would here call a legend of self-projections; British Columbia's answer to Colette, Thomas is a writer of very specific witness whose world is bounded by family, flora, fauna, and that intertidal life whose symbolic soundings resonate especially distinctly for women and upon whose meanings she has both predicated and titled one novel. Part of her interest (possibly even a large part) lies in her public invitation to have the heroines of her prose be identified with the author of that prose.[3]

This may well have been the Canadian response to its women writers in the sixties and seventies. Like Margaret Atwood and Marian Engels, Thomas was first patronized by reviewers as a kind of latter-day 'scribbling lady' at the same time as her readership (like theirs) grew because of the emerging interest in Canadian writing.[4] Born of middle-class New England parents in a dissolving domestic and economic unit, she was to propel herself away, traveling from and to places: out of New York state to

England, to Canada, to Africa. With the birth of three daughters and a separation and then divorce from her husband, her connection to British Columbia's Galiano Island, (a ferry ride away from the city of Vancouver) and the Canadian West Coast grew to be a firm and felt commitment.[5] Yet the voyaging impulse in her has remained strong, the outward and visible counterpoint to those inward journeys of the creative imagination. Looking through the fiction, we can see figured the landscapes to which she has traveled, their contours frequently distorted by a questing, self-conscious, and distracted narrator. From work to work, one kind of female protagonist recurs, as do the reiterative narrative episodes she inhabits.

"Everything Thomas writes is a companion piece to everything else," observes a fellow Canadian, Margaret Atwood. "More than most writers, [Thomas] is constantly weaving and reweaving, cross-referencing, over-lapping, even repeating her materials."[6] In the linked narratives, we meet the presiding figure of the author's imagination—a woman longing for the pastoral domesticity of husband, children and island life, yet bolted into voyage and action by sexual love and an equally uncontrollable passion for words, words as puzzles, words as refrains, words as wizards. We also encounter the presiding preoccupations that surface, fleshed or told from various vantages in the various books: the lost child, the madhouse, the male abandoner, the process of female creativity, the act of writing with its dislocatory distortions.

Audrey Thomas is never the inventor; having little of the fabulist in her, she seldom spins the kinds of plots that, for instance, Margaret Drabble, Toni Morrison, Doris Lessing, Margaret Lawrence, or Iris Murdoch can create. Rather she is a storyteller who filters a good part of her fictional world through the retrospective consciousness of her chief creation: a narrating self. "Your books are absolutely self-centered,"[7] accuses *Latakia's* Michael, charging that novel's prolific writer Rachel with the very insularity critics have ascribed to Thomas. Fictively self-indicted as she may be, the novels and shorter fiction alike seem to slide across each other's borders as stories are told and retold with slightly different empha-ses. Thomas's attraction to the etymology of words and her pointed play with puns, nursery rhymes, literary refrains, and intertextual allusion add to the overall sense of the fiction's narcissistic circuitry and its dissolution of conventional boundaries between what has actually happened and what is being imagined. "Writers are terrible liars,"[8] as the first line of the story, "Initram" (from Thomas's ironically titled second collection *Ladies and Escorts*) willfully announces.

All in all, hers is a narrative technique that relies on disrupting the linearity of sequence as well as sentence. My argument in this essay is that Audrey Thomas's "transgressive"[9] method amounts to more than mannered and self-indulgent experiment. Rather, its very discontinuity allows the random movement of memory its own depiction. Conversely, memory shapes method, a point underscored by one of the voices in "If One Green Bottle . . . " (the title—and important—story from Thomas's first collection, *Ten Green Bottles*), who observes: "the whole thing should have been revised . . . rewritten . . . we knew it from the first."[10] What makes these memory works especially intriguing is the author's way of burrowing into a female "I" that navigates sight as well as site. To explore the geography of the inner life is to reach the shores not only of identity but its place in space. For Thomas believes what she has her writer/heroine in *Intertidal Life* determine when—reading the "voyages of exploration, about the search for the Northwest Passage, about brave bold men in their rickety boats"—she wonders: "The turn of women, now, to go exploring?" (*I*, 69).[11]

For Thomas, writing about self inevitably embraces the metaphor of exploration, its trajectory of search shaping the interrogations of her consuming interests: female identity, female sexuality, female socialization, female physiology and—above all—female creativity. Insight also inevitably embraces sighting the site where domestic sphere can become powerful female space.

> The mothers don't need mirrors—they have created creatures in their own image.
>
> Audrey Thomas[12]

> My first "real" story . . . *had* to be written, it seemed . . . the only way I could organize the horror . . . of a six-months long . . . miscarriage in a hospital in Africa.
>
> Audrey Thomas[13]

A prolonged miscarriage is the central event in Thomas's first shorter fiction, "If One Green Bottle, . . . " (in *Ten Green Bottles*, 1967), just as a horrific mummified homunculus on public display in a Mexican museum is the central symbol in a later story, "The More Little Mummy in the World," from her second collection, *Ladies and Escorts*, 1977. Similarly, Thomas's first novel, *Mrs. Blood* (1970), and her third, *Blown Figures* (1974), are requiems for the lost child, retelling the painful experience from the fractured perspective of Isobel Carpenter, the narrator of each novel. The same Isobel Carpenter also narrates *Songs My Mother Taught Me* (1973), the trilogy's first volume and one that chronicles its protagonist's childhood, adolescence, and young adulthood in New York state during the forties and fifties. In what appears to be a conventional first-person female bildungsroman (divided chronologically into the "Songs of Innocence" of childhood and the "Songs of Experience" of adolescence), the book sketches Isobel's efforts to elude the conventional world offered to her by her embittered mother, a departure successfully embarked upon in the narrator's seventeenth year when she takes a job as an aide in a lunatic asylum. There she rids herself of her "mind's virginity" at the same time as she shakes off her body's innocence through sexual initiation.

Any examination of *Songs My Mother Taught Me*, *Mrs. Blood*, and *Blown Figures* must begin (as one critic suggests) "with the strong centre of consciousness or perspective which is characteristic of them. This centre is either Isobel's own voice, the 'I' of personal communication and dream-thought intelligence, or the more limited narration used in *Blown Figures* where the narration moves away from the character infrequently while remaining in the third person."[14] Two voices predominate in *Songs My Mother Taught Me*—the narrator referring to herself as "I" as well as "she"—and this strategic doubling[15] will again be adopted by Thomas in *Mrs. Blood*, the novel whose narrative action involves an unnamed narrator seeing herself in two figures: Mrs. Thing, Feminine Mystique wife of an Englishman teaching at the University of Ghana, and Mrs. Blood, Female Eunuch memory-mordant, reliving past erotic adventures and the guilt attached in that epoch to female sexuality. A miscarriage forms the bloody base of this novel, the memory of which propels a solitary Isobel some five years later back to Africa in the trilogy's third volume, *Blown Figures*. Thematically situated somewhere between the adolescent longings of *Songs My Mother Taught Me* and the maternal disintegrations of *Mrs. Blood*, the Isobel Carpenter of *Blown Figures* has several mutating personae, their multiplicity contributing to her unreliable witnessing of her own unraveling. Miscarriage, maternity, sexuality: each remembrance blows the protagonist further into Africa and through a psychic journey, whose steps are less actual and material than overcharged and psychological.

However determined are the novel's ambitions to infect its imagined world with a disease of contending points of view and a plague of contentious interpolated plots (newspaper articles, cartoons, billboards, personal columns, recipes, nursery rhymes, African chants and rituals, advertisements), *Blown Figures* exhausts.[16] "Epitome of [the] narrative mannerisms Thomas has used and would use,"[17] its failure as an engaging and affecting novel seems aptly enough summarized in the comments of another of Thomas's female protagonists: Rachel, the writer who narrates the novel *Latakia* (1979). "Yes, the pain is there and very real, but where is the organization? She is at the beginning of a long, long road" (*L*, 46).

Latakia and its earlier companion, *Munchmeyer and Prospero on the Island* (1971), are novels distant from the Isobel Carpenter trilogy to the degree that each is a kunstlerroman, or portrait of the (female) artist.[18] Both *Latakia's* Rachel and *Munchmeyer and Prospero on the Island's* Miranda are writer/narrators whose shared obsession with the nature of writing focuses on how storytelling can go about telling the truth. Both are islanded (and eye/I–landed): Rachel in Crete is writing "the longest love-letter in the world" (*L*, 191) to her departed lover, and Miranda is spinning her diary/novel on the West Coast's Magdalena Island. Each discovers that the site set aside for their creativity offers insight into that creativity. Though neither Miranda nor Rachel extrapolates the fact from her worried work with words, doubling—both as fictional device and as imaginative response to experience—lies at the very heart of the creative process. The "artist almost always lives in a Double Now" (*L*, 127), Rachel comments: in two places at once, two characters at once, two different times at once.

A quick sampling of *Munchmeyer and Prospero on the Island* illustrates how much in evidence are Thomas's favored doubling techniques for reflecting memory's transformation of fact into imaginative artifact. These include interleaved diaries, interpolated dreams and fantasies, echoes of episodes from other of Thomas's stories, labyrinthine echoes of and allusions to other literatures. (Miranda's name and the book's title, for example, becomes the wedge through which Shakespeare's interrogations of art and reality in *The Tempest* are rewoven.[19]) Dominating is the strategy of the story told and re-told, a narrative doubling so subtle here that the novel is divisible into two novella: *Munchmeyer* and *Prospero on the Island*, the latter being Miranda's diary about writing a novel. Toward *Prospero's* conclusion, we discover that the novel Miranda is writing is *Munchmeyer*—a novel about a male writing a diary about trying to write a novel. Thus female/male doubling in *Munchmeyer and Prospero on the Island* ends with the jest of a female author, Audrey Thomas, dissolving conventional gendered oppositions at the same time as she so inverts conventional male/female relations by having a fictional female writer invent (and so control) the character's fictional male counterpart.

Textual analyses involving this degree of formal explication reward only to the extent that they underscore how tenacious in Thomas's work is what she has called "this terrible gap between men and women."[20] *Intertidal Life* (1984) is ship of such a state, wonderful by way of its marriage of Thomas's pervasive themes to her persistent narrative strategies. Again, we are introduced to a familiar: Isobel has shifted to Alice, but the latter constructs the same stories in silence, mirror-doubling herself between journal entries in the first person and a novella in the third person where Alice represents herself as "she". In retrospective memory of her husband's departure seven years before, Alice "writes a story of abandonment, of island isolation, of water, of the moon, of maps and guides and learning to read—in short, a story of exploration."[21] It is not just the geography of her life that needs remapping, caught as she is between the tides of past and present, marriage and divorce, mothering and writing. There is a compulsion to reexplore that topography delineated by the ancient relations between men and women and to rename under the flag of female its once conquered continents. As Alice observes, comparing women's estate to the imperial colonization of countries:

> Women have let men define them, taken their names . . . just like a . . . newly settled region: *British* Columbia, *British* Guiana . . . *New* Jersey, *New* France. . . . I understand African nations taking new names. (*I*, 717)

The female landscape most repatriated in *Intertidal Life* is that of family life. Here a single mother's generative relation to her three daughters is realized in such rooted detail as soup making, wood cutting, fire stoking and garden planting. Though motherhood pulls as strongly on Alice Hoyle as moon on tide, its psychic space is never enclosure but rather expanding sphere. Indeed, her island-encircled house is likened not to a marooned circlet of female restriction but to a forging ship, a resolute metaphor in a novel filled with references to voyage, tide, and sea change. *Intertidal Life* teaches that explored-female and female explorer are mirrored-doubles, not warrior-antagonists, and the novel's celebratory spirit marks a new departure in the Thomas oeuvre. To borrow from Thomas's habit of truthtelling through pun[s]manship: no more should memories be mummified; nor too should mothers be others.

> Who can see the "other" in mother? Calling the school—
> "Hello, this is Hannah's mummy." "This is Anne's
> mummy." . . . All wrapped up in her family.
> Audrey Thomas (*I*, 13)[22]
>
> Why must I always search for similarities?
> Audrey Thomas (*MPI*, 101)

Audrey Thomas's craft has always been guided by an ironic shifting of boon, a maneuver never so apparent as in her shorter fiction. A look at one story can perhaps convey how characteristic is the wry ridiculing of gendered roles and codes. Some might typify as feminist her exposure of inherited conventions; she would amplify such scrutiny so as to include men as well as women—and especially the daughters of mothers. As the incantation from one story sings: "'Let her be strong,' [the mother] thought. 'Let her be strong and yet still loving.'"[23]

"Crossing the Rubicon" is the final story in Thomas's collection of fiction, a volume titled almost tautologically as *Real Mothers*.[24] Among a handful of shorter fictions by Thomas—and one must include here "Natural History" with its anticipatory rehearsal of the themes and landscapes of *Intertidal Life*—"Crossing the Rubicon" has an almost spendthrift capacity to combine Thomas's flair for the self-projective with a set of narrative moves that enhance the blurring of autobiography and fiction: doubling and memory's mapping of sight through site.

The shorter fiction's outward plot seems disarmingly simple. An unnamed narrator tries to write a story, which "I do not particularly want to write. But it nags at me, whines, rubs against the side of my leg, begs for attention."[25] At the same time, the narrator places that story's writing in her here and now, here being Canada's West Coast and now being one day before Valentine's, 13 February 1980. As for the story's here and now, they are Montreal on a fine October morning. "My story . . . will begin with a woman on a Number 24 bus, heading East along Sherbrooke Street. She is on her way to meet a man who used to be her lover" (CR, 158).

The weaving together of the twinned tales—that of the unnamed narrator ("I") and that of her central character ("She")—is set in motion by Valentine's Day rituals, as a single mother helps her daughter make cupcakes for the boys at school. "'KISS ME' . . . 'BE GOOD TO ME' . . . 'LOVE ME'" (CR, 157), sigh mottoes on the heart-shaped candies, voicing the very scripts and romantic codes against which the narrator wants her character to fight.

Appropriately enough in a story whose title and first line initiate two among several allusions to Julius Caesar, "Crossing the Rubicon" is a declaration of war, committing its heroine by way of an irrevocable gesture in defiance of romantic enslavement to Caesar's fate: that of conquering or perishing.[26] As a text about memory, "Crossing the Rubicon" also declares war against chronological narrative, the narrator crossing through (by my count) seven layers of the past—in sites as distant as Rome, Vancouver, Montreal, and upstate New York—to bring their booty back to the present and the task of writing (so righting) the embattled story. "Right now, I want to play soothsayer and call out to her, 'Beware, beware,'" muses the narrator as she imagines her fictional double at a crucial point in her encounter with her former lover. "Walk away. Run. Leave well enough alone" (CR, 161), she warns.

Doubled as the "I" and the "she" most certainly are, the narrator's second self here enacts what secret sharers from Conrad down have done: like others of Thomas's doubles, she performs those unconventional acts the more compliant self cannot. "Crossing the Rubicon's" final paragraph shows a woman walking away from her lover, then exuberantly running. Traffic signals command in an imperial and foreign tongue: "Arretez." She defies this ruling too, crossing—as Caesar did—her own rubicon. Such a turning away by this woman in love from the old codes for the woman in love is summed up by the I/Eye of Thomas's autobiographical projection in three—limpidly simple—final sentences. "And she doesn't look back. In my story, that is. She doesn't look back" (CR, 168).

She doesn't look back. Audrey Thomas certainly does, looking back on literary lineages just as she looks back on her own life. From her first book, *Ten Green Bottles* (1967), to her more recent work, *The Wild Blue Yonder* (1990), Thomas has depicted both the privileges and the privations of mothers, wives, and lovers. Like "Crossing the Rubicon's" narrator—indeed, like Thomas herself—each realizes she cannot wholly reject traditional roles; the foundations of custom and belief still stand sturdy. However, they can be enjoined by their author to revise conventional fictions of femininity and so transform women's future relations to their inheritances.

Routing his first enemies, Caesar trumpeted *Veni, Vidi, Vici*. His fabled boast seems suitable script for closing comment. Novelist of memory and triumphant Eye/I of sight and site, Audrey Thomas might herself say, "I came. I saw. I conquered." And my bet—based on the practice of a novelist who can twist "ménage à trois" to a ribald "ménage à twat" (CR, 162)—has it that she would no sooner say Caesar's sentence than start playing with the male pun.

Writings by Audrey Callahan Thomas

NOVELS

Mrs. Blood. Vancouver: Talon Books, 1970, 1975; Indianapolis: Bobbs-Merrill, 1970.
Munchmeyer and Prospero on the Island. Indianapolis: Bobbs-Merrill, 1971.
Songs My Mother Taught Me. Vancouver: Talon Books, 1973; Indianapolis: Bobbs-Merrill, 1973; New York: Ballantine Books, 1974.
Blown Figures. Vancouver: Talon Books, 1974; New York: Knopf, 1975.
Latakia. Vancouver: Talon Books, 1979.
Intertidal Life. Toronto: Stoddart, 1984; New York: Beaufort Books, 1984.

COLLECTED SHORT STORIES

Ten Green Bottles. Indianapolis: Bobbs-Merrill, 1967; Ottawa: Oberon Press, 1977.
Ladies and Escorts. Ottawa: Oberon Press, 1977.
Real Mothers. Vancouver: Talon Books, 1981.
"Two in the Bush" and Other Stories. Toronto: McClelland & Stewart, 1981.
Goodbye Harold, Good Luck. Toronto: Viking, 1986; Markham, Ont.: Penguin Books, 1987.
The Wild Blue Yonder. Markham, Ont.; New York, N.Y.: Viking, 1990.

UNCOLLECTED STORIES, ARTICLES, REVIEWS

"Through a Glass Darkly: Canadian Art Criticism." *Canadian Literature* 46 (Autumn 1970): 62–72.

"The New Adventures of Elisabeth Hopkins: Discovered, At 80, To Be an Artistic Talent." *Maclean's*, August 1975: 54, 56–57.

"African Journal Entries." *Capilano Review* 7 (1975): 55–62.

"'My Craft and Sullen Art': The Writers Speak—Is There a Feminine Voice in Literature?" *Atlantis* 4:1 (1978): 152–54.

"Clean Monday; or, Wintering in Athens." *Capilano Review* 13 (1978): 68–87.

"An Open Letter to Dorothy Livesay." *Room of One's Own* 5:3 (1980): 71–73.

"Graven Images: A Memoir." *Capilano Review* 20 (1981): 44–51.

"Spring Break." *Chatelaine*, March 1981: 40–41.

"Spaghetti and Meatballs for Christmas?" *Chatelaine*, December 1981: 70–71.

"Untouchables." *Room of One's Own* 7:3 (1982): 2–17.

"Basmati Rice: An Essay about Words." *Canadian Literature* 100 (Spring 1984): 312–17.

"Trash." In *Vancouver Fiction*, ed. David Watmough. Winlaw, B.C.: Polestar Press, 1985.

"A Fine Romance, My Dear, This Is." *Canadian Literature* 108 (Spring 1986): 5–12.

MISCELLANY

Foreword. To *Canadian Short Fiction Anthology*. Ed. Cathy Ford. Vancouver: Intermedia, 1976.

9. Canadian Identity and Women's Voices: The Fiction of Sandra Birdsell and Carol Shields

Sandra Birdsell and Carol Shields figure predominantly among women writing in the wake of "the flowering of Canadian fiction,"[1] a term used by Linda Hutcheon and others to define the state of Canadian literature since the 1960s. Responding to the call to explore Canadian identity using postmodernist techniques,[2] Birdsell and Shields depict fictional women who may be profitably viewed as metaphorical of the Canadian condition.[3] However, I suggest that the two writers differ, finally, in their views of Canadians and of their relationships to the world beyond the Canada borders, as well as in their convictions regarding the situations of Canadian women. The Canadian-born Sandra Birdsell, inventing a mythical Canadian town as her setting, presents a microcosm peopled largely by first- and second-generation immigrants who move as essentially solitary individuals lacking meaningful relationships with family and with community.

In contrast, the American-born Carol Shields (who has made Canada her home since 1957) moves easily back and forth across the border between Canada and the United States, featuring international as well as Canadian characters and demonstrating their similarities as well as their differences. Shields seems less concerned than Birdsell with the "Canandianness" of her characters. Here is a humanist approach which blurs both national boundaries and, in postmodern fashion, the lines separating literary genres. She depicts people who, although fallible and aware of the "unknowability"[4] of others, are fully, generously drawn and develop an increased awareness, however imperfect, of their identities, and of their relationships to family and community. As these two writers demonstrate different pictures of Canadian men and women, they illustrate Coral Ann Howells's point about the multivoiced aspect of Canadian fiction by women: unlike America, which has an identity, Canada's "problem of identity may not be the problem of having no identity but rather of having multiple identities, so that any single national self-image is reductive and always open to revision."[5]

Sandra Birdsell, who has been writing for ten years,[6] writes of disjointed family relationships, concentrating particularly on characters she sees as outsiders whether because of gender, ethnicity, or religion. She feels especially angry about the disadvantaged situation of women, which may be viewed as metaphorical of the condition of all outsiders who must dwell on the fringes of society. Birdsell's two published novels depict the residents of Agassiz, which contains a mixture of all the ethnic Canadians—particularly Native American, Metis, Mexican, South American, French, British, German, Russian. Birdsell's are working-class people, primarily women immigrants and their daughters trying to define themselves both in relation to their contemporary English-speaking world and to their ethnic heritage. None of her characters displays a strong interest in either reading or writing and, significantly, titles of books are rarely invoked. Appropriately, then, Birdsell uses her women characters' nonverbal talents—music and art rather than writing—to suggest their emerging self-consciousness. Over all, the mood in Birdsell's work is realistic, even pessimistic, and the tone somber.

A flood provides the starting point for Birdsell's recently published *Agassiz: A Novel in Stories.*[7] Therein, Birdsell presents the fragmented but realistically rendered family of Mika and Maurice Lafreniere, beginning with the catastrophe (based on the great Manitoba flood of 1950) and ending with their grown children and grandchildren. *Agassiz* opens with Maurice Lafreniere, whose sobriquet, Old Man River, suggests not only the strength and endurance of his Native American heritage but also his degraded status. He lives a lie, never telling his wife Mika or his six children that he is part Native American, not merely French as he has led them to believe. The opening pages of the novel signal his potential to make a name for himself, but that potential is repeatedly undercut by his painful denial of his ancestry. His suppression of the insistent image of his Native American mother not only contributes to his own fractured identity and feelings of failure but adumbrates the silenced and degraded position of women which he, along with the other men in the novel, helps to perpetuate.

Because Maurice is too drunk to tell Mika of his Indian background as he intends early in the novel, she mistakes his inarticulateness for sexual desire, and she refuses: "And the anger had come rushing, thick and violent. He'd wanted to smash into her breasts with his fists but instead, he'd taken her by force, without using precautions, with a grinding punishing force that he felt in his own muscles that morning" (37). But the next morning, feeling guilty, he offers to fix the kitchen window. Mika is all he has: "She was what he could put his hands on and touch. But he knew, for some reason, it would never be enough" (41).

Only death finally allows him to embrace the heritage of which his family never learns; neither Mika nor Truda can understand his last words, for he speaks in a tongue they cannot comprehend. Although Maurice is a peripheral character compared to his wife and daughters, his lack of identity, his feelings of loss, and his rape of his wife Mika underscore the dominant themes of self-doubt, loneliness, and violence which permeate the book. His uneasy, unarticulated secret underscores the miscommunications which effectively isolate Maurice, Mika, and their three eldest daughters Betty, Lureen and Truda.

In a recent interview, Birdsell said that she wrote her stories out of a sense of anger "at what had been done to me as a woman by . . . a man, and by the institution of marriage, and by the church."⁸ And certainly her works depict women as victims. Mika, an immigrant born in Russia to a German father and a Russian mother, worked as a maid to a wealthy family and taught herself to read and write English. Although Mika, with her educated father, feels superior to Maurice, she too has been thwarted in her desires. Her German Mennonite father rules her life, and we eventually learn that he forbade her to marry her first love. Significantly, Mika appears in several scenes with her father, never really with her mother. As she is expecting her sixth child, she rebels from marriage and motherhood to engage in an affair with an itinerant laborer, only to be thwarted once again by her father, who cows her into submission by quoting from the bible and threatening to expose her in church. Unhappy and constricted, she tries to do her best for her daughters, but despite her good intentions, she remains incapable of envisioning for them any life other than hers.

Her message to her daughters is contradictory. She emphasizes the importance of their education but she also instructs them to conform: they must marry, have children, and suffer as she has suffered. Unhappy in her marriage to Maurice, who womanizes and drinks too much, Mika ends up, like her mother, adhering to the Mennonite beliefs which have oppressed her. At one of her weekly religious meetings, a women's organization which includes her daughter Betty, mother and daughter listen to the tale of a thirteen-year-old Russian girl who, after enduring a gang-rape, took her own life. Mika blurts out her certainty that suicide is "unpardonable": "Knowing that keeps me going. Otherwise I would have done it myself long ago" (62). Betty feels shocked and disillusioned with her mother's statement: she explicitly learns not only of her mother's despair, but of the stunning powerlessness of these women who until this moment she has believed could "surround her and protect her" (58–59).

Just as Mika's daughters have no real knowledge of her aspirations and disappointments, she remains unaware of theirs. Mika never knows, for instance, that Betty is the victim of sexual abuse at the hands of a man on a neighboring farm, of a loveless seduction by a high-school boyfriend, and, just before graduation, of rape by a Royal Canadian Mounted Police officer. This last violation results in her pregnancy and virtual expulsion from the family. Never fulfilling the potential implied by her intelligence, her school awards, or her instinctive love of music, Betty becomes pregnant again and marries a Mennonite country-western bass guitar player. Lureen, knowing that her mother prefers the blonde, blue-eyed Betty to herself, consciously sides with her father whose dark looks she has inherited: she loathes her mother's German-Russian Mennonite heritage, choosing instead to identify with what she believes to be her father's French ancestry. Lureen refuses to sympathize with her mother when Maurice leaves her at night: "Fix your hair, put on some makeup. Don't be such a drag, I said. And maybe he would stay home with you" (262). Ironically, when her alcoholic husband leaves Lureen for another woman, Lureen neglects her youngest child much as her mother neglected her and finds herself totally unprepared for independence, "flat broke without a job, starting over at forty" (313). Truda, overweight and afraid to be alone, believes her poor vision to be caused by her excessive crying when, as a child, she was "abandoned" by her parents who literally farmed her out for six months after the crisis of the flood. Although Truda initially wishes both to marry and to attend art school, she follows her mother's advice: "I had to get married and so you have to, too" (151). Truda marries, only to leave her husband on realizing that he never intends to have children.

If in Birdsell's work the major women characters are in fact metaphors for the problems that plague Canada, the implications are bleak indeed, as the characters are still unsure of themselves, still searching, unable or unwilling to communicate their thoughts and to make sense of their experiences and feelings. Like their mother, the daughters live lives bereft of any sense of achievement or fulfillment, ultimately seeming able merely to endure.

Birdsell's technique involves multiple perspectives with minimal information, challenging her postmodern readers to fill in the gaps. The narratives of the five members of this family demonstrate each character's memories, frustrations, and impressions of one another; but all remain essentially separate, understanding neither themselves nor each other. Birdsell explains that in her writing "people have always, always been my initial interest. So that I mostly start pieces of fiction with an idea of a person, and not an idea for a story."[9] However, in the words of one reviewer of *Agassiz*, "Unfortunately, as time passes, identities tend to blur; . . . to the reader many of these characters look and sound alike."[10] In fact, Birdsell's minimalist style and withholding of (sometimes essential) information occasionally mystifies even the most cooperative reader (for instance, the similarities between Mika and Betty are suggested through related images of their sheared hair, but we never learn exactly why Betty snipped off her braids). Birdsell acknowledges, "I hate plot, actually," and admits that this dislike accounts for her difficulties with endings and for some readers' complaints about the "shapeless" aspect of her stories. For this reason she believes that the stories make more sense when used together, as they are in *Agassiz*.[11] (McCormack 20)

When Birdsell responds to criticism of the "tremendous pessimism" in her stories peopled with "trapped characters,"[12] she denies the charges: "A lot of things that happen to us *are* inevitable; we can't do anything about them, especially as women." Birdsell describes her attitude not as one of pessimism but of "positive realism."[13] In the reunion with her daughters and their children, Mika dwells on her dim memory of a story her grandmother told her—which she recollects as a dark story of a Russian woman who was buried alive—and Mika passes it on to her own granddaughter. This image constitutes the end of the book, an unquestionably despondent summation of her life as wife, mother, and grandmother.

Although Birdsell says that she was "quite angry" while writing the stories that comprise Agassiz but that her new work is "different" (21), her anger and pessimism seem to permeate *The Missing Child*. It is a relentlessly dark, harrowing, apocalyptic novel of Agassiz women whose childhood memories reveal male violence, sexual abuse, and murder, a novel which again unfolds during a flood—purposely caused by angry dispossessed Native Americans—which, by the end, engulfs everyone in town.

Agassiz contains a large cast of characters representing many ethnic groups and religious denominations. The European immigrants have staked out their communities, but the mixed-blood people are homeless. "Those who have become French or English are invisible. The others wander through bushland, along the edges of the hills, or near the shore of the north waters" (6). Howells's observations about Margaret Laurence's prairie town of Manaawaka or Alice Munro's southwest Ontario towns of Jubilee and Hanratty apply equally to Birdsell's Agassiz: they are places "where the enclosed community defines itself against the surrounding wilderness and where the edges of the town . . . provide that wasteland occupied by the more marginal members of the community."[14] (16). A corollary to the traditional fictional use of the Canadian wilderness theme is the "garrison mentality" noted by Northrup Frye and others.[15] In this case the town is a metaphor for Canada itself: with its vast ethnic population and its "undesirable" ethnics lurking around the fringes, the town invokes the "garrison mentality" of the whites, who even in the 1950s look nervously over their shoulders when an Indian walks into town. Over all looms the theme of white male dominance and violence. Women are objects of derision and sexual contempt: laughing white men repeatedly refer to a submissive housekeeper as having "jelly for brains"; white men reject the Native American June's friendly offer of a drink because they "Don't take a hand-out from no squaw" (58),[16] and before raping and murdering Sandra Adams, Sonny Erickson thinks of June's daughter Robin as a "bloody half-breed cunt" (71).

Minnie is the central character, a woman who suffers from amnesia. Signaled by the painful sound of a little girl's cries and a haunting image of a white, strawberry-printed dress, the fragmented pieces of her memory gradually return to reveal a horrific childhood event: the little girl was Wanda, Minnie's twin, and Minnie watched from a hiding place as Wanda was brutally raped by a man in a white suit who then broke her neck and threw her into the river. Now the river is angry, "turning brown with irritation," dissatisfied because "it was at one time so much more than a river which the people spit into, curse, and refuse to drink, a breeding place for mosquitoes" (5). And before the novel ends the river will spew up one more victim; Sandra Adams, the motherless seventeen-year old choir girl whose raped and murdered body is, like Minnie's sister Wanda's unceremoniously dumped as so much refuse.

The town of Agassiz bears a welcoming sign inscribed with the words,

"Drive Carefully, We Love Our Children"—but as the novel opens these words have been "scoured and defaced" (5). The entire book constitutes an ironic exposure of this motto. Agassiz, a town settled by white men on land stolen from Indians, loves neither its children nor its women nor any who fail to conform to institutionalized white male morals and standards. The "missing child" of the title is a boy, but Birdsell undercuts the town's concern with his disappearance (he is found safely, tied to a tree by another boy) with her emphases on the true missing children: the violated little girls who, if they are not killed, grow up to become powerless women.

Thus, while Minnie's memory of the rape and murder of her sister is central, it reverberates in the similar tales of the other women in the novel: they come from Russia, Germany, England, Mexico, and all eventually reveal past memories wherein they (or their sisters) were sexually violated or murdered. Powerless to prevent the violence, most of them either have no mothers or were abandoned by mothers. The day after Sandra's body is discovered, Minnie molds a clay figure of the dead girl which is immediately crushed by Sandra's father. Minnie thinks,

> Once I had a sister Her name was Annie . . . Sandra . . . Wanda. I had a girl once; you could be her. One tiny hand emerged from the ruined figure, imprinted now with the whorls and lines of a man's fingertips. She turned the lump of clay over and there was her own face, cheeks pinched together and lips puckered, as though she'd just blown out the candles on a birthday cake. Once, I was a girl. (291) [Birdsell's ellipses]

Birdsell's Canada is filled with anger, prejudice, and a sense that the experiment is not working. Until women gain strength and self-respect, the pattern will continue, producing more little girls whose mothers are incapable of protecting or guiding them. Unless women and children and, by extension, all marginalized citizens, are treated equally, Birdsell's implied solution is to obliterate completely the currently existing structures. The situation for women is intolerable, and in the final scene Minnie dives into the river and swims away. Memory, central to the book, brings only Minnie's understanding that, were she to have a choice, she "would never, never again, choose to be born" (7).

Carol Shields, too, uses memory in her works, agreeing that "in a sense all my books have been about retrieval from the past.[17] She has been publishing since the mid-1970s, and is, quite simply, a brilliant writer who has not gained the recognition she deserves in the United States. Extremely well known in Canada, she is valued by such Canadian contemporaries as Alice Munro and Janette Turner Hospital, who praise *Various Miracles*, her short story collection.[18] For the 1990 British publication of *Swann*, Margaret Atwood named the novel "one of the best" of the year—"deft, funny, poignant, surprising, and beautifully shaped."[19]

Almost immediately Carol Shields's style commands our attention and invites our admiration for her fresh and original imagery and metaphor; her wry humor; her refusal to descend into pathos; and her consistent respect for individual human beings, the "ordinary" as well as the intellectual person. Because Shields comprehends the mysterious and secretive core at the heart of every individual, she writes no romantically happy endings. Nonetheless, she valorizes the will to surmount obstacles and move beyond mere survival.

Central to Shields's art are her compelling portraits of women characters who attempt to fathom the nature of happiness, of love, and of their own identities. Shields recalls her dilemma when she first began to write:

> I wanted to write the kind of novel I couldn't find on the library shelf. Where were the novels about the kind of women I knew, women who had a reflective life, a moral system, women who had a recognizable domestic context, a loyalty to their families, a love for their children? (Most of the novels written during this period were about women who left their families, who struck off in search of "freedom," whatever that is.)[20]

She certainly depicts women full of doubts and questions; biographer Judith Martin of *Small Ceremonies*, and her poet-sister Charleen of *The Box Garden*, for instance, share memories of a constricting mother. Yet both sisters also recall brighter memories which sustain them. Shields also concentrates on women's relationships, especially those between and among mothers and daughters and sisters. Key to establishing their identities are stories, books, language, and the question of individual interpretation.

Although her most remarkable characters are women, all of them are profoundly human as, women and men together, they grapple with the onslaughts and ravages of fallibility and happenstance. Therefore, although Shields unhesitatingly dramatizes male attitudes of superiority and condescension toward women, few of her men are villains. As she has noted, "men and women are more alike than we think, responding similarly to experience, but perhaps expressing those responses differently. The language of men and women has been differently conditioned, as we all know" (De Roo, 42). Thus she wrote *Happenstance* from Jack

Bowman's point of view and *A Fairly Conventional Woman* from his wife Brenda's perspective. In fact, language is one of Shields' most compelling concerns—not only its failure, its abuses, its gaps, but also the "sudden way it connects us to one another" and the way it seems, to her, "a kind of proof of our spiritual nature" (De Roo, 45).

The connection between gender and language fascinates Shields, who has experimented with all major forms of literature: biography as well as novels, short stories as well as poetry, drama as well as nonfiction. "Stunning, and distressing" are her words to describe the energy wasted on "genre classification," for she prefers "to think that these categories of reader response are breaking down as rapidly as the boundaries between genres, and that this process has been accelerated by feminist writing" (De Roo, 38, 39). Her settings and characters demonstrate that she is equally at home in several countries; indeed, as her repeated references to our "green planet" attest, an internationally human quality inheres in her writings.

In fact, at a time when she had difficulties with *Swann*, her novel which experiments daringly not only with genre, but with gender difference and with the making of art itself, she stopped and wrote the stories which comprise *Various Miracles*. The results, she says, were "dazzling— anything was allowed, everything was allowed" (De Roo, 41). *Various Miracles* contains many short stories which echo and underscore the themes of women's identity, especially the closeness of women's relationships, the impelling nature of words, and the transcendent nature of humanity. Of the twenty-one stories therein, five stand out to reiterate those concerns and Shields's own remarkable abilities. The book opens with the title story, a paean to commonality in places as different as Morocco, Montana, France, South America, and England, and ends on the other familiar Shields note: the final story, entitled "Others," closes the collection with a baffling sense of the impossibility of truly knowing others; it mitigates against the happy-ending syndrome. Commenting on her "misappropriated" use of the book's epigraph from Emily Dickinson's "Tell all the truth but tell it slant," Shields explains, "I am talking about approaching stories from subversive directions; my 'slant' involves angles of perspective, voice, and layered perception and structure" (De Roo, 49).

"Mrs. Turner Cutting the Grass"[21] is memorable for the way it charters the life of an ordinary woman in an ordinary Winnipeg suburb. The effect is achieved not only through detailing her remarkable life, but through juxtaposing the events of that life to that of a rather smarmy academic, poet and professor of British poetry at a small Massachusetts college. As the story opens, Mrs. Turner, mowing her lawn, is the object of despair to her neighbors, who cannot bear the thought of the pesticides she uses on her grass; and to the teenage girls returning from the nearby high school, who shudder at the sight of the cellulite on her thighs. At the very beginning, however, the narrator intrudes to tell us that Mrs. Turner has no idea that she causes these concerns; Mrs. Turner, Girlie Ferguson, as she was called, has lived a life full of small individual dramas and, having survived them all, she now enjoys her life to the fullest. After discovering Girlie, then 18 years old, with a married man in the local hotel, her father humiliated her by pounding on the door and yelling out his anger. Girlie ran away from home to New York, where she met a man with "skin like ebony" who lived with her until their child was born. Abandoned by her lover and seeing nothing else to do, Girlie placed her baby on the porch of a prosperous house in Brooklyn Heights and, assuring herself that she had done the best she could under the circumstances, returned home.

There, however, as her father again tried to dominate her life, she left home to marry Gordon Turner, a man who loved "every inch of his wife" and who felt no concern about Girlie's past (VM, 23). When he died he bequeathed her the house whose grass she is cutting and enough money so that she could take at least one trip a year with her two sisters. And Girlie has been everywhere—Disneyland as well as Disney World, the American South, Europe, Mexico, and, most recently, Japan, where she has eaten uncooked fish and a fried chrysanthemum, enjoying herself immensely. To the intellectual professor, Girlie and her sisters appear the epitome of vulgarity, and he writes a poem to that effect, regaling his audiences of crass undergraduate students, who also look at Mrs. Turner and her ilk with condescension and amusement. But again the narrator intrudes: these three sisters have weathered their lives, including an angry dominating father and a mother who never once interfered on their behalf, and now they travel about the world. Mrs. Turner may not know the words for certain ideas—but if she knew the word "commonality" she would embrace it, for this is what she has observed in her travels: humans eating, sleeping, working, growing things. This male professor has no concept of her life, so different from his—and herein lies the genius of this story, for the narrator ensures that we understand: intruding again at the end, she points out that Mrs. Turner is happy—the implication is that after enduring her affair, the humiliation by her father, the abandonment by her lover, and a placid marriage to a decent husband who apparently inspired affection if not love, Mrs. Turner has survived and transcended this mortal life to enjoy herself. Unable "to imagine that anyone could wish her harm," she "shines" for us from the pages of her story (27).

"Flitting Behavior" is one of Shields's stories whose male subject is ironically unaware of his selfish treatment of his wife Louise, who lies dying of a terminal disease in an upper room while Meershank dallies downstairs with his forty-year-old editor Maybelle Spritz. True, he has only once slept with Maybelle—on the day when he learns of his wife's illness—but he rationalizes his behavior as his reaction to the way her dying will upset his life. In between the lines of his reminiscences of his meeting, courtship, and marriage to Louise—lines which suggest her primness as opposed to his expansive and ebullient comic talent—we learn that Louise was his reader, his editor, his business manager, in fact his support in all ways, while Meershank continued to write his best-selling comic works absurdly titled, for example, *Snow Drift and Won Ton Soup* and *Walloping Westward*. In these works the narrator adroitly reveals that Meershank has based several of his unflatteringly portrayed women characters on Louise, as well as on one of his daughters, Sonya, who is director of women's studies at a university in London, Ontario. Although one critic has reported that Louise "never read" her husband's works, the narrator informs us that he misinterpreted her statement: in fact, Louise read everything Meershank wrote, but "never *laughed*" at it (62). Now, shut up in an airless room, her imminent death is signaled by the loud explosions of the Victoria Day fireworks as her husband sips brandy and eats ripe, juicy peaches with Maybelle.

Maybelle, sympathetically portrayed as a realist who understands the exact nature of her status with Meershank, calls the daughters whom she has never met to tell them their mother is dying. The bond between mother and daughters is sensed rather than explained, for their responses are swift and immediate: Sonya declares, "I'll be there in three hours flat," while Angelica, who must board a plane, pleads, "Tell her to wait for me" (62). Maybelle, a well-meaning woman, imagines herself embodied in both daughters as they speed to their mother's bedside, and in the doctor who enters the room, and in Louise herself as, with her, she notes that the windows of the stifling room are finally opened to admit the scent of the mock-orange blossoms. She does not, however, attempt to enter Meershank's thoughts.

After Louise's death, Meershank, the two daughters, and Maybelle congregate on the veranda to interpret the dying words of Louise. One daughter thought she said, "The locked door of the room"; the other, "The wok cringes in the womb," both serio-comic feminine interpretations of their mother's life—but Meershank is described through an auctorial intrusion: "a blundering old fool in shirtsleeves, heard, incredibly, 'The sock is out of tune.'" Maybelle wishes to bring order to these fragments, and "through some unsecured back door in her imagination she comes up with 'The mock orange is in bloom'" (65). The suggestive quality of the gorgeous heady scent of mock orange as Louise departs her life, as well as the "mocking" quality inherent in its name, remain with the reader as the story closes on these four temporarily united in the death of a wife and mother.

Three stories in particular delineate the centrality of stories in the lives of women and men: "Poaching," "Scenes," and "Invitations." In "Poaching," the unnamed narrator and her husband Dobey are experimenting with the stories of others: they drive around England, picking up hitchhikers, having agreed to listen to their stories: "We would dwindle, grow deliberately thin, almost invisible, and live like aerial plants off the packed fragments and fictions of the hitchhikers we picked up" (78). They pick up a solitary Venezuelan woman, the description of whom shows Shields's use of and belief in the power of language at its best:

Yes, she adored to travel alone. She liked the song of her own thoughts. She was made fat by the sight of mountains. The Welsh sky was blue like a cushion. She was eager to embrace rides from strangers. She liked to open wide windows so she could commune with the wind. She was a doctor, a specialist in bones, but alas, alas, she was not in love with her profession. She was in love with the English language because every word could be picked up and spun like a coin on the table top. (79)

The narrator and Dobey agree to three points: Never to talk, never to judge, and always to believe what the storytellers say, no matter how improbable. But near the end, the narrator grows restless: she wants to tell her own story, to "float" it "on the air" in order to determine whether "it's true or the opposite of true" (80). And when she queries Dobey about his theory that within all human lives are caves and descending steps, protesting that after all the effort "there may be nothing" when they reach the bottom, he responds, "How will we know if we don't look" (80), a theory to which Shields herself apparently subscribes as she privileges us with glimpses of those inner lives and inner secrets of her characters.

These inner lives are frequently described in "Scenes," another story containing a hallmark of Shields's approach. The narrator reveals that Frances has always valued a mirror bequeathed to her by her grandmother; in recalling her own childhood she wonders about her own two daughters, who seem to live easy lives empty of childhood fears and insecurities. Like a majority of Shields's women, she recalls the terror and "exquisite" sadness of childhood (83), seeing in them forces to overcome and to make her strong in the process. She also recalls scenes of ecstasy: learning to read, for example, was "like falling into a mystery deeper than the mystery of airwaves or the halo around the head of the baby Jesus" (84); hearing foreign languages opened up the world and impelled her to study language at the university; and recalling the time she completed twenty-seven perfect free throws conjures up this incomparably satisfying memory: "Each time the ball went through the hoop she felt an additional oval of surprise grow round her body" (87).

All these, she knows, are merely fragments, seemingly useless information which unlocks no mysteries, constitutes no real stories. And yet in fact Frances understands "perfectly well" that life consists of such fragments, "one fitting against the next like English paving-stones." Other times "she thinks of them as little keys on a chain, keys that open nothing, but simply exist for the beauty of their toothed edges and the way they chime in her pocket" (90).

Again, these images contain and demonstrate much of Shields's technique: her art consists of taking such fragments so that we understand that they are part of an individual life, that all life is made up of such scenes. In the concluding lines she recalls the way she and her mother performed their yearly Easter ritual of coloring and decorating eggs, the best of which could be viewed and admired, one at a time, fitting perfectly into the palm of her hand, "this little egg that was round like the world" (90).

The pleasure of solitary reading, the importance of books, of words, especially to women, is demonstrated in Shields's story "Invitations." After receiving several invitations, each more exciting than the next, aimed at celebrating her literary success, the author-character decides to accept none, instead staying at home with her coffee and Jane Austen's *Mansfield Park*. People passing by that night see "a woman sitting calmly in an arc of lamplight, turning over—one by one—the soft pages of a thick book" (141). The passersby who observe her through her window "were seized by a twist of pain, which was really a kind of nostalgia for their childhood and for a simplified time when they, too, had been bonded to the books they read and to certain golden rooms which they remembered as being complete and as perfect as stage settings" (142).

Although space precludes an examination of Shields's many books, her two most recent novels published in the United States, *Swann* (1989),[22] and *The Republic of Love* (1992), deserve particular mention. They demonstrate her astonishing and seemingly unabated versatility as well as her ongoing fascination with the nature of language, of gender relations and differences, of the process of creating art and culture and, in Shields's words, "who gets to name them."[23] Her continued interest in the role of women who write is evident in her creation of Sarah Maloney, the literature professor in *Swann* whose feminist doctoral dissertation becomes a national bestseller, and who "discovers" the work of Mary Swann, a dead Canadian poet. An academic whodunit on the surface, the text incorporates the genres of film-writing, poetry, and biography, and explores not only academic hypocrisy but also the human inability to comprehend fully an individual life or to penetrate its mysteries.

Carol Gerson's observation is apt here: "The early Canadian woman poet has deviously begun to reenter our literature in fictional form" in Shields's Mary Swann and in Alice Munro's Almeda Joynt Roth.[24] Of relevance to Sarah Maloney is Lorna Irvine's point about Audrey Thomas's Alice, the main character of *Intertidal Life*: "Just as she can articulate her emotions and her investigation of the role of women in society, Alice can also write about writing."[25] And *Swann*'s emphasis on literary foremothers is amplified by Shields's treatment of the relation between Sarah and her real mother:

> When my mother and I are in the same room we work magic on each other: I grow impossibly cheerful and am guilty of reimagined naivete and other in-dulgent stunts, and my mother's sad, helpless dithering becomes a song of succour. Within minutes, we're peddling away, the two of us, a genetic sew-ing machine that runs on limitless love. Its my belief that between mothers and daughters there is a kind of blood-hyphen that is, finally, indissoluble. (47)

The relation not only provides a basis for Sarah's interest in Mary Swann, but also helps her become a strong, confident reader, writer, protector of women's words, and mother of her own child. Shields herself has stated that she grew up by reading texts not mainly from her "father's library" but from her "mother's bookshelf."[26] And in the words of Wayne Fraser,

Carol Shields, Audrey Thomas, Alice Munro, and others are the literary "daughters" of earlier Canadian women writers who now, "excellent writers" themselves, explore the lives of contemporary Canadian "girls and women."[27]

Ultimately, Shields's is a hopeful vision which includes men and women recognizing and working out their differences. Her works contain plentiful examples of misunderstandings, bigotry, misogyny. But they also contain "reaffirming" moments when we suddenly see our commonality. "I have always been compelled," says Shields, "and comforted, too, by the idea of the transcendental moment, that each of us is allotted a few random instances in which we are able to glimpse a kind of pattern in the universe."[28] For this reason one is unsurprised that her most recent novel, *The Republic of Love*, provides sheer delight, for, in the words of one reviewer, "Shields uses a tender, upbeat touch to bring two amiable wounded souls together," suggesting that "it takes courage in a cynical age to risk loving."[29]

Together with Sandra Birdsell, Carol Shields is a writer whose gendered perspective provides essential insights into contemporary Canadian life and to the continuing effort to define Canadian identity. By illuminating the reality of women's history of entrapment and violation, as well as its obverse—the reality of women's achievements and contributions to revisioning the status quo—the very difference in their voices is essential. The identity of Canada, or of any other nation, is impossible to define without their voices. As women, Birdsell and Shields provide the multiplicity of voices and views—their own and those of their fictional characters—necessary to defining both their own worlds and their places within the international community.

Writings by Sandra Birdsell and Carol Shields

Birdsell

NOVELS

Agassiz: A Novel in Stories. Minneapolis: Milkweed Editions, 1991. Originally published as *Agassiz Stories*. Winnipeg: Turnstone Press, 1990.
The Missing Child: A Novel. Toronto: Lester & Orpen Dennys, 1989.

COLLECTED SHORT STORIES

Ladies of the House. Winnipeg: Turnstone Press, 1984.
Night Travellers. Winnipeg: Turnstone Press, 1982.

SHIELDS

NOVELS

Small Ceremonies. Toronto: McGraw-Hill Ryerson, 1976.
The Box Garden. Toronto: McGraw-Hill Ryerson, 1977.
Happenstance. Toronto: Macmillan of Canada, 1980.
A Fairly Conventional Woman. Toronto: Macmillan of Canada, 1982. Published in England with *Happenstance* as *Happenstance.* London: Fourth Estate, 1991.
Swann. New York: Viking, 1989. Published in England as *Mary Swann.* London: Fourth Estate, 1990. Published in Canada as *Swann: A Mystery.* Toronto: Stoddart: 1987.
The Republic of Love. New York: Viking, 1992.

COLLECTED SHORT STORIES

Various Miracles. New York: Penguin Books, 1989. Published in Canada by Stoddart, 1985.
The Orange Fish. Toronto: Random House, 1989.

POETRY

Intersect: Poems. Ottawa: Borealis Press, 1974.
Others: Poems. Ottawa: Borealis Press, 1975.

NONFICTION AND LITERARY CRITICISM

With Clara Thomas, and Donna E. Smyth. "Thinking Back through Our Mothers' Libraries: Tradition in Canadian Women's Writing." In *Re(Dis)covering Our Foremothers: Nineteenth-Century Canadian Women Writers*, ed. Lorraine McMullen, 9–13. Ottawa: University of Ottawa Press, 1989.
Susanna Moodie: Voice and Vision. Ottawa: Borealis Press, 1977.

PLAYS

Departures and Arrivals. Winnipeg: Blizzard Publishing, 1990.

HEATHER ZWICKER

10. Canadian Women of Color in the New World Order: Marlene Nourbese Philip, Joy Kogawa, and Beatrice Culleton Fight Their Way Home

The phrase *Canadian women of color* is a tense one, but it captures exactly the tensions I want to explore in this essay. Whereas "women of color" emphasizes marginalization and difference, "Canadian" tends to domesticate difference by gathering it into a geographical and historical entity which is itself situated in a larger territorial division of the world. What I will argue is that writing by women of color is essential to any sustainable definition of *Canadian*, not merely by expanding the term *Canadian* to include women of color in a pluralist sense, but by blowing wide open any easy notion of what constitutes a national tag like *Canadian*.

The term *women of color* is a relatively new category designed to provide a basis for solidarity among women of various racial and ethnic identities different from the white, Protestant Euro-Canadian popularly believed to characterize Canada.[1] The term does not denote visible difference— many women of color are fair-skinned, mixed-blood, or can "pass" as white—but is a form of self-identification that recognizes marginalization and affirms difference. Inasmuch as the term operates as a self-conscious basis for solidarity by foregrounding the racism that constructs women of color as "other," the term is useful. But, to my mind, it has two problems. First, it tends to homogenize the enormous heterogeneity among Japanese Canadian, Native Canadian, Caribbean Canadian, and Chinese Canadian women, to name just a few "hyphenated" national identities. Second, the term does not foreground the experience of immigration that is constitutive, at some historical moment, of Canadian identity.

The editors of *Feminist Organizing for Change: The Contemporary Women's Movement in Canada* call the link between immigration and people of color "one of the most insidious forms of racism" because it encourages the idea "that the problems of race are really temporary problems of assimilation."[2] I do not believe that assimilation is either possible or desirable, though clearly it is the goal of official multiculturalism of the kind advocated by Canada's Ministry of Multiculturalism, which has a mandate to celebrate and a tendency to police multiculturalism.[3] I mean the term *immigration* in a large sense of settling in a country not one's own, whether alienation from ownership is a result of natality or systemic racism. This expanded definition excludes those who are technically immigrants but for whom, by reason of privilege based on class, race, or gender—unofficial "favored nation" status—assimilation is not an issue. On the other hand, it includes Native Canadians, for whom the history of colonialism and perpetuation of systemic racism interrupt any easy equation between Native and Canada. Though the land might originally (and properly) have belonged to Native Canadians, they, like immigrants, have to fight to make it home.[4] I want to use the uneasy links between "women of color" and "immigrant" that I believe the novels of Marlene Nourbese Philip, Joy Kogawa, and Beatrice Culleton provoke, in order to explore and explode the way Canada is constructed and reconstructed.

For Canada cannot be taken for granted: its geography and history are marked within and demarcated from without by unequal relationships of power. In a phrase as offensive as it is telling, George Bush and his cronies describe contemporary international relations as "the New World Order." The phrase quotes Hitler's regime of "New Order" in the quincentenary of European imperialism to locate hegemony in the so-called New World.[5] Although I am fundamentally skeptical of U.S. policy, I think the "new world" trope can be used subversively precisely because it foregrounds the experience of immigration described above. Making oneself at home in the new world necessitates a radical rethinking of national identity, because the elements that conventionally constitute national identity— history, natality, family, and place—no longer fall neatly into the territorial and historical entity that we know as Canada.[6]

"Home" is not simply a place, but a place one makes one's own; it is both a geographical given and a discursive construct. Places have their effects on us, but we are also continually ascribing meaning to particular places. In their essay titled "Feminist Politics: What's Home Got to Do With It?" Biddy Martin and Chandra Mohanty offer a useful way of defining home. [7] They start from the position that there is no single meaning to any place nor any single defining attribute to a person: as they put it, "Individuals do not fit neatly into unidimensional, self-identical categories" (205). As a complex subject, one may be simultaneously at home and not at home; furthermore, in the contemporary world, people frequently relocate from one place to another, always moving through spaces that constrain but never contain them. This notion of transience is important for conceptualizing new-world identity: people bear the imprints of their origins, but move from them to absorb and create new identities in new places. Hence the phrase *Caribbean Canadian* signifies a meaningful place of origin, even while it looks ahead to the new home. But just as *Caribbean* marks a site that is lost, *Canadian* signifies a location that is never easily reached, because it is always preceded by its significant modifier, *Caribbean* (or *French*, or *Japanese*, or *Ukrainian*). Once the population of Canada is divided up by such appellations, it becomes clear that there is no such thing as simple "Canadian": Canada is based on ethnic diversity. Even though British and French ethnicity still dominate Canada, they account together for less than 50 percent of the Canadian population. Fully 30 percent of Canadians in the 1986 census claimed "multiple ethnic origins," and by the year 2000 at least 10 percent of Canadians will be people of color. [8]

The idea of a subject in continual transition works against an easy identity of self with place in both the past and the future, but there is always a tension between this rootlessness and the desire for stability. The problem facing Canadians is that of making themselves *at* home by making themselves *a* home. This process is an act of attributing meaning to place. Homes as locations "acquire meaning and function as sites of personal and historical struggle," Martin and Mohanty argue (196). The apparent stability of places is always cross-cut by the histories of struggle congealed in them—in Canada, struggles against racism and exclusion. It is not by avoiding the struggles that inhere in a place, but rather by taking part in them, that a meaningful home is created. The safest community is "that which is struggled for, chosen, and hence unstable by definition; it is not based on 'sameness,' and there is no perfect fit. But," Martin and Mohanty go on to stress, "there is agency as opposed to passivity" (208–09). Community ultimately is not simply place, but also history, written with an eye to both political priorities and human needs. To quote Martin and Mohanty at some length:

Community, then, is the product of work, of struggle; it is inherently unstable, contextual; it has to be constantly reevaluated in relation to critical political priorities; and it is the product of interpretation, interpretation based on an attention to history, to the concrete, to what Foucault has called subjugated knowledges. There is also, however, a strong suggestion that community is related to experience, to history. For if identity and community are not the product of essential connections, neither are they merely the product of political urgency or necessity. . . . they are a constant recontextualizing of the relationship between personal/group history and political priorities. (210)

Tracing the connection between "the purely experiential" and "the theoretical oversight of personal and collective histories" is, it seems to me, the work of fiction (210). The fleshing out of history, the writing of oneself into social texts, is an act of imagination. The Canadian writers I will discuss in the remainder of the essay record desire for and fear of the nation called Canada, experiences of alienation from it and profound love. Throughout their novels, we are reminded that we cannot take this place called Canada for granted.

Of course, few of the novels operate so schematically as this emphasis on place suggests. Rather, the concept *home* is rendered quite narrow, often domestically, taking family members for national subjects and describing history as memory. Perhaps the most schematic of the novels is Marlene Nourbese Philip's *Harriet's Daughter*. The story centers on the friendship between two girls, Margaret and Zulma. Margaret, the first-person narrator, is a second-generation Canadian whose father is from Barbados and whose mother is Jamaican. For Margaret, Toronto is home. Her best friend, Zulma, has recently arrived in Toronto, to live with her mother and stepfather, from Tobago, where she lived with her grandmother. Zulma's compelling desire is to return to the Tobago that she loves. The plot of the story, in brief, traces Margaret's attempts to help Zulma get back to Tobago, even while she battles her own father's threats to send her to Barbados for what he calls "some 'Good West Indian Discipline.'"[9] In the course of enabling Zulma to choose her own home, Margaret defines her own social identity differently from the familial identity she is born into.

The figurative device by which Nourbese Philip deftly ties together Margaret's resolution to stay in Canada and Zulma's determination to return to Tobago is the Underground Railroad. It starts out as a game played by kids at Margaret's school: some students are arbitrarily slaves, others slave-owners or dogs. The object of the game is for the slaves to make it to a designated place called Freedom without being caught by the slave-owners and dogs. Hence place and liberty are linked from the outset of the game, and Margaret and Zulma have the same goal in their lives as they have in the game: making it "home-free." Zulma's return to Tobago constitutes a historical completion of the escape from slavery by reversing the middle passage. Significantly, the destination of Zulma's voyage home is not Africa, but the Caribbean fulcral point between Africa and the New world—the main stage on which the ugly colonial violence of genocide and slavery, as well as the genesis of American revolutions, was played out. By making the West Indies the site of return, Nourbese Philip foregrounds struggle and resists an idealization of racial origin.

She similarly refuses to idealize Canada by foregrounding choice as a constitutive element of home. Although both Margaret and Zulma choose as home the countries in which they were born, the connection between place and family breaks down: while Zulma's attachment is to her grandmother, not her mother, Margaret chooses to remain with her birth family. What such a formulation implies is the importance of self-determination as a constitutive element of freedom. [10] Furthermore, to extend the historical Underground Railroad suggests that the escape from oppression to freedom is an ongoing struggle that cannot end in a specific location, like Canada. Rather, the attempt to arrive at some home-free location always continues in changed and changing forms: it is what Martin and Mohanty call a "[site] of personal and historical struggle" (196).

A similar insistence on choice informs Margaret's subjective self-determination. Alongside her efforts to help Zulma and inextricable from the Underground Railroad game, Margaret rewrites her identity. She has been named by her father, an oppressive patriarch, for his mother, whom Margaret has never met but who comes to represent the "'Good West Indian Discipline'" that Margaret's father repeatedly threatens her with. She is named, essentially, within the patriarchy. Determined to distinguish herself from her familially inherited role, Margaret renames herself. The name she chooses is Harriet, out of admiration for Harriet Tubman and in remembrance of Harriet Blewchamp, a woman who survived concentration camps, employed Margaret's mother, and bequeathed to Margaret her books and letters, as well as a trust fund. Choosing to be identified as Harriet, then, is a self-conscious move on Margaret's part to write herself into the most important historical events of the last two centuries from an explicitly feminist point of view.

Margaret's family and friends address her as Harriet for the bulk of the novel. Ultimately, however, a borrowed identity, even one which is so positively imbued with history, is an incomplete stage of subjective self-determination: rebelliousness is, in a sense, its own form of bondage. The success of getting Zulma back to Tobago—in effect, fulfilling her role as Harriet Tubman—is paradoxically the point at which Margaret reclaims her birth name. Although at the beginning of the novel she refers to herself as "me, Harriet, as leader," she comes to read her actions as something she has "done . . . as Margaret" (*HD*, 1, 130). The complexity of resuming her birth name lies in the process of redefinition that informs it: having written herself into the grand narrative of history and enacted a historical role in the life of her friend, Margaret has forged a social identity that can never be collapsed back into the familial identity she was born with. Resuming her own name is not at all a renunciation of the feminist impulses that led her to adopt the name Harriet, but rather their necessary completion. The implication is that feminist action does not inhere in a few historical identities, but continually reappears in everyday women with everyday names. [11] Margaret's socially and historically constructed identity is not just narrowly familial, but analogous to national identity. To be born in Canada is not enough to constitute Canadianness: meaningful national identity, in the terms of Nourbese Philip's novel, is a personal and historical struggle.

Struggle as a constitutive element of national identity is even more evident in Joy Kogawa's *Obasan*, which tells the story of a Japanese Canadian family's internment during World War II. Unlike Nourbese Philip, Kogawa takes Canada not as a choice, but as inevitable: rather than telling the story of the first generation of immigrants, as Zulma represents, Kogawa writes about the Nisei, second-generation Japanese Canadians for whom relocation is not a matter of choice but of racist governmental policy. The problem Kogawa addresses is, how do you make a country your own when it disowns you?

There is no simple answer. In fact, the novel exemplifies what Martin and Mohanty call "the tension between the desire for home, for synchrony, for sameness, and the realization of the repressions and violence that make home, harmony, sameness imaginable, and that enforce it" (208). On the one hand, Naomi has violent dreams of dismemberment: of her legs being sawed in half, of being chased by superhuman beings with hinged metal arms, and, always, of soldiers—the most direct manifestation of the national state apparatus. On the other hand, these dreams take place against the backdrop of Canadian natality:

> Where do any of us come from in this cold country? Oh Canada, whether it is admitted or not, we come from you we come from you. From the same soil, the slugs and slime and bogs and twigs and roots. We come from the country that plucks its people out like weeds and flings them into the roadside. We grow in ditches and sloughs, untended and spindly. We erupt in the valleys and mountainsides, in small towns and back alleys, sprouting upside-down on the prairies, our hair wild as spiders' legs, our feet rooted nowhere. We grow where we are not seen, we flourish where we are not heard, the thick undergrowth of an unlikely planting. [12]

In this passage, Kogawa differentiates home as place—the relentlessly verdant national soil that keeps making Canadians of people—from home as political entity, where the undesirable are weeded out. Occupation alone cannot make a home: those unnamed in the history of a place remain unknown and are consequently mistaken for weeds rather than new strains. Kogawa's metaphor implies an ideal vision of Canada as a garden of many species, all of which deserve to be tended. This pluralist position is reiterated by Rough Lock Bill, a man of unspecified ethnicity [13] who saves Naomi's life, literally and, from an ideological point of view, figuratively (*O*, 143). He says to the young Naomi, "'Never met a kid didn't like stories. Red skin, yellow skin, white skin, any skin. . . . Don't make sense, do it, all this fuss about skin?'" (*O*, 145).

Of course, the fuss isn't just about skin, but about stories—about which history, whose history, is recorded, and how it is used—and this is where the pluralist solution runs into trouble. Pluralist history presupposes that several versions of the past exist, and that minority positions need only to be unveiled and included in order to rectify the discrimination that hides them. This in turn presupposes that history *can* be told, that language is expressive rather than mystifying, and that alternate histories, once told, can be heard.

The novel enters this contentious territory by sustaining a debate between Naomi's two aunts, Emily and Obasan. Naomi herself registers a deep ambivalence, by turns suspicious of Emily's stridency and frustrated with Obasan's silence. Aunt Emily, the academic, articulates the commonsensical pro-history position that talking is good, that it lessens pain and aids healing. Habakkuk 2:2, "Write the vision and make it plain," is her slogan (*O*, 31). History, according to Aunt Emily, is never singular, neutral, or objective. Says she: "'There's no strength in seeing all sides unless you can act where real measurable injustice exists.'" (*O*, 35). Hers is an unarguable position, as far as it goes: if oppression takes the form of exclusion, the appropriate solution is inclusion. But she presupposes that the story of internment can be told and, more problematically, that it can be heard and used to modify conventional histories of Canada.

Aunt Emily's optimism is easy to understand: in living out World War II in Toronto, she escaped internment. Those who lived through it, represented by the deaf Obasan in her world of silence, add important correctives to Emily's valorization of speech. Against Emily's Old Testament credo, the interned community rely on the forgiveness phrase of the Lord's Prayer: "Forgive us our trespasses as we forgive those who trespass against us." Their position is that there are some wounds that never heal, some things too painful to talk about: "What is past recall is past pain" (*O*, 45). History cannot express the truth of past pain because language is inadequate to the task. The same language that writes history, even alternative history, also wrote the Orders-in-Council that initiated internment, and calls internment camps "Interior Housing Projects" (*O*, 34). Furthermore, the silence of the interned community suggests a radical questioning of the usefulness of historical visibility. Although certainly historical invisibility is a product of racism, from the perspective of those discriminated against on the basis of visible difference, invisibility can seem safe. To "grow where we are not seen, . . . flourish where we are not heard" can be a form of adaptation, a way of surviving (226). If a true history can never be written, and visibility is no guarantee of ending discrimination, what is the point of history at all?

> "Life is so short," [Naomi] said sighing, "the past so long. Shouldn't we turn the page and go on?"
> "The past is the future," Aunt Emily shot back. (42)

Although Naomi agrees with Aunt Emily, she universalizes the lesson: "What is done, Aunt Emily, is done, is it not? And no doubt it will all happen again, over and over with different faces and names, variations on the same theme" (*O*, 199). Though doubtless Naomi is right, such a version of history silences the nationally and personally specific: greed, selfishness and hatred might be "as constant as the human condition," but they take specific forms in particular historical moments (*O*, 199). It is the emphasis on historical specificity, with attention to the lessons about silence taught by the internment survivors, that inform the novel's ultimate stance toward history.

The final, jarring revelation of the plot is that Naomi's mother was critically disfigured in the bombing of Nagasaki. Naomi's mother, represented only in black and white photographs, has been an enigmatic silence throughout the novel (that is, disfigured). And yet, hers is a significant silence, a silence that contains history within it. In her charred skin and maggot-infested wounds, Naomi's mother literally embodies more history than all of Aunt Emily's conference papers and documents. The challenge for Naomi is to interpret her mother's silence:

> Silent mother, you do not speak or write. You do not reach through the night to enter morning, but remain in the voicelessness. From the extremity of much dying, the only sound that reaches me now is the sigh of your remembered breath, a wordless word. How shall I attend that speech, Mother, how shall I trace that wave? (241)

The ability to hear her mother's silence takes place through concentrated listening, through a willingness and an effort to hear. "Mother. I am listening. Assist me to hear you," Naomi asks (*O*, 240). Hearing is not automatically attendant on the articulation of historical events; it requires determination.

At this point Naomi's own ethnicity becomes significant. If family symbolizes national identity, any possible return to the motherland is slain with Naomi's mother. Naomi is explicitly not Japanese, but Japanese Canadian: a full Canadian citizen who is also an intermediary between two cultures. As someone who sets out to hear what is written in silence, Naomi gives us an important lesson about the equal importance of listening to telling. Easy pluralism is impossible because history is predicated on silences that point to what exceeds the expressive possibilities of language. Inasmuch as the novel follows Naomi's discovery of her mother's loss, the novel foregrounds as history the process of constructing history, the process of coming to hear its silences as well as its words.

Beatrice Culleton's first-person fictional autobiography *In Search of April Raintree* makes a similar point. The novel tells the story of two Metis sisters, April and Cheryl Raintree. Separated very young and placed in different foster homes, the sisters also choose very different lives for themselves: April, the older and fairer-skinned sister, assimilates into white society, while Cheryl, who cannot pass as white, adopts a militant political identity at a very young age and grows up to work for Native Canadians at a Friendship Centre. Tragically,[14] it is Cheryl who turns to alcohol and eventually commits suicide, while April, in uncovering the chain of events and emotions that led to her sister's death, arrives at a politically informed self-determination. In the course of telling this story, Culleton radically revises conventional notions of the family and its relation to the nation, and argues, like Kogawa, for the importance of personal history in the construction of the national.

For immigrants, the disjuncture between family and nation is explicit: at some level, members of the same family have different nationalities. But there is no simple fit between family and nation in Culleton's work. The family is de-naturalized from the outset of the novel by the intervention of the state, which takes April and Cheryl away from their natural parents and puts them in foster homes. The sisters have opposite responses to this deprivation of family. April renounces familial ties completely, telling friends at school that her parents were killed in a plane crash. She disavows connections to community, to foster families, and even lets lapse her relationship to Cheryl. Cheryl, on the other hand, reaches to restore the natural family. She tries to locate her birth parents, and forges ties to the Indian community. Metis identity, for her, is inherent ("'The Indian blood runs through your veins,'" she tells April) and communal: she feels most alive at the Pow Wow she and April attend.[15] But ultimately Culleton suggests that such a version of being Indian is insufficient to the racist day, by juxtaposing the Pow Wow with the court hearing for April's rapists. The symmetry is telling: the character who will survive has to be able to mediate both ceremonies. The emphasis on mediation (but not assimilation—April tries but renounces that) is reminiscent of Nourbese Philip's choice of the Caribbean rather than Africa as a site of return: there is no going back to any pure origin. Metis and Creole, not Indian or African, symbolize survival in the "new world."

April's ability to embody a truly mixed-blood identity takes place through historical discovery and political commitment. The importance of history is evident from the outset of the novel—it opens with the word "Memories"—and the process of remembering is explicitly connected to survival (*SAR*, 9). Says April, as explanation for telling her life story, "I always felt most of my memories were better avoided but now I think it's best to go back in my life before I go forward" (*SAR*, 9). It is essential, too, Culleton suggests, that this process of remembering not elide personal pain. Cheryl continually rails against official representations of Native people in school curricula: "'Your history books are full of lies,'" she tells the school principal, and she writes revisionist essays on Louis Riel not as a traitor but as a freedom fighter (*SAR*, 58). However, it is not such impersonal history, but the very personal record of her sister's life that spurs April's move to political identity. [16] Just as it is the horrific account of the death of Naomi's mother in *Obasan* that finally brings Naomi to historical consciousness, it is the record of how racism hurts people that brings about political mobilization in *In Search of April Raintree*.

April's ultimate self-determination takes place through reconstituting a family. The first aspect of this reconstituted family is political: in reading through Cheryl's journals, April comes to understand the racism and impoverishment her darker-skinned sister endured. April's sympathy for her birth sister grows into larger political affiliation with "[her] people" (*SAR*, 228). The family is not only national, but also more narrowly domestic: April adopts the son Cheryl has left behind, Henry Liberty. The novel closes with April's arrival at political consciousness:

> As I stared at Henry Lee, I remembered that during the night I had used the words 'MY PEOPLE, OUR PEOPLE' and meant them. The denial had been lifted from my spirit. It was tragic that it had taken Cheryl's death to bring me to accept my identity. But no, Cheryl had once said, 'All life dies to give new life.' Cheryl had died. But for Henry Lee and me, there would be a tomorrow. And it would be better. I would strive for it. For my sister and her son. For my parents. For my people. (*SAR*, 228)

What Culleton does in this volatile closing passage is unite classical tragedy with national revolutionary consciousness. The psychic and familial chaos wrought by Cheryl's suicide is healed by the promise of Liberty born as the next generation. But the family is not and, given the story that precedes it, cannot be defined by simple natality. First, the son is not April's, but Cheryl's; second, it has no father. The domestic family has nothing to do with commonly available images of the nuclear family, but it is stronger for the commitment that stands behind April's conscious dedication. This mother-son relationship acts as a trope for Metis nationhood in the larger sense. April as Metis matriarch has to exist in both Indian and white societies, and must negotiate the relationship of the past to the present in order to construct a viable future. This places her at a radical crossroads, a point that is defined only by the myriad crisscrossing of lines. It is a hard place, but it is the only place for sustainable constructions of the nation. [17]

Ultimately, I see this as the lesson of all three writers I have discussed. I have argued for their importance as theorists of the new-world nation that sustains and is sustained by difference, that is constructed geographically and historically through struggle, that eschews ethnic purity but can never forget racism. Affiliation, political commitment, provisional alliances, struggle—these, I have suggested, are the bases of sustainable national identity. There may be no roots, but there is routedness, and it is essential, I believe, on our way into the future, to pay attention to the radical.

Writings by Marlene Nourbese Philip, Joy Kogawa, and Beatrice Culleton

Nourbese Philip

FICTION

Harriet's Daughter. London: Heinemann, 1988.
Looking for Livingstone: An Odyssey of Silence. Stratford, Ont.: The Mercury Press.

POETRY

Thorns. Stratford, Ont.: Williams-Wallace Press, 1980.
Salmon Courage. Stratford, Ont.: Williams-Wallace Press, 1983.
She Tries Her Tongue; Her Silence Softly Breaks. Charlottetown, P.E.I.: Ragweed Press, 1989.

KOGAWA

FICTION

Obasan. Harmondsworth, Eng.: Penguin, 1981; Boston: Godine, 1982.
Woman in the Woods. Oakville, Ont.: Mosaic Press, 1985.
Naomi's Road. Toronto: Oxford University Press, 1986.
Itsuka. Toronto: Lewster & Orpen Dennys, 1991; Toronto: Viking Press, 1992.

POETRY

A Choice of Dreams. Toronto: McClelland & Stewart, 1974.
Jericho Road. Toronto: McClelland & Stewart, 1977.
The Splintered Moon. Fredericton, N.B.: Fiddlehead Poetry, 1967.

CULLETON

FICTION

In Search of April Raintree. Winnipeg: Pemmican Press, 1983.
April Raintree. Winnipeg: Pemmican Press, 1984.
Spirit of the White Bison. Illus., Robert Kakaygeesick. Winnipeg: Pemmican Press, 1985.

Notes

Notes to Chapter I

1. David Stouck, "Alice Munro," in *Major Canadian Authors*, 2d ed. (Lincoln: University of Nebraska Press, 1988), 257–59.

2. 14 October 1990, 8:5.

3. E. D. Blodgett, *Alice Munro* (Boston: Twayne, 1988), 6.

4. Ildikó dePapp Carrington, *Controlling the Uncontrollable: The Fiction of Alice Munro* (DeKalb: Northern Illinois University Press, 1989), 16.

5. John Metcalf, "A Conversation with Alice Munro," *Journal of Canadian Fiction* 1:4 (1972): 56.

6. Harold Horwood, "Interview with Alice Munro," in *The Art of Alice Munro*, ed. Judith Miller (Waterloo: University of Waterloo Press, 1984), 135.

7. Interview by Peter Gzowski, *Morningside*, CBC Radio, 2 June 1987.

8. Blodgett, *Alice Munro*, 10.

9. Peter Kemp, *London Sunday Times*, 14 October 1990, 8:5.

10. References to Munro's collections are drawn from the following readily available paperback editions: *DHS* (*Dance of the Happy Shades*, Penguin, 1968); *LGW* (*Lives of Girls and Women*, Penguin, 1971); *SIBMTY* (*Something I've Been Meaning to Tell You*, Penguin, 1974); *BM* (*The Beggar Maid*, Penguin, 1978); *MJ* (*The Moons of Jupiter*, Knopf, 1983); *PL* (*The Progress of Love*, Penguin, 1987); and *FMY* (*Friend of My Youth*, Vintage, 1991).

11. Carrington, *Controlling*, 202.

12. Some narrator/protagonists who are *not* intelligent women include the appropriately named Dick in "Thanks for the Ride" (*DHS*); Helen, the obtuse jilted salesclerk in "Postcard" (*DHS*); Edie, the young and naive maid in "How I Met My Husband" (*SIBMTY*); Mr. Lougheed, a sensitive and lonely pensioner in "Walking on Water" (*SIBMTY*); Colin, the put-upon older brother in "Monsieur les Deux Chapeux" (*PL*); and the wealthy widower Sam, still looking for past happiness in "The Moon in the Orange Street Skating Rink" (*PL*).

13. Horwood interview, 131.

14. Eudora Welty, *One Writer's Beginnings* (Cambridge: Harvard University Press, 1984), 44.

15. Horwood interview, 132.

16. Blodgett, *Alice Munro*, 33.

17. Munro frequently connects water and sex in her stories, often with an implied or overt threat of danger. Garnet French, to whom Del Jordan has lost her virginity, tries to baptize/drown her in "Baptizing" (*LGW*). Et likens her sister Char's "big and swollen" look to the sight of her drowned brother Sandy when she catches Char tangled with her lover, Blaikie Noble, in "Something I've Been Meaning to Tell You" (*SIBMTY*, 10–11). The seductive pilot of "How I Met My Husband" (*SIBMTY*) is named Chris Watters; in "The Found Boat" (*SIBMTY*), the spring-swollen Wawanash River is the site of a pre-pubescent sexual encounter between Clayton and Eva when, during their nude bathing, he spits a mouthful of river water at her and hits her breasts (136). Rose's crush on Cora in "Privilege" (*BM*), the beginning of sexual love, is compared to "the high tide; . . . the flash flood" (35). Rose later encounters on the train to Toronto the "minister" who masturbates her after telling her of a flock of wild swans he'd seen on a pond; his hand is able "to get the ferns to rustle and the streams to flow" ("Wild Swans," *BM*, 64). The menstruating "poetess" Alemeda, ill and distracted both by the obscene racket on Pearl Street and her attraction to Jarvis Poulter, "channels" all her feelings into the composition of a poem about the river, "Meneseteung," which for her becomes the river—as a basin of grape juice for the jelly she's been making overflows its basin and runs across her kitchen floor, staining it a purple that will never come out (*FMY*, 70). In this stunning image, Munro links flowing water with creativity, both sexual and poetic.

18. Carrington, *Controlling*, 89.

19. Ibid., 156.

20. Stouck, "Alice Munro," 260.

21. J. R. (Tim) Struthers, "The Real Material: An Interview with Alice Munro," in *Probable Fictions: Alice Munro's Narrative Acts*, ed. Louis K. MacKendrick (Downsview, Ont.: ECW, 1983), 24.

22. Blodgett, *Alice Munro*, 85.

23. Robert Towers, "Short Satisfactions," *New York Times Book Review*, 17 May 1990, 38.

24. Joan Didion, *The White Album* (New York: Simon and Schuster, 1979), 11.

25. *The New Yorker*, 10 February 1992, 30–40.

26. Geoff Hancock, "An Interview with Alice Munro," *Canadian Fiction Magazine* 43 (1982): 94.

Notes to Chapter 3

1. Hébert's awards include the Prix David, the Prix de Québec, the Prix France-Canada, the Prix Duvernay, the Governor General's Award for Poets, the Molson Prize, and the Prix de Libraires de France.

2. An extensive library search reveals that with the exception of some brief reviews in popular publications of translations of her recent novels there are no articles on Hébert in journals devoted to general literary or feminist analysis. Studies appear in Canadian publications, American journals of Canadian study, and journals aimed at teachers of French or comparative literature.

3. On the assumption that my readers will be primarily English speakers, I have listed the translations and their dates of publication first, followed by the original French titles and dates of initial publication.

4. Not only is this work based on an "actual event that took place many years ago," according to Hébert's headnote to the novel, it was an event that took place in the neighborhood where Hébert's grandmother lived; the murdered man was, in fact, a distant relative of Hébert's mother, whose maiden name was Tache, and the author explained in an interview that an important source for her treatment of the events was extensive family discussion recalled from her childhood. See Delbert W. Russell, *Anne Hébert* (Boston: Twayne, 1983), 74–80, for an account of Hébert's personal connection with the story and for a survey of the historical events upon which the novel is based.

5. This popular novel was also adapted by Hébert for a critically acclaimed 1973 film of the same title, starring Genevieve Bujold and directed by Claude Jutras.

6. Of related interest is John Lennox's discussion of gothic elements in the novel, in "Dark Journeys: *Kamorouska* and *Deliverance*," *Essays on Canadian Writing* 12 (Fall 1978): 84–104.

7. John G. Cawelti, *Adventure, Mystery, and Romance: Formula Stories as Art and Popular Culture* (Chicago: University of Chicago Press, 1976), 44–45.

8. William Flint Thrall et al., "Tragedy," in *A Handbook to Literature* (New York: Odyssey, 1960), 488.

9. I use a spaced ellipsis (. . .) to indicate my own omissions; the unspaced ellipsis (...) indicates an ellipsis included in the text. Page numbers from the English translations of Anne Hébert's works of fiction are given in parentheses in the text.

10. His literary criticism includes *De livres en livres* (Montreal: Carrier, 1929), *Et d'un livre à l'autre* (Montreal: Levesque, 1932), and *Les Lettres au Canada francais* (Montreal: Levesque, 1936). According to Russell, his criticism sought "the merits of even the weakest works, in the belief that only a positive encouragement of literature would lead to the creation of a mature French-Canadian literature" (117 n. 1).

11. Lorraine Weir, "Anne Hébert," in *Dictionary of Literary Biography 68: Canadian Writers, 1920–1959*, ed. W. H. New, 167 (Detroit: Gale Research).

12. Norah Story and Joyce Marshall, "Hébert, Anne," in *Supplement to the Oxford Companion to Canadian History and Literature*, ed. William Toye, 109 (Toronto: Oxford University Press, 1973).

13. Hébert reports that she had read a newspaper account of the murder of his mother by a young man studying for the priesthood. Ibid., 25.

14. Edmund Wilson, *Axel's Castle: A Study of Imaginative Literature of 1870 to 1930* (New York: Scribners, 1931), 21.

15. Hébert's poetry, very much in the symbolist tradition, has been compared to that of Paul Verlaine. Susan L. Rosenstreich, "The Marginal Poetics of Anne Hébert," in *Traditionalism, Nationalism, and Feminism: Women Writers of Quebec*, ed. Paula Gilbert Lewis, 65 (Westport, Conn.: Greenwood Press, 1985).

16. Because of their belief in the uniqueness of inner experience, symbolists were accused of self-referential obscurity, substituting a "rimed rebus for poetry"; they maintained, however, that their complex and subtle poems should be "an enigma for the vulgar, chamber-music for the initiated." "Symbolism," in *The Reader's Companion to World Literature*, ed. Calvin S. Brown, 432 (New York: NAL, 1956).

17. Weir, "Anne Hébert, 173.

18. Maurice Cagnon, *The French Novel of Quebec* (Boston: Twayne, 1986), 16.

19. Marie-Claire Blais, another contemporary Quebec writer remarks with regard to French-Canadian literary heritage: "Any nostalgia we may feel for their vitality of language is not unmixed with irritation as we remember the outrageous censorship they had to submit to, and the narrowness that was a product of their social and cultural milieu." Introduction, *The Oxford Book of French-Canadian Short Stories*, ed. Richard Teleky, xi (Toronto: Oxford University Press, 1983).

20. Hébert's treatment of the region of Kamouraska as a zone of unwarranted license in the novel of that title is another instance of her interrogation of traditional French-Canadian literary convention. Traditionally, the northern regions, the *pays d'en haut*, represent a myth of the French frontier, a primary site of the "purity of Canadian nature" and "the love of the true freedom." Jack Warwick, *The Long Journey: Literary Themes of French Canada* (Toronto: University of Toronto Press, 1968), vii.

21. Ibid., 18.

22. Anne Hébert, "Poetry Broken Solitude," in *Poems*, trans. Alan Brown, 48 (Don Mills, Ontario: Musson, 1975).

23. Jansenism, a Catholic reform movement especially influential in France during the seventeenth and eighteenth centuries, was based on a philosophy of predestination. It advocated simplicity of living and rigid adherence to moral principle, and encouraged mysticism.

24. Weir, "Anne Hébert," 166–67. Russell, *Anne Hébert*, also cites several franchophone critics who also hold this view (119 n. 18).

25. See Russell, *Anne Hébert*, 91–95, for an analysis of the scholarly sources and notes on the history of witchcraft that Hébert appended to the original French version of the novel. This material has been omitted from the English translation.

Notes to Chapter 4

1. Margaret Atwood, *Bodily Harm* (New York: Bantam, 1982), 11.

2. Margaret Atwood, *Survival* (Toronto: Anansi, 1972), 245. Further page references are given in the text.

3. Margaret Atwood, *The Edible Woman* (New York: Fawcett, 1969), 7.

4. Margaret Atwood, *Lady Oracle* (New York: Fawcett, 1976), 3. Further page references are given in the text.

5. Jessie Givner writes, "The mirrors in *Lady Oracle* display a multiplicity of divisions, a complete fragmentation or dispersion of the self" ("Mirror Images in Margaret Atwood's *Lady Oracle*," *Studies in Canadian Literature* 14:1 [1989]: 141).

6. *Bodily Harm*, 26. Further page references are given in the text.

7. "At last she knows that the ability to identify oneself with another woman, to connect to another person in empathetic touch, is the only real antidote to what she has seen and experienced." Roberta Rubenstein, "Pandora's Box and Female Survival: Mar-

garet Atwood's *Bodily Harm*," in *Critical Essays on Margaret Atwood*, ed. Judith McCombs, 273 (Boston: G. K. Hall, 1988).

8. Margaret Atwood, *A Handmaid's Tale* (New York: Fawcett, 1985), 65. Further page references are given in the text.

9. Judith Thurman, "When You Wish upon a Star," *The New Yorker*, 29 May 1989, 110.

10. Virginia Woolf, *To the Lighthouse* (New York: Harcourt, Brace, Jovanovich, 1927), 209.

11. Margaret Atwood, *Cat's Eye* (New York: Bantam, 1989), 427. Further page references are given in the text.

Notes to Chapter 5

1. Marie-Claire Blais, *Deaf to the City*, trans. Carol Dunlop (Woodstock: The Overlook Press, 1981). Subsequent quotations are denoted by *DC* and page numbers in the text.

2. Gaston Bachelard, *The Poetics of Reverie: Childhood Language, and the Cosmos* (Boston: Beacon Press, 1960). Subsequent quotations are denoted by *PR* and page numbers in the text.

3. Louise Wetherbee Phelps, "Practical Wisdom and the Geography of Knowledge in Composition," *College English* 52:8 (December 1991): 865. Subsequent quotations are denoted by *PW* and page numbers in the text.

Notes to Chapter 6

1. Janette Turner Hospital, in *Homeland*, ed. George Papellinas, 18 (Sydney: Allen & Unwin, 1991).

2. Mickey Pearlman, "Interview with Janette Turner Hospital," in *Listen to Their Voices*, 56 (New York: W. W. Norton, 1993).

3. Coral Ann Howells, *Private and Fictional Worlds: Canadian Women Novelists of the 1970's and 1980's* (London: Methuen, 1987), 9.

4. Robert Kroetsch, *The Lovely Treachery of Words: Essays Selected and New* (Toronto: Oxford University Press, 1989), 67.

5. Judith Timson, review of *The Tiger in the Tiger Pit*, *Chatelaine* 56 (January 1983): 4.

6. Pearlman, "Interview," 56. *Listen to Their Voices*, N.Y.: W. W. Norton, 1993.

7. Elspeth Cameron, "Borders," *Saturday Night* 101 (April 1986): 57.

8. In this essay, Janette Turner Hospital's novels are identified in the following way, and page numbers are given in parentheses in the text: *IS* (*The Ivory Swing*, New York:

Bantam, 1984); *TTP* (*The Tiger in the Tiger Pit*, London: Virago, 1991); *B* (*Borderline*, New York: Bantam, 1987); *C* (*Charades*, New York: Bantam, 1989); *LM* (*The Last Magician*, Queensland, Australia: University of Queensland Press, 1992).

9. Pearlman, "Interview," 52. *Listen to Their Voices*, New York: W. W. Norton, 1993.

10. Gerry Turcotte, "Janette Turner Hospital: *Dislocations, Borderline, Charades*," in *Writers in Action: The Writer's Choice Evenings*, 85 (Sydney: Currency Press, 1990).

11. Ibid., 72.

12. Candida Baker, "Interview with Janette Turner Hospital," in *Yacker 2: Australian Writers Talk about Their Work*, 275 (Sydney: Pan Books, 1987).

13. Janette Turner Hospital, "Letter to a New York Editor," *Meanjin* 47 (Spring 1988): 561.

14. Elizabeth Neild, "Disjointed Lives," *The Women's Review of Books* 6 (July 1989): 34.

15. Lee Grove, "Star-Crossed," *Boston Magazine* 77 (December 1985), 123.

16. Hospital, "Letter," 562.

17. Ibid., 561.

18. Hospital, Ibid., 561–62.

19. Turcotte, "Hospital," 66.

20. Pearlman, "Interview," 56.

Notes to Chapter 7

Patricia Chapman and Leah Shafer assisted in preparing the bibliography for this chapter.

1. Carolyn Heilbrun, "A Response to *Writing and Sexual Difference*," in *Writing and Sexual Difference*, ed. Elizabeth Abel., 293 (quoting Myra Jehlen).

2. "Jack of Hearts," in *The Elizabeth Stories*, 43 (New York: Penguin Books, 1988). Subsequent references will appear in the text, giving the name of the story being quoted and the page number (e.g., "King of Hearts," 43).

3. The form is an appropriate one for Huggan, one readily available to her, as "the linked-but-broken series of stories . . . had become a familiar pattern" in Canada by the 1960s (W. H. New, *A History of Canadian Literature* [London: Macmillan Education Ltd., 1989], 250). Kathryn Chittick points out that "this genre of linked short stories has emerged most distinctly of course since Munro published *Lives of Girls and Women* and *Who Do You Think You Are?*" (review of *The Elizabeth Stories* and Sandra Birdsell's *Ladies of the House*, in *The Fiddlehead* 145 [Autumn 1985]: 91). Michelle Gadpaille further notes that "in the early 1980s the influence of acclaimed writers such as Alice Munro began to be felt in the fiction of a younger group of writers. Isabel Huggan . . . did for 'Garten,' Ontario, what Munro did for Jubilee" (*The Canadian Short Story* [Toronto: Oxford University Press, 1988], 108).

4. Kim Heron, "Do We Really Escape?" brief interview, *The New York Times Book Review*, 12 July 1987: 11.

5. Nancy Chodorow, *The Reproduction of Mothering: Psychoanalysis and the Sociology of Gender* (Berkeley and Los Angeles: University of California Press, 1978), 7.

6. Michiko Kakutani (*New York Times* review, 23 May 1987: 11) badly misreads the relationship between Elizabeth, her mother, and feminine identity when she says that Elizabeth's mother "attempts to restore her sense of femininity by buying her her first brassiere." Her mother buys the bra in order to keep Elizabeth's too early and too pronounced femininity from showing; Elizabeth once again has done it wrong; her mother once again rubs salt into the wound.

7. Susan Gubar describes the difficulty of women who, taught to think of their beauty as the only artistic product of which they are capable, are unable to realize their identities by themselves ("'The Blank Page' and the Issues of Female Creativity," in *The New Feminist Criticism*, ed. Elaine Showalter, 296–97 (New York: Pantheon Books, 1985).

8. "Canada appears repeatedly [in Canadian literature] as a place of exile . . . ; it is not so much that the country houses exiles, though that is part of the 'exile syndrome', but that Canada is a society in which foreigness [sic] and familiarity are one" (W. H. New, *A History of Canadian Literature* [London: Macmillan Education Ltd., 1989], 245). Elizabeth has always been an exile, a foreigner in her own home town. The American elicits her warmest feelings.

9. Liza Potvin, "*The Elizabeth Stories* and Women's Autobiographical Strategies," *Studies in Canadian Literature* 14:2 (1989): 7.

10. Elaine Showalter speaks particularly succinctly of the much-recognized silence imposed on women by a patriarchal society: "The problem is not that language is insufficient to express women's consciousness but that women have been denied the full resources of language and have been forced into silence, euphemism, or circumlocution" ("Women's Criticism," in *Writing and Sexual Difference*, ed. Elizabeth Abel, 23 [Chicago: The University of Chicago Press, 1982].

11. "Sometimes childhood just doesn't work out the way it should." Carolyn See writes an excellent descripton of how this theme plays itself out for Elizabeth and her mother (*Los Angeles Times*, 2 August 1987: 3.

12. Gubar, "Blank Page," 305–06.

13. *The Whirlpool*, 1986 (Boston: David R. Godine, 1990), 188. Subsequent references will appear in the text (e.g., *Wh*, 188).

14. As some reviewers have noted, Urquhart takes a conventional line when she develops the theme of Canadian nationality and its attendant antagonism to America. But David serves as more than the enactment of Canadian nationalism and the garrison mentality; he also enacts the theme of male obsession with theories of life that exclude or try to reshape a feminine world. In this case his own whirlpool of obsession with America is particularly appropriate in that America indeed lies directly across the river—as Fleda lies next to him in bed. He constructs his own visions of both from an unreclaimable, unreliveable past.

15. The Browning framework appears as a separate story in *Storm Glass*; see the Huggan bibliography.

16. On Gubar, see n. 7.

17. Most readers will recognize that, as Alice Van Wart and other reviewers have said,

art uses symbolic meaning rather than plot and character development to show her meaning: "The characters remain puppets acting out their fates" (*The Canadian Forum*, August/September 1987: 48). Given the central controlling symbol of the whirlpool, Urquhart's method seems appropriate.

18. Urquhart modeled Maud on her husband's grandmother. This grandmother was the widow of an undertaker and kept a record of "floaters" pulled from the river (Geoff Hancock, "An Interview with Jane Urquhart," *Canadian Fiction Magazine* 55 [1986]: 29). Urquhart used another historical source for Fleda: "Parts of this novel were inspired and informed by Julia Cruikshank's diary, published in 1915 and entitled *Whirlpool Heights: The Dream-House on the Niagara River* (*Wh*, 215). Urquhart notes that "the past is a memory but it is a memory that is alive" (Hancock interview, 34).

19. Urquhart's treatment of language recalls, of course, for those who care about such matters, French linguistic theory and the arbitrary nature of signs. But readers need not be versed in theory to recognize that Urquhart's treatment of language through Fleda and the child dramatically highlights women's increasing attention to the connection between words and the world in which they find themselves.

20. *Changing Heaven* (Toronto: McClelland & Stewart, 1990), 1. Subsequent references will appear in the text (e.g., *CH*, 1).

21. Urquhart says she herself is "very interested in the work of the Brontës. I read *Jane Eyre* and *Wuthering Heights* when I was nine and I feel precisely the same way about those books today as I did then." (Hancock interview, 25)

22. Review of *The Elizabeth Stories* and Sandra Birdsell's *Ladies of the House*, 93.

23. Potvin, "Autobiographical," 1.

24. One must note, of course, that Patrick and David manage their obsessions no better than does Fleda. They are, however, free to make more choices; they themselves are the object of no one else's obsessions.

25. *CM: Canadian Materials for Schools and Libraries* (Ottawa: Canadian Library Association) 18 (July 1990): 190.

26. *Writing a Woman's Life*, 130.

27. Robert E. Spiller et al., *Literary History of the United States* (New York: Macmillan, 1974) 1: 1216, speaking of Willa Cather.

Notes to Chapter 8

1. Audrey Thomas, *Intertidal Life* (New York: Beaufort Books, 1984), 89. Subsequent references will taken from this edition, page numbers being indicated in textual parentheses.

2. Audrey Thomas, *Mrs. Blood* (Vancouver: Talon Books, 1975), 33.

3. "I never write about anybody but myself," Thomas told the eminent critic George Bowering (Bowering, "Songs and Wisdom: An Interview with Ardrey Thomas," *Open*

Letter [Spring 1979]: 14). And to another interviewer, Thomas insisted: "I'm an auto-biographical writer" (Eleanor Wachtel, "The Guts of *Mrs. Blood*," *Books in Canada*, November 1979: 5).

4. In this context, especially telling is Thomas's comments on her efforts at the University of British Columbia to pursue a Ph.D. in English while simultaneously publishing her first collection of stories. Consulting the department's chair, she was advised by him that it would be inappropriate for a graduate student to "write a non-academic book." Remembering—some twenty-five years later—how assaultive of en-deavor such an patriarchal atmosphere was, Thomas expostulated to an interviewer: "If you wanted to get an inferiority complex . . . you went to graduate school in the early sixties, late fifties. As a mother, as a *wife* . . . I was simply not taken seriously" (Eleanor Wachtel, "An Interview with Audrey Thomas," *A Room of One's Own*, March 1986: 41, 42).

5. On the vexing issue of national identity, Thomas has more than once indicated her displeasure at being described as an American living in Canada. Some twenty-six years after emigrating to the Canadian West Coast, she queried: "Why don't [reviewers] say a Canadian born in the States?" Wachtel interview, 56.

6. Margaret Atwood, "Audrey Thomas: 'Ten Green Bottles,' 'Ladies and Escorts,'" in *Second Words: Selected Critical Prose* (Toronto: House of Anansi Press, 1982), 268.

7. Audrey Thomas, *Latakia* (Vancouver: Talon Books, 1979), 118. Subsequent refer-ences will be taken from this edition, page numbers being indicated in textual parenthe-ses.

8. Audrey Thomas, "Initram," in *Ladies and Escorts* (Ottawa: Oberon Press, 1977), 88.

9. Susan Rudy Dorscht, "On Blowing Figures . . . and Bleeding: Poststructuralist Feminism and the 'Writing' of Audrey Thomas," *Canadian Fiction Magazine* (1986): 8.

10. Audrey Thomas, "If One Green Bottle . . . ," in *Ten Green Bottles* (Ottawa: Ob-eron Press, 1977), 3.

11. Thomas has frequently described (as well as placed) the situations of later twentieth-century middle-class women through the metaphors of voyage, whose end may be only as important as the act of voyaging. "A search for self is like looking for the northwest passage," she remarked. "[A]ll those guys were sent out from England and Spain . . . [but] in their terms it didn't exist . . . so what did they get out of all that to-ing and fro-ing and travelling up Vancouver Island looking for some way to get across? What they got was doing it . . . the search" (Wachtel interview, 49).

12. Audrey Thomas, *Munchmeyer and Prospero on the Island* (New York: Bobbs Merrill, 1971), 46. Subsequent references will be taken from this edition, page numbers being indicated in textual parentheses.

13. Audrey Thomas, "'My Craft and Sullen Art': The Writers Speak—Is There a Feminine Voice in Literature?" *Atlantis* (1978): 153.

14. Robert Diotte, "The Romance of Penelope: Audrey Thomas's Isobel Carpenter Trilogy," *Canadian Literature* (Autumn 1980): 60–61.

15. Thomas's preoccupation with the dividing and intersection of narrative voices has been called a "splitting" technique in a ground-breaking article on the author's practices

(Joan Coldwell, "Memory Organized: The Novels of Audrey Thomas," *Canadian Literature* [Spring 1982]: 47). Coldwell's analysis stresses the warring derangement of the divided self; I prefer to view division as doubling where the totalized subject (the self) always includes the other.

16. George Bowering, among others, would not agree; his reverent, exceptionally clever review of *Blown Figures* has become staple nourishment in analyses of Thomas. To my mind, the review is more paean of praise than critical exegesis; most consistently quoted is Bowering's play with the title's ambiguity: "What are figures and what is blown? There are fly-blown corpses, and corpses once were figures." And etc. ("The Site of Blood," *Canadian Literature* [Summer 1975]: 76).

17. Louis MacKendrick, "A Peopled Labyrinth of Walls: Audrey Thomas' *Blown Figures*," in *Present Tense: A Critical Anthology*, ed. John Moss (Toronto: NC Press, 1985), 169.

18. Notably, each central consciousness has a name both symbolic of and other than Isobel, though several references in each work tie the Miranda of *Munchmeyer and Prospero on the Island* and the Rachel of *Latakia* back to Isobel and to Isobel's projection and inscription of Audrey Thomas's remembrance of things past.

19. Thomas's cheery declaration about *Munchmeyer and Prospero on the Island*—I "loved writing it, I had more fun writing that book than any book I've ever written" (Bowering, "Songs and Wisdom," 26)—should come as little surprise, given her evident delight in having swamped the book with the kind of literary pyrotechnics now called intertexual and extratextual.

20. Elizabeth Komisar, "Audrey Thomas: A Review/Interview," *Open Letter* (Fall 1975): 61.

21. Lorna Irvine, "Sailing the Oceans of the World," *Quad.: New Directions in Canadian Writing* (Spring–Summer 1987): 28.

22. In *Intertidal Life*, Alice Hoyle's name carries allusions, including the punning whole/hole and the various associations of mirroring and voyaging, that refer deliberately to *Alice in Wonderland* and *Alice Through the Looking Glass*. What may be less apparent is the degree to which Thomas has drawn upon the doubling strategy: Alice's two daughters here have names which mirror one another, Hannah being the Hebrew for Ann[a]e. For intriguing discussions of the name Anna, see Mickey Pearlman, ed., *The Anna Book: Searching for Anne in Literary History* (Westport Conn: Greenwood Publishing, 1992).

23. Audrey Thomas, "Natural History," in *Real Mothers* (Vancouver: Talon Books, 1981), 33.

24. The titles of Thomas's short-story collections insist upon ironic inversions, just as do the cartoon-like colored illustrations on their covers; each sets up a stereotypical female image that will be debunked in the stories. See Pauline Butling's discussion, "Thomas and Her Rag-Bag," *Canadian Literature* (Autumn 1984): 197.

25. Audrey Thomas, "Crossing the Rubicon," in *Real Mothers* (Vancouver: Talon Books, 1981): 155. Subsequent references will be taken from this edition, page numbers being indicated in textual parentheses.

26. "Today is the ides of February, February 13th" (*CR*, 155), observes the story's opening sentence. Discovering the happy coincidence that in February the ides fall on the thirteenth (that is, one day before Valentine's) and not—as in the Ides of March—on

the 15th, Thomas can borrow from *Julius Caesar* to forewarn her enthralled heroine of the deadly dangers inherent in a day devoted to enshrining romantic love.

Notes to Chapter 9

1. Linda Hutcheon, *The Canadian Postmodern: A Study of Contemporary English-Canadian Fiction* (Toronto: Oxford University Press, 1988), 1. Hutcheon comments that the reasons for this flowering were diverse: "Nationalist sentiment, government support for publishers and artists, and the general feeling that in cultural terms Canada has finally ceased to be what Earle Birney once called 'a highschool land/deadset in adolescence'." See also, for example, Stanley Fogel, *A Tale of Two Countries: Contemporary Fiction in English Canada and the United States* (Toronto: ECW Press, 1984), 4, citing Harold Horwood, author and past president of the Canadian Writers' Union; according to Horwood, "The 'Canadian renaissance' compares to that of the United States in the mid-nineteenth century."

2. For varying points of view on the issues of identity and postmodernism, see, for example, Northrup Frye, "Journey Without Arrival, A Personal Point of View," *The Globe and Mail*, 6 April 1976: 7, quoted in Fogel, *Two Countries*, 8, Rejean Ducharme, *Le Nez qui vogue* (Paris: Gallimard, 1966), 12, quoted in E. D. Blodgett, "After Pierre Berton What? In Search of a Canadian Literature," *Essays on Canadian Writing* 30 (Winter 1984–85): 60–80; and Margaret Atwood, *Survival: A Thematic Guide to Canadian Literature*. Toronto: House of Anansi, 1972, pp. 18–19, quoted in Fogel, p. 18.

3. For discussions of women as metaphor in Canadian fiction, see, among others, Hutcheon, *Canadian Postmodern*, 5–6; Lorna Irvine, *Sub/Version: Canadian Fiction by Women* (Toronto: 1986), 3–17 passim; Coral Ann Howells, *Private and Fictional Words: Canadian Women Novelists of the 1970s and 1980s* (London and New York: Methuen, 1987), 2–11, passim; and Barbara Hill Rigney, *Madness and Sexual Politics in the Feminist Novel* (Madison: University of Wisconsin Press, 1978), 100.

4. Harvey De Roo, "A Little Like Flying: An Interview With Carol Shields," *West Coast Review* 23:3 (1988): 38–56, 43.

5. Howells, *Private and Fictional Words*, 26.

6. Birdsell studied creative writing at the universities of Winnipeg and Manitoba. She served as writer in residence at Centennial Library in Winnipeg and, in 1987–88, at the University of Waterloo. Winner of the Lampert Aware for New Fiction, the National Magazine Award for short fiction, and the Canadian Book Information Centre's 45 Below Award, she has also received awards from the Manitoba Arts Council and the Canada Council. Birdsell is author of two volumes of short stories, *Night Travellers* (1982) and *Ladies of the Night* (1984). She has also written two novels, *The Missing Child* (1989), set in the mythical town of Agassiz, and *Agassiz: A Novel in Stories* (1991); two plays, *The Revival* and *A Prairie Boy's Winter*, both produced by Prairie Theatre Exchange; and two film scripts for National Film Board: *From the Heart* (1985) and *Places Not Our Own* (1986).

7. Originally published in Canada as *Agassiz Stories* (Toronto: Turnstone Press, 1990). With virtually no changes, the novel comprises the stories previously published in *Night Travellers* and *Ladies of the Night*.

8. Eric McCormack, with Kim Jernigan and Peter Hinchcliffe, "A Conversation With Sandra Birdsell," *New Quarterly* (Summer 1988): 8–22, 12. McCormack's ellipses.

9. Ibid., 11.

10. Sharon Oard Warner, review of *Agassiz: A Novel in Stories*, *New York Times Book Review*, 5 May 1991.

11. McCormack, "Conversation," 20.

12. Ibid., 13, 11.

13. Ibid., 11, 12.

14. Howells, *Private and Fictional Words*, 16.

15. For discussions of this theme in Canadian literature, see, for example, Fogel, *Two Countries*, 27, who discusses critics who continue to disagree about parochialism and the appropriateness of continued use of the "survival in a garrison" theme. E. D. Blodgett, "Conclusion," in *Literary History of Canada: Canadian Literature in English*, ed., Carl F. Klinch (Toronto: University of Toronto Press, 1965), 830, quotes Northrup Frye on "garrison mentality." See also D. G. Jones, *Butterfly on Rock: A Study of Themes and Images in Canadian Literature* (Toronto: University of Toronto Press, 1970), 8.

16. Birdsell has stated that she admires Louise Erdrich's *Love Medicine*, perhaps because she and Erdrich share "similar background, the geographical area and culture" (McCormack, "Conversations," 9–10). Erdrich's influence may be seen not only in her use of interconnected short stories to evoke the lives of present-day North Dakota Native Americans but also in her endearing, doomed alcoholic character named June. And Minnie's trapeze artist, circus mother's flight certainly echoes the mother's flight in Erdrich's *The Beet Queen*.

17. DeRoo interview, 43.

18. Alice Munro compares Shields's stories to "the beautiful broken light of a prism," while Janette Turner Hospital has praised this "wonderful writer" as "wry, witty, wise, and fiercely intelligent." Quoted in the opening page of Carol Shields, *Various Miracles* (New York: Penguin Books, 1989).

19. Quoted on the front and back covers of the British edition of *Swann*, in Britain titled *Mary Swann* (London: Fourth Estate, 1990). Shields is the author of several other novels: *The Box Garden* (1977), companion to *Small Ceremonies; Happenstance* (1980) and its companion *A Fairly Conventional Woman* (1982); *Swann* (1989); and *The Republic of Love* (1992). Additionally Shields has published two short-story collections, *Various Miracles* (1985) and *The Orange Fish* (1989); two poetry collections, *Others* and *Intersect* (1974); and a critical book, *Susanna Moodie: Voice and Vision* (1977). Winner of the 1976 Canadian Authors' Association Award for Fiction for *Small Ceremonies*, a Book-of-the-Month-Club Alternate Selection, Shields also won the 1983 Canadian Broadcasting Company Drama Award in for her play *Departures and Arrivals*, published in 1990.

20. DeRoo interview, 41.

21. For an incisive reading of Shields's subversive technique in this story, see Simone Vauthier, "On Carol Shields' 'Mrs. Turner Cutting the Grass,'" *Commonwealth* 11:2 (1989): 63–74.

22. Published in Canada as *Swann: A Mystery* (1987), and in England as *Mary Swann* (1990). For an analysis of *Swann* as a feminist revision of the detective novel, see Barbara Goddard, "Sleuthing: Feminists Re/Writing the Detective Novel," *Signature: Journal of Theory and Canadian Literature* 1 (Summer 1989): 45–80.

23. DeRoo interview, 40.

24. Carol Gerson, "Anthologies and the Canon of Early Canadian Women Writers," in Lorraine McMullen, *Re(Dis)covering Our Foremothers: Nineteenth-Century Canadian Women Writers*, 55–70 (Ottawa: University of Ottawa Press, 1989), 63.

25. Lorna Irvine, "Sailing the Oceans of the World," *New Quarterly: New Directions in Canadian Writing* 7 (1987): 50–56. Numerous other similarities occur between Shields's Sarah and Thomas's Alice. Sarah says, "I want my brain to be all sinew and thrum, chime and clerestory, crouch and attack" (*Swann*, 28). "Alice's mind was the heavyweight champion of the world in the disguise of the Scorpio Housewife. Washing the dishes, she let her mind off the leash, let it run and snuffle." (*Intertidal*, 226). Moreover, Shields and Thomas place special emphasis on their characters' love of Virginia Woolf. And for both women, reading and writing are connected with pregnancy and birth.

26. Carol Shields, with Clara Thomas and Donna E. Smyth, "Thinking Back Through Our Mothers' Libraries: Tradition in Canadian Women's Writing," in *Re(Dis)covering Our Foremothers: Nineteenth-Century Canadian Women Writers*, ed. Lorraine McMullen, 9–13 (Ottawa: University of Ottawa Press, 1989) 12.

27. Wayne Fraser, *The Dominion of Women: The Personal and the Political in Canadian Women's Literature* (Westport, Conn: Greenwood Press, 1991), 176.

28. DeRoo interview, 46.

29. Andy Solomon, "A Celebration of Romantic Love," *Boston Globe*, 2 February 1992: B47.

Notes to Chapter 10

This paper is at some level a collaborative project. I would like to thank Jana Sequoya, Brian Gore, Mark Simpson, and Stephen Slemon for their discussions and comments, and women of color over the last fifteen years for the courage and thoughtfulness that made this project even thinkable. Its flaws, of course, are mine alone.

1. The term is certainly imported from the United States, but I have not been able to trace its first use there or here. It is common by 1981, the publication date of the watershed *This Bridge Called My Back: Writings by Radical Women of Color*, eds. Cherrie Moraga and Gloria Anzaldua (Watertown, Mass.: Persephone Press, 1981; New York: Kitchen Table Women of Color Press, 1983).

2. Conversely, of course, not all immigrants identify as women of color. Nancy Adamson, Linda Briskin, and Margaret McPhail, eds., *Feminist Organizing for Change: The Contemporary Women's Movement in Canada* (Toronto: Oxford University Press, 1988), 107. See also Marlene Nourbese Philip, "Solitary Dialogue" (*Broadside* 7:5 [March 1986]) and *Resources for Feminist Research*, Special Issue on Immigrant Women, 16:1

(March 1987). I am aware that the argument I am about to make is volatile in the face of these critiques, but I think that, first, the novels invite thinking about Canada in terms other than natality, and, second, that it is essential to think about Canada in an international frame.

3. This kind of multiculturalism reaches its zenith at festivals like Heritage Days, a public festival at which all kinds of ethnicities occupy separate tents in a single public park and celebrate diversity by selling ethnic food and trinkets. Masked in this carnival are the struggles over which ethnicities get represented and which don't, who represents any given ethnic category, who has how much space and where, and, of course, who gets how much money, from whom, and for what purposes. I am much more interested in multiculturalism which talks specifically about struggles against discrimination and exclusion, as do Nourbese Philip, Kogawa, and Culleton.

4. It is no accident, I think, that the Canadian national anthem provocatively differentiates "our home" from "native land": in a not very new variation on a very old theme, Indian people get the land, while white people get the homes.

5. And does the phrase unintentionally echo "brave new world" as well? For etymology, see William Safire, *Safire's Political Dictionary* (New York: Random House, 1978), 459. Woodrow Wilson used the phrase before Hitler, suggesting a historical extension of cooperation between the United States and Germany.

6. Simply put, much of the history of Canadian people takes place outside Canada's borders, as it passes through families that straddle countries and even continents.

7. Martin, Biddy and Chandra Talpade Mohanty, "Feminist Politics: What's Home Got to Do With It?" in *Feminist Studies/Critical Studies*, ed. Teresa de Lauretis (Bloomington: Indiana University Press, 1986), 191–212. Subsequent references to the essay will be included parenthetically in the text.

8. For these and other statistics, see Harry H. Hiller, *Canadian Society: A Macro Analysis* (Scarborough, Ont.: Prentice-Hall Canada). Hiller's figures suggest even more diversity among younger Canadians.

9. Marlene Nourbese Philip, *Harriet's Daughter* (London: Heinemann, 1988), 6. Subsequent references to the novel will be included parenthetically in the text.

10. Current debates over Québecois secession and Native Canadian demands demonstrate that self-determination is central to conceptions of Canada.

11. It is significant, too, that Margaret in mythology is the patron saint of childbearing women; Margaret moves from identifying herself as another woman's daughter to owning a procreative role herself. The shift might be read as a literalization of Harriet Tubman's role as deliverer of her people.

12. Joy Kogawa, *Obasan* (Harmondsworth: Penguin, 1983), 226. Subsequent references to the novel will be included parenthetically in the text.

13. Rough Lock Bill's toe is "dark as a walnut," and the way he pronounces *cement*— "see-ment"—sounds U.S.-American, but his stories are about Native Canadians (141).

14. I mean this word in its literary sense: Cheryl is a hero who falls from a great height, not because of any tragic flaw but from exhaustion at fighting the racist war of attrition that is life in Canadian society for Metis people. I will return to the idea of tragedy and its implications.

15. Beatrice Culleton, *In Search of April Raintree* (Winnipeg: Pemmican Publica-

tions), 167. Subsequent references to the novel will be included parenthetically in the text.

16. Of course, the clever irony of the novel is that we get the sociopolitical history, too. I don't want to suggest that histories of individual pain can or ought to replace social and political histories, but they are an indispensable supplement because they mobilize people—readers, for instance. This seems to me the importance of politically astute fiction.

17. The well-used trope holds particularly well for Canada, it seems to me. Canadians are by and large a border people; twenty-eight million Canadians live in 10 percent of the nation's 10 million square kilometers, mostly in a hundred-mile strip along the U.S. border. See Hiller, *Canadian Society*, 11.

Contributors

Katherine K. Gottschalk (Ph.D., University of Chicago) is Director of Freshman Writing Seminars in Cornell University's John S. Knight Writing Program. She has published "Paralyzed in the Present: Susan Fromberg Schaeffer's Mothers, or Daughters," in *Mother Puzzles: Daughters and Mothers in Contemporary American Literature*; "Stephen King's Dark and Terrible Mother, Annie Wilkes," in *The Anna Book: Searching for Anna in Literary History*; and "Training TAs Across the Curriculum to Teach Writing: Embracing Diversity," in *Preparing the Professoriate of Tomorrow to Teach: Selected Readings in TA Training*, eds. Jody Nyquist et al. She is also a coeditor and author of *Teaching Prose: A Guide for Writing Instructors.*

Georgeann Murphy (Ph.D., Tulane University) is an Associate Professor of Dramatic Arts and English at Centre College in Danville, Kentucky, where she teaches, directs, and writes. She has published articles on the relationship between Shakespeare and the commedia del l'arte and on the concept of chastity in *A Midsummer Night's Dream*, and is currently working on both a study of Shakespearean comedy and a collection of short stories.

Mickey Pearlman (Ph.D., Graduate School of the City University of New York) is the editor of *American Women Writing Fiction: Memory, Identity, Family, Space*, of *Mother Puzzles: Daughters and Mothers in Contemporary American Literature*, and of *The Anna Book: Searching for Anna in Literary History*. She is the coauthor of *Inter/View: Talks with America's Writing Women* (in paperback as *A Voice of One's Own*) and of *Tillie Olsen*. She is the author of *Listen to Their Voices: 20 Interviews With Women Who Write*, of *Reinventing Reality: Muriel Spark's Novels*, and is now editing a collection of twenty original essays, *Regarding Friendship*, by contemporary authors.

Margaret K. Schramm (Ph.D., University of Pennsylvania) is an Associate Professor in the Department of English at Hartwick College. She has published articles on Ann Beattie, Ellen Gilchrist, George Orwell, John Osborne, and Grace Paley. She is the author of "The Quest for the Ideal Mother in Sula" in *The Anna Book: Searching for Anna in Literary History*.

Diane Simmons is a doctoral candidate in English at the Graduate School of the City University of New York. Her second novel, *Dreams Like Thunder*, was published in 1992 by Story Line Press. She is working on a study of the Caribbean writer Jamaica Kincaid to be published by Twayne/Macmillan.

Virginia Tiger (Ph.D., University of British Columbia) is Professor of English and Associate Dean of the Faculty of Arts and Sciences at Rutgers University–Newark. Author of *William Golding: The Dark Fields of Discovery* and *Everywoman*, she co-edited *Critical Essays on Doris Lessing* and has published articles on Golding and Lessing in *Modern Fiction Studies*, *Twentieth Century Litery* and *Style*.

Martha M. Vertreace (Associate Professor and poet-in-residence, Kennedy-King College) is the author of *Second House from the Corner* and *Under a Cat's Eye Moon*. Substantial collections of her poems appear in *Spoon River Anthology* (Winter 1988) and *Benchmark Anthology of Contemporary Illinois Poetry*. Recent fiction appears in *Oyez, Willow Review, Caprice, Womanwarp*, and *Writer's Bar-B-Q*. Recent articles include "Muse . . . Revisions," in *Reading to Writing: Form and Meaning*; "Toni Cade Bambara: The Dance of Character and Community," in *American Women Writing Fiction: Memory, Identity, Family, Space*, and "Secrets Left to Tell: Creativity and Continuity in the Mother/Daughter Dyad," in *Mother Puzzles: Daughters and Mothers in Contemporary American Literature*.

Abby H. P. Werlock (Ph.D., University of Sussex, England) is the author (with Mickey Pearlman) of *Tillie Olsen* and has published articles on the female heroes in the novels of Chandler, Cooper, Faulkner, Hemingway, Steinbeck, and Wharton. The recipient of fellowships from the National Endowment for the Humanities and the Joyce Foundation of Chicago, she has also written on mother-daughter relationships and mixed marriages in American fiction. She teaches American literature and women's studies at St. Olaf College.

Marilyn C. Wesley (Ph.D., Syracuse University) teaches literature, theory, and women's studies at Hartwick College in Oneonta, New York. She has published articles on Joyce Carol Oates's fiction in *Studies in Short Fiction, Essays on Literature, LIT, Critique,* and *Women's Studies.* Her book *Refusal and Transgression in Joyce Carol Oates's Family Fiction* is forthcoming. She is currently at work on a study of the trope of the woman traveler in American literature.

Roberta White (Ph.D., Stanford University) is N.E.H. Professor of Humanities at Centre College. She is the author of "Anna's Quotidian Love: Sue Miller's *The Good Mother*" in *Mother Puzzles: Daughters and Mothers in Contemporary American Literature,* and of "John Berryman's Anne" in *The Anna Book: Searching for Anna in Literary History.*

Heather Zwicker is a displaced Canadian and a Ph.D. candidate at Stanford University. She is working on a dissertation titled "New National Narratives for a New World Order: Contemporary Canadian and Irish Fiction."

Index